ALFRED BINET

MODERN IDEAS ABOUT CHILDREN

Translated from
the French
by
Suzanne Heisler

I.S.B.N. 0-9617054-1-8
L.C. NO. 86-162049

ERRATA

Table of contents, page 6; Chapter 4, II, Audition.

Preface I, page 9, line 1, 1982 *not* 1892.
          page 10, line 1, no comma after mental orthopedics.

The measurement of achievement, page 36, line 15.
          There can be little wrong with it; [add comma]

The measurement of Intelligence, page 101, § 2, line 4.
          The average limit of the intelligence of adults [no comma after adults]

The measurement of Memory in school children, page 128, § 6, line 5. word-for-word learning [add hyphen]

The perversions of Memory, page 136. Footnote not italicized.

Remarks on a few types of intelligence. page 180, § 2, line 7. Souriau [not Sourian]

Moral education, page 215, line 4. desert [not dessert]

*DEDICATED
TO THE CHILDREN
OF THE WORLD*

ACKNOWLEDGMENTS

The writer is indebted to Dr. Robert Thrapp, Lecturer, Frederic Burk Foundation at San Francisco State University, for suggesting the topic of this study, for his many helpful comments and his encouragements while it was in preparation; also to other members of the Special Education Department who, in one way or another, have facilitated our work; to Rev. Father Oziol, Director, Institut Médico-Pédagogique, Marvejols, France, for his assistance in securing the original text and for his unflagging interest in our efforts; to Dr. Kenwood Bartelme, Psychologist, and Professor of Psychology at San Francisco State University, for taking the time to read and to criticize the manuscript (although he is of course not responsible for any of its faults), for his advice as to the literature relevant to some psychological aspects of this work and for his constant support throughout this venture; to Mrs. Betty Gardiner for her expert typing and editing of the manuscript and for her many helpful suggestions.

Finally, the author is indebted to Binet's granddaughters (who still live in Paris), to Professor Avanzini, President of the Société Binet (formerly the Binet Foundation), and to his assistant, Dr. Claude Kohler, for their encouragement and help in publishing this translation; and to Professor Paul Fraisse for his contribution of a current evaluation of Binet in the Preface.

S. H.

TABLE OF CONTENTS

PREFACE I

The modern ideas of 1909 are still modern in 1892. Alfred Binet wanted to make teachers of his time aware of the individual differences which exist in children. The task has not been completed. As the author points out, he reviews a medley of research, observations, and memories. A carefully observed, particular fact opens new horizons to him. A typical student is never confronted with a teacher created from a unique mold. Individual differences spring forth from all directions, and it becomes the task of pedagogy to discover each child's true aptitudes so as to tailor its teachings to the child's needs.

From the start we are far removed from any dualism. Alfred Binet asks that we take the child's body into consideration. He quickly discovers a relationship between psychological poverty and physiological deficiencies. Binet already sees that one must understand the child in terms of his socio-economic background. A caste system still exists, he says, in spite of the 1789 revolution. The teacher must take this into account, just as he must be concerned with possible visual and auditory defects. As far as these technical problems are concerned, no didactics; instead, he offers a harvest of anecdotes and introduces simple rules which prevent overlooking real problems.

Of course, Binet dwells more particularly on the question of intellectual aptitudes. In these pages filled with nuances, the author of the famous Binet-Simon test seems very different from the dogmatic Binet mummified by history. He says little about his tests except to contrast two kinds : those which take into account the results — or performance, as we would say today — and those which are a pretext for only introspective analyses of a process. Of course, he defends only the first ! He thinks that intelligence must be analyzed into four steps : comprehension, invention, direction, and censorship. (Today we would substitute "knowledge of results" for the term "censorship.") In reality, intelligence is a looped process which is revealed by different tests. But Binet asks that results not be interpreted globally, for each child is an individual, although correlations may exist between aptitudes.

His interest focuses on the discrepancies which tests may reveal between aptitude and school results. He then challenges the teacher not to be satisfied with making a report, especially a report of inadequacy; the teacher must make every effort to correct a problem, and — like Americans of the same period — Binet says that the main pedagogical task is to help the student "learn how to learn." One must create true mental orthopedics, which make the child an active individual instead of only a listener. The goal, he says, can be reached, and he derives his belief from what he has learned while working with abnormal children.

The chapter on memory is of a prodigious richness. Binet anticipates much of what will be precisely stated later. He sees the pros and cons of too systematic a recourse to memory. He distinguishes — without naming them — short-term memory and long-term memory. He already raises questions about the so very contemporary and still unresolved problem of the best time of day for memorization exercises; today we would speak of the question of scholastic rhythm undifferentiated from circadian rhythm.

Confronted with the specificity of aptitude, Binet takes an eclectic position. It is true that there are correlations, but he sees many special aptitudes which will not fit into any of the various past or present classifications: music, drawing, but also spelling, which involves visual memory, mental arithmetic, and mathematics. Where intelligence is concerned, he sees children locating themselves between the extreme poles of three different types. He indeed differentiates three axes:
— the conscious vs. the unconscious;
— the objective vs. the subjective;
— the practician vs. the literary (verbal type).
The study of the objective and the subjective, which relates Binet to Witkin, is particularly interesting to Binet because his two daughters, Armande and Marguerite, are located at both extremes of the axis. But having watched his daughters develop, he remarked that there is no strict determinism.

The chapter on laziness may appear to be the most dated; it is actually one of the most modern. Binet spontaneously believes in laziness like practically all those who say that laziness does not exist. Consequently, he starts looking for lazy children, and he finds practically none. The causes of laziness are many, and the alert teacher must get to the real root of the problem as often as he can.

This brings us to moral education. Binet asks a lot from teachers: not only to set an example, but also to make every effort to awaken in the child ideas and feelings — and also actions, of solidarity, for instance. "To give lessons in solidarity is good; to teach it by having it practiced is better."

I hope the reader will experience as much pleasure in reading this book as I have experienced in re-reading it myself. This scientist, who goes about schools the way a naturalist goes about the countryside, is forever making us aware of new problems. He teaches us to examine the world of children with a new eye. His imagination suggests to him how an observation can become objectified. What an example for teachers, but also what a responsibility!

Professor Paul Fraisse, Director
Laboratory of Comparative and
Experimental Psychology

Paris, 1982

PREFACE II

A year before his death at the age of fifty-four, Alfred Binet published *Modern Ideas About Children*. The book represents, among other things, a review of the interests and achievements that made Binet such a significant figure in education and psychology and, to my mind, a model for the investigation of individual differences in both its conceptual and methodological approaches. Many of the factors that nineteenth-century experimental psychology had attributed to "error" became for Binet the means of understanding the developing child. Throughout the book he emphasizes the crucial importance of variations in the physical, intellectual, and characterological as diagnostic indicators for the proper assessment of children's performance.

The book itself is a mixture of theory, empirical observation and anecdotes that illustrates Binet's impatience with traditional pedagogy and his innovative proposals for reform and change. Like his contemporary Sigmund Freud, Binet is often at his best when he is "clinical," that is, when he uses an exhaustive case to underline a general observation. These observations sometimes have a prophetic modern ring, as, for example, when he proposes that ethnological differences may have important implications for educational policy. Indeed this book, far from being out of date, offers a multitude of reminders of the many problems of assessment and educational policy that remain as lively today as they were at his death.

This book has remained unavailable to the mono-lingual American for three quarters of a century, and we have Suzanne Heisler to thank for remedying this. She has rendered a painstaking and highly readable translation of the text, as well as a succinct and scholarly review of Binet's life and work.

Dr. Kenwood Bartelme
Professor of Psychology
San Francisco State University

San Francisco, California, 1983

12

FOREWORD

This project was undertaken for two reasons : first, *Les idées modernes sur les enfants* had never before been translated into English and in our view this book is a valuable historical document ; secondly, it is a work which should prove to be of great interest to teachers and one which we feel can make an important contribution to education even today.

Its author, Alfred Binet, was born in Nice, France, on July 8th, 1857. His mother was a successful artist. His father, his grandfather, and a great-grandfather were physicians. Binet was evidently impelled to follow the predominantly scientific family tradition, for after obtaining his *baccalauréat* at the Lycée Louis-le-Grand in Paris and before completing the law studies he undertook upon graduation from high school, he oriented himself towards the sciences and soon became involved in experimentation. In 1879, at the age of 21 and the day after completing the first part of his law studies, he published what was considered in academic circles a very interesting paper entitled " The Psychic Life of Micro-organisms " *(Revue Philosophique,* Vol. XXIV, p. 449). In 1884, still while studying law but with this aspect of his training almost completed, he submitted a first paper on " The Fusion of Images "[1] to the Director of the *Revue Philosophique,* Th. Ribot, who published the article and encouraged Binet to continue his work in psychology. Binet took his advice and while working for a degree in the natural sciences *(licence es sciences),* he collaborated on research in psychopathology at the Salpêtrière, one of Paris's psychiatric hospitals. He also undertook independent studies in physiology and in psychology which eventually led to the publication of his first book, *The Psychology of Reasoning; Experimental Research in Hypnotism* (1886); also *Animal Magnetism* (1887),[2] and *The Alterations of the Personality* (1892).[3]

A chance encounter in 1891 led to his nomination to be Assistant, then Associate Director of the Psychological Laboratory which had just been created at the Sorbonne, and he immediately became the most active member in it. He was named Director of the Laboratory in 1899 and retained this post until his death.

In 1894, the same year he submitted his thesis for the Doctorate in the Natural Sciences, entitled "Contribution to the Study of the Sub-intestinal Nervous System of Insects," he published his *Introduction to Experimental Psychology;*[4] then *The Psychology of Great Calculators and Chessplayers;*[5] also the initial volume of the first French psychological journal, *Année Psychologique;*[6] and finally, his first research on the psychology of dramatic authors, which, along with his analysis of master calculators, helped set the stage for Binet's later work on normal subjects and individual differences.

By 1894, Binet the experimental psychologist had achieved maturity, and we see his work branch out in many directions as he applies his findings to various fields. We become familiar with another dimension of his personality : his altruistic turn of mind, his social and educational preoccupations. In Bertrand's words : "It gets to be difficult to differentiate the theoretician from the born educator in Binet."

Starting in 1897, he became interested in the practical problems arising in the schools as a result of individual differences found in children. This culminated in 1900 in the creation of the "Free Society for the Psychological Study of the Child" by Buisson, and soon afterward of an "Experimental Pedagogy Laboratory," Rue Grange-aux-Belles, by Vaney; also in the elaboration of the first intelligence scale in 1905. Around 1900, Binet left the Laboratory part of the time to conduct experiments in schools and in summer camps. He undertook studies on attention and on distraction, this enigma which is of such great importance in education. He started perfecting the test method, using two parallel and complementary types of investigation : psychology and scientific pedagogy. While involved in these activities, Binet published numerous important papers in *Année Psychologique,* and also several books : *Suggestibility* (1900) ;[7] *The Experimental Study of Intelligence* (1903);[8] *The Soul and the Body* (1906).[9] Also in 1906 a paper entitled "The Science of Testimony," which appeared in the *Revue Philosophique,* marked the beginning of Binet's research in criminology, with Charcot's collaboration. Then in 1907, Binet and Simon published *Abnormal Children.*[10] In 1908, Binet did not contribute anything to *Année Psychologique.* Bertrand explains this silence :

> We know that a full year of rest was imposed upon him because of ill health and it is probably this one. Volume XIII of *L'Année* which corresponds to this period does not contain a single line from him.

In 1909, Binet began a survey on the teaching of philosophy. He also became an art critic and, just as earlier he had analysed dramatic authors, he now analysed artists, Rembrandt and Styka in particular.

Finally, during the last few years of his life, Binet undertook serious medical studies with the aim of proving scientifically that the child is not a "homunculus" but a unique being, from both the physical and the intellectual point of view. His school anthropology program was based on these studies.

In all the works mentioned above, Binet had laid the foundation for *Modern Ideas about Children,* which appeared in 1911 shortly before his death. The goal of education, says the author, is to form minds which become increasingly powerful, well balanced, penetrating, while at the same time strengthening, freeing, and exalting souls, and, he adds, when this goal of fostering the harmonious development of body, mind, and conscience takes precedence over preparing children for examinations, humanity will have taken a huge step forward. Bertrand has called this book Binet's "testament." It is this testament, still in large part unexecuted, which we present to you now on page 17.

1. See Robert H. Pollack and Margaret W. Brenner, eds, *The Experimental Study of Alfred Binet* (New York : Springer Publishing Co., 1969).

For 2, 3, 4, 5, 6, 7, 8, 9, 10, see Theta H. Wolf's comprehensive study, *Alfred Binet* (Chicago : University of Chicago Press, 1973).

CHAPTER ONE

The purpose of this book

This book is a review. I have written it to express, as sincerely as I can, what I feel thirty years of experimental work, conducted mainly in the United States, in Germany, and a little in France, have taught us about matters relevant to education. In it will be found résumés and conclusions of those studies which have been called — sometimes with enthusiasm, sometimes with contempt — "scientific," "modern," "experimental," "physiological," "psychological," or even "pedological," * a newly coined word. I tried to evaluate the many published works and to establish which ideas can be put into educational practice, which must be rejected, and to what extent the new methods can be expected to improve pedagogy. This is one of the most important questions which face our times. I have tried to examine it as objectively as I could.

Unfortunately it was not possible for me to encompass the complete and vast domain of education within the narrow framework of this book. It has been necessary to set limits to the subject in order to deal with it with precision and in detail. I have selected those areas which appear to be of the greatest interest and to represent the most pressing need. It must therefore be clear to all my readers at this time that this book will not answer all questions concerning the education of children or young people which can be asked from the point of view of a father, a teacher, or a sociologist. These questions are extremely numerous and can be divided into three main categories : 1) the educational programs; 2) the teaching methods; and 3) the children's aptitudes.

Let us orient ourselves by examining briefly these three important areas.

1. A program is a detailed list of subjects offered in schools. It is the program which is most often the object of public scrutiny. It is set

---

* Pedology : scientific pedagogy. This word may have been coined by E. Blum (*Revue Philosophique*, 1898), who used it in his critique of Binet's work, *La fatigue intellectuelle*.

up by the state, and attention becomes automatically focused upon it every time that, for political, economic or other reasons, something curiously and tendentiously called "an educational crisis" occurs in our country; the same thought immediately comes to everyone's mind: there is only one resource, only one remedy — change the program!

This attitude can be criticized only to the extent that it is exclusive, for there is no denying that curriculum contents have an enormous influence on the education of intelligence and on the effectiveness of instruction. The philosophy embodied in the program partially reveals the goal that is aimed for. About the value of this goal, its absolute value and more especially its value in relation to the times and the particular society involved, very serious questions are raised. For instance, one may ask what should be emphasized in the training of children? Should we stress more especially knowledge or intelligence? Intelligence or also the will? The will or also physical fitness? In other words, should we adopt as our model the type of sedentary, thoughtful intellectual who is formed by the study of the humanities, who tends more and more to become a civil servant and later to retire? Or the man-of-action type, the businessman, the industrialist, the agronomist and even the settler or colonist; the man filled with initiative who relies only on himself and for whom the material results of action take precedence over intellectual development?

Another question fits into the same category since it also involves an ideal of education: Should we more especially develop in the child such social aptitudes as discipline, gregariousness, solidarity, devotion to community interests and a host of other similar excellent qualities which are highly social; or should we, on the contrary, encourage everything which favors the development of the individual, of his personality, of his inner life, that is to say, personal and critical judgment, independence?

These beautiful questions, which have been the object of discussion at various times, are not part of our program, but we shall touch upon them often. What we can say about them here is that two conditions must be met if we do not wish them to remain vague and banal formulae, only used as the subjects of literary dissertations and homilies. First, we must establish the relative value of the various proposed ideals of education, taking into account the environment, the times, the ethnology, the needs and aspirations of the society to be educated. That which is good to an Anglo-Saxon nation may be detestable to a Latin nation; that which is good for a particular group, a particular class, a particular child may not be appropriate for others. This could become the object of a very long discussion from the point of view of psychology, pedagogy, and especially sociology.

Secondly, we must determine how education needs to be conceived if it is going to satisfy fully the chosen educational ideal, and this is no easy matter. It is not sufficient to state principles, to give moral directions, to make eloquent appeals to everyone's good will; the teaching task must be organized in such a way that the educational ideal is reflected in the educational procedures.

2. After the programs are the methods. We use the term "method" in its broadest sense to include all acts, all procedures, all organizations which contribute from far or near to the teaching process. In this sense, the choice of teachers, their previous training, the way they are selected are already an integral part of the methods. More directly related, perhaps, are the regulations which govern the duration of study periods and the presentation of the various subject matters. To determine the proper length of study periods we shall consider the total number of hours spent in school and the total number of vacation days; we shall also consider the dates and the length of vacation breaks, for while they undoubtedly provide a rest, they also allow absence of practice and forgetting if they are too prolonged. With regard to presentation, we shall consider the level of difficulty and the dryness of the material offered when setting up study plans, for should not the more abstract subjects be presented early in the day when, after a night's rest, the child's mind is most alert? We shall also distribute lessons so as to provide for the alternation of intellectual and physical work, so effective when it is well understood. As we attempt to revive interest by this alternation, we shall strive to avoid the inefficient scattering of energy and attention which could result from having the children endlessly dash about. We shall avoid even more the error of attempting to relieve fatigue resulting from one type of activity by having students engage in another type of activity so strenuously that it becomes a second source of fatigue adding itself to the first. Nothing is worse, really, than trying to correct an excess of intellectual work by an excess of physical exercise. All these questions are dominated by the important consideration of the overwork and intellectual fatigue of school children. We are happy to think that with regard to this problem experimental psychology has already obtained appreciable results.

If we still lack the means to recognize the early signs of fatigue in a particular student, if especially we are only beginning to guess at some of the important laws which govern the hygiene of intellectual work, we at least already possess the means to study and evaluate the collective fatigue of a whole class. Consequently, when we so desire we can use this knowledge to insure a rational distribution of school work hours in accordance with the children's ages and their class level.

But all this is comparatively accessory to another matter which constitutes the core of teaching methods, that is to say the very form of that teaching. There are many ways of getting an idea across, or of

instilling a new habit. One can use the various sensory modalities —
sight, hearing, touch — or one can use speech. Some methods are good;
some are detestable.

Our universities have long been reproached for their excessive
reliance upon the oral method. It addresses itself uniquely to the verbal
function, turning every lesson into a language exercise, setting as the
goal of all education a well-learned lesson which can be recited. This is
a serious error. The goal of teaching is to develop satisfactory ways of
acting and thinking; it is also to turn these ways of acting and thinking
into habits which will permit a better adaptation of the individual to his
environment. The only value of school is as preparation for life; all
teaching is sterile which remains verbal, for verbalism is only symbol-
ism and life is not a mere word.

Another defect of university teaching is that it makes the student
passive; it turns him into a receptacle, like an urn, into which one pours
education. It is necessary that the student be active, that what is taught
stimulates him to responses which show a modification, a perfecting of
his behavior and which are a proof that his intelligence and character
were affected and improved as a result.

And above all, the last and gravest question raised by this study of
methods can be represented by an equation: let the left side of the
equation show the number of hours, days, years that a child spends in
school sitting on a bench; let the right side show the benefits derived
from school by the child. One must ask: "Was it worth it for him?
Do the acquired instruction and education compensate for the time
spent in school and the work done?" Clearly there would be much to
say about this, much to criticize. But this is not our domain and with
regret we set it aside. We are not dealing here with teaching methods, at
least in general; but from time to time we shall find it necessary to
make incursions into the analysis of methods, for it is difficult to set
up rigid boundaries between related questions.

3. Finally, having made the necessary distinctions and set up the
necessary limitations, let us talk about our chosen theme. We said
earlier that the third area pedagogy can be divided into is called "Children's aptitudes."

For it is a fact that, theoretically, a complete exposé of education
includes three subdivisions: What is being taught — the program. How
we teach — the method. Who is being taught — the child. We shall
therefore look at pedagogy as it relates to children and school children
— more particularly boys of six to fourteen years of age. We shall try to
find out who they are and what is involved in the art of getting to know
them. We shall show that our aim in the pursuit of this art is not to give
ourselves the charming pleasure of penetrating into their souls and of

20

playing around with their ideas and their emotions, but to discover their real aptitudes and make it possible to tailor education to their needs. This is one of the most neglected areas in education and I don't mind saying that many pedagogues would be surprised to hear that it exists.

In the hundred books published annually on education, one is hard put to find a single page on which individual differences in children are mentioned. For these poorly informed pedagogues the child is a negligible quantity. It seems to be taken for granted, *a priori,* that he is nothing other than a miniature man endowed with varying degrees of all adult faculties. A typical child is assumed to exist whom all children resemble, more or less. Thus, all existing differences are ignored, not only in children's characters or in the way they feel but also in the way they think and in their intellectual aptitudes. Many educators commit this error; they have in front of them a class composed of from forty to sixty pupils, sometimes more. At the time they dispense knowledge to their young audience, their attention is focused on the value of the teaching itself, viewed *in abstracto,* in the absolute. No thought is given to the quality of the children's receptivity, to the children's characters or aptitudes, or to the necessity of adapting their teaching to the needs and abilities of individual students.

Their class is a herd, the elements of which never become differentiated. All children are given the same education. All are treated in the same way: those who have a good memory, for instance, are treated the same as those who have a poor one. Educators give little thought to the individuals in their classes, and I was often surprised to observe that they either ignored their pupils' ages or considered the matter unimportant. If chance has placed a child of nine and a child of twelve side by side on the same bench, they will demand the same effort from both children, will administer the same punishment for the same error. This represents a very unfair application of the law which demands that justice be equal for all.

In relation to this I remember an experience which stands out in my memory because it proved to me that an excellent professor may be a mediocre observer. I asked a teacher one day to identify the most intelligent student in his class; he gave me the name of a twelve-year-old child. The average normal age for this class was ten, and had the designated pupil been normal in his intellectual development, he would not have been in the class but in a much higher one. He was actually two years below grade level in academic achievement and probably in intelligence. What a strange error not to take the child's age into account but to present this retardate — for that is what he was — as the most intelligent of forty children!

I'll give another example of the tendency of teachers to ignore individual differences in their students. It is a simple, easy-to-understand example, and it may come as a surprise that such an error could have been made. Many school children have visual or auditory deficiencies; it is understandable that they derive little benefit from teachings which they cannot perceive. Dr. Simon and I conducted a study in the schools of Paris. The vision of a large number of children was examined and many — more than 5 per cent — were found to have visual deficiency. Would you believe that in most cases the teachers were unaware of the problem? The students were sitting too far from the pulpit or from the blackboard to be able to hear or see correctly; but since, as a rule, children do not complain, the thought of getting these children closer to the pulpit or to the blackboard had never occurred to the teachers. I was able to intervene successfully and, thanks to Mr. Liard's cooperation, am assured that all elementary school teachers in the Paris school district conduct yearly pedagogic examinations of vision.

I shall end with another example related to the psychology of what may be called "the tail of classes." Each large class contains a certain number of students who are invariably failing exams and who derive little benefit from the teaching they are exposed to. They remain as unaffected by it as the beggars who warm up in winter in Le Louvre remain unaffected by the beauty of the Rembrandts. Nothing is more interesting than to study the psychology of this group of pupils. They must be examined individually and we must know why they occupy this inferior rank in the class. Is it due to low intelligence? To lack of character? Can their condition be improved? These questions are of great social significance and we must constantly strive to decrease the number of these failures so that they do not become permanent. But I wonder how many teachers have ever seriously studied these children and have tried to help them. How many have asked themselves: If these students do so poorly, could it be my fault as much as theirs?

I am convinced that some excellent teachers have been concerned about this problem. But I also know from experience that many do not see in it a question to be studied, a professional duty to be accomplished. They seem implicitly to admit that in a class where some students are first, some must be last; that it is a natural phenomenon, inevitable, and not the concern of teachers any more than the existence of rich and poor in society is. What an error again!

And since it is good always to give real, concrete, living examples, I shall describe what I observed about ten years ago in a provincial Teachers' College. My friend and collaborator Victor Henri and I were conducting an experiment on a class of student teachers. This class was not composed exclusively of brilliant subjects. The top students in the class had keen minds, but those who occupied the lowest rank were

22

truly dull individuals who would have been better behind a plow than in a professor's chair. The Inspecteur d'Academie told me about the deplorable reason for this state of affairs. The district was rich and included many chateaux. Intelligent young people who wanted to command good salaries preferred entering the service of aristocratic families to entering the teaching profession. Since it was very difficult to find prospective teachers, it was necessary not to be too demanding and to take what was available. It was on this class, composed of sixteen students, that I conducted a series of experiments during a whole winter, and it was then that an important fact became revealed to me. The ratings given the students by the director of the school were in agreement with the results of all my tests which resembled academic tasks and which demanded literary ability or the handling of general ideas. But certain subtests tapped quite different abilities : vision in space, for instance, or a particular kind of manual dexterity, or discrimination of small differences in sensation. In these trials we were not concerned with academic skills but with manual skills and practical life situations. Surprise! The poor students, those slow, dull-witted individuals, succeeded as well and even better than the top students on these empirical tasks, in spite of the fact that these tasks were of a rather high level of difficulty. And I understood then what an error it was to judge those individuals on the basis of tests which were not designed to evaluate their particular abilities, and especially to give them an education ill-suited to their intellectual type.

I hope to have said enough, if not to convince my readers, at least to have impressed upon them the idea that a problem which well deserves investigation may have been neglected. As for myself, twenty-five years of experimentation in schools have led me to believe that the most important task of teaching and education is the identification of children's aptitudes. The child's aptitudes must dictate the kind of education he will receive and the profession toward which he will be oriented. A study of the psychology of the individual must precede teaching.

Of course, a true statement carried to extremes may become false. Teaching should not be adapted uniquely to the aptitudes of each individual, for we are not alone on this earth ; we are living in an era, in an environment, among other individuals and in a world to which we must adapt ourselves. Adjustment is the sovereign law of life. Instruction and education, the goal of which is to facilitate this adjustment, must necessarily take two factors into account : the environment and its demands ; the human being and his resources.

It may happen that these factors are not entirely compatible and that a compromise is necessary. The problem is not a simple one. Some retarded children, for instance, find it hard to learn to read and reading is a chore for them. Their natural tendencies would direct them toward an entirely different domain, and if we looked only at their psychological make-up, we would teach them to handle the hammer rather than to handle a book. This would be good psychology, but very poor sociology. In our modern society the number of illiterates is becoming infinitely small. Reading and writing play such an important role, in large communities especially, that the illiterate is at a great disadvantage. Because of this, and whenever it is possible, it is necessary to insist that the retardate make the effort of learning to read, taking into consideration the environment in which he is going to live.

Some educators and psychologists have recently become impressed with the importance of individual differences. In a violent reaction against present-day routine, some of the most zealous ones have gone so far as to demand "customized schools" or to present "customized schools" as the educational ideal. The teaching in this kind of school would be so individualized as to take into account the physical, intellectual and moral personality of each student. If we demand so much, we shall obtain nothing. Public education can only be collective, presented by one teacher to several pupils at the same time. Collective is the opposite of individual; it is ready-made, not custom-made clothing. Collective teaching should not be rejected completely, for it has numerous advantages we cannot do without; without it there can be neither imitation, nor emulation, nor esprit de corps, and these are powerful stimulants leading to progress. We prefer some of the less radical solutions and we recommend the following. In the numerous schools where the law imposes the organization of parallel classes, it would be possible to consider the repartition of students in these classes according to their aptitudes. In some of them literature would be emphasized, in others it would be science, in others still it would be crafts. We have only given examples, but these examples should, of course, be carefully studied. This type of program is in fact the one which was implemented in the secondary schools with the advent of the cycle system. A similar system could be tried at the elementary school level. We could make sure that the repartition of pupils in classes is not done indiscriminately; that is to say, to satisfy the often blind wishes of students or their families. I believe that, without going against anybody's will, a well-informed teacher would be in a position to give useful advice, especially if he has made it a point to study the child's abilities very closely. Indeed, my carefully considered opinion is that we don't really need new ministerial regulations. What would be infinitely more useful would be for teachers at all levels not to remain systematically ignorant with regard to these questions of individual differences, to stop looking upon them with suspicion, to become interested in them and take them into consideration in teaching. A new spirit must prevail in our schools and this spirit must result from a rapprochement between the teacher

24

and his students. The administration can make this rapprochement easier by decreasing the number of overcrowded classrooms, for it is evident that a teacher who must teach sixty children cannot find the time to get to know them individually and loses interest in this type of study. To facilitate work, not to hamper it, not to make it impossible, is all one can reasonably ask from an intelligent administration. The rest depends on the educator's initiative. We would like to see informal discussions take place after class. We would like to see the teacher in the schoolyard during recess once in a while; we would like him to become a coach, an organizer of games; we would like his character, the sympathy he inspires, to be such that he is often chosen as referee. And most of all, we would like him to inspire confidence so that children would feel free to confide in him if need be. These practices are widespread among priests and among British professors. It is also much to be desired that the teacher learn about the psychology of individual differences; that he know the methods used; that he be adept at the art of asking questions without making suggestions; and that he be familiar with the most common types of child mentalities so as to be able to classify his students whenever feasible, for it is with the help of these classifications that the best diagnoses are made. And finally, what must be asked from teachers is that they adopt firmly the attitude of experimenters when it is necessary. We encourage them to administer, when in doubt, some of these mental tests which reveal an aptitude, an ability. In the course of this work, when we describe in detail some useful and practical mental tests, we shall also list the numerous rules which must be observed if they are going to be used wisely, either for experimentation or for interpretation after experimentation. It will be readily understood that this new role pre-supposes a new way of thinking, a new kind of training, tending to make the professor something he rarely is : he is a teacher; he must also become an observer. These are two very different attitudes, and experience has taught me how very independent they are from each other. I have met excellent educators who endlessly created innovative methods of teaching and had good control of their classes. The progress they helped their students make educationally and even intellectually cannot be denied. But these teachers were not observers; they could tell us almost nothing about the history, the aptitudes, the character of their pupils, and consequently what they knew remained their personal property, was uncommunicable. Seguin, the famous professor of the retarded, was one of these teachers. He wrote books which contain nothing. I have known others, also with keen minds, who participated in my research in observation but interrupted it constantly by ill-timed interventions which proved to me they had not understood the difference between teaching and observing. When the task was only to see, to observe, to judge, that is to verify a fact or a state of affairs, they were obsessed with the need to straighten out, to correct, to teach. They resembled those examiners who, instead of being satisfied with asking questions, constantly want to lecture to the examinee.

As we have seen, the training needed to be a good observer is very different from that needed to be a professor. Let us add that the former type of training cannot be improvised and, especially, it cannot be acquired uniquely by listening to lectures. I would even admit — in a low voice — that the often excellent lectures given almost everywhere these days about pedagogy, which aim to enhance its prestige in the minds of many people who are bored by it or who look upon it with contempt, appear to me to have a serious drawback : they stress the lesson learned and language development, something which is already the plague of education. It would be much better, in my opinion, to give object lessons, to offer practical experience in pedagogy or psychology of individual differences, which would put student teachers in the presence of real problems and would enable them to study a child's mental characteristics and to identify the methods to be applied to him. To this practical pedagogical work I would add another type of help : pedagogical consultations given by specialists as examples for teaching. These consultations appear to me to be so important that I have published a few in this volume.[1] Along this line of thought, I am afraid everything remains to be done, but certainly everything *will* be done. It is imperative. The children's welfare depends upon it. My only aim in writing this book is to foster the development of this movement.

1. I might add that the Pedagogical Laboratory which I created four years ago in a Paris elementary school, Rue Grange-aux-Belles, where the director of the school, Mr. Vaney, has been my faithful and conscientious collaborator, is open liberally to those who desire to be given pedagogic consultations about particular children. I take this opportunity to thank all those who have facilitated our research in experimental psychology in this environment, and more particularly my friends Mr. Bedorez, Directeur de l'Enseignement Primaire de la Seine, and Mr. Belot, Inspecteur Primaire.

CHAPTER TWO

The child in school

I. The Criterion of a Good Education

When talking about the education, the instruction and the formation of the mind, one must never lose sight of the fact that : (1) all human activity is subject to a sovereign law — that which governs the adaptation of the individual to his environment; and (2) the aim of the education given young people is to facilitate this adaptation. The value of education can only be determined by answering the paramount question : Has the individual's capacity for adjustment been improved? This is our criterion of pedagogy. Let us add that in order to apply this criterion correctly to a teaching situation, it is very important to take into account both the individual's welfare and the welfare of the society to which he belongs. In order for education to be judged effective it must not only increase the contribution of a particular individual, but also enable society to profit from that increase in contribution. If this were not so, such pernicious or even criminal teachings as swindling and thievery would have to be considered good so long as the training was effective in forming students of such caliber that they would never be caught by police and would all make fortunes.

In our social milieu we cannot judge the value of anything without taking equally into consideration the welfare both of the individual and of society. With the acceptance of this principle, it follows that a study is necessary to decide if an education program has been well conceived, if the teaching methods used are to be retained, and if both the program and the method have been well adapted to the students' aptitudes. This study should follow up students in life, to find out what has become of them, appraise their condition and compare their performance with that of other students who have received either different training or no training at all, for the effectiveness of schooling is judged on the basis of post-school performance. Schools have no other reasons to exist. Their merit cannot be established — or can only be incompletely established — on the basis of examination results. One must have lost sight of the overall picture to see prizes and high grades as the goal of education. The error is often made by school children. They know

27

hardly anything about life yet, and for them life is school. They think only about adjusting to the school situation, which they see as an end in itself rather than as a preparation. When they are given a lesson to learn, they view it as a recitation exercise; they think that when the lesson has been recited and the grade obtained, everything can be forgotten. They think homework is done to merit rewards and that the only consequence of being lazy is getting the dunce hat or being kept after school.

It is only much later that the child's mind reaches beyond the school walls and that he thinks about the useful but long-range consequences of the education he has received. This broadening of his horizon is a natural law of mental development. I often wonder if there has not been an untimely arrest of this natural development in many teachers. Are they not also viewing school as a self-sufficient environment and thinking that students are made for schools instead of schools for students? And are not the parents from certain social classes laboring under the same illusion when they insist on a diploma for their children because it represents a means of distinction between the bourgeoisie and the proletariat? Do they not feel that the diploma as such is endowed with a mysterious virtue?

It is true that from time to time some critics ironically adopt the opposite view and deny the importance of school success. According to them, the worst students in a class are the ones who succeed best in life. Examples are readily given. Everyone knows the story of Merimée, the brilliant novelist, who was once a dunce. Young Darwin was also called a dunce. A short time ago Maurice Donnay used his charming and malicious verve to sing the glory of the one who had been twenty-third in his class. But had he really the right to ridicule secondary education in this way? He told me that his school years were spent in a dream-like state in which he thought about very few things. He misrepresents himself; by his own admittance he won two prizes while at the *lycée,* one in physical education and one in catechism. Is this not proof of a perfectly harmonious development of body and of soul?

The truth cannot be sought in a happy medium between these two extreme opinions. The latter, which shows contempt for the education provided by the schools and for the schools' system of evaluation, is pure fantasy, since it is based only on anecdotes. We do not wish for a complete reversal of opinion as such. Rather we hope, first of all, that the problem will be examined from the simple point of view that school has value only as preparation for life; and, second, that the merit of this preparation will not be judged on the basis of approximations or chance observations. We are surprised to find that follow-up studies regarding the type of education given and the eventual fate of school children are lacking. Statistical data or, to express it more accurately, a serious and in-depth study complemented by a statistical analysis should have been made long ago to make it possible for us to see if the education given is effective or if it should be modified. Generally the most important job is the one we think about least; but it also happens that because it is so necessary, it eventually imposes itself on our attention. This can be seen now. The need for control that we have discussed is becoming apparent. On one hand, what is referred to as a "crisis of apprenticeship" has erupted at the elementary school level and it raises questions about the value of the school curriculum; on the other hand, technical schools have been created for some time now, as well as courses, workshops and a thousand different means of giving the young apprentice needed professional training. These have not always been successful, it is true; errors have often been made and the schools, financed at great expense, have turned out civil servants instead of workers. But it does not matter. If the remedy has not yet been found, we at least have become conscious of the problem and have understood that in order to judge or evaluate schools we must look at real life. Post-school educational programs, too — for which much has already been spent and which have also so often missed their goal — prove that the desirability of evaluating education as preparation for life is understood. Little by little those generous but too schematic ideas which state that instruction is good in itself and that reading is effective moral teaching will be given up. It is becoming understood that instruction is only a means, a means which must be used to improve the adaptation of the individual to his environment; consequently, there is no type of instruction which in itself can be recommended as the unique truth. Instruction, being a means, must vary with the individual, his temperament, and the economic world in which he will struggle for life. Studies of adjustment will be substituted more and more for the kind of abstract study of programs now being made, and instruction will be modified in view of the well-defined goals to be attained.

Having no other resource than myself, I tried to undertake on a small scale the investigation I recommend so highly, and the results have shown me that the problem to be solved is not as simple as I first believed. I contacted a rural teacher who had been teaching in the same village for twenty-five years and who knew every one of its inhabitants. At my request this teacher, Mr. Limosin, set up a list of one hundred former students, of whom the first half had graduated from grammar school (passed the comprehensive final examination), and the second half had not. He found out what had become of these former students since they had left school, and he located them on a scale ranging from 1 tc 10 according to their social situation and their degree of success. A village official also rated the former students, locating them on the scale independently of the teacher, and although their evaluations differed by one or two points from time to time, they gave essentially the same results. The students who had passed the examination received an average rating of 7, which indicated that their social condition was good; while the other students' average ratings ranged from 3 to 5, which meant that their social condition ranged from mediocre to bad.

My first thought when I received these results was that they were all to the credit of the primary school; it seemed that in the small village studied, primary school provided an excellent preparation for life, since the students who had graduated were those who had fought most successfully in life. After thinking about it awhile, I feel less sure of the accuracy of this conclusion and now believe it to be very exaggerated. What appears to me to be proven is that one succeeds in life because of three important factors : health, intelligence, and character. We might add to this a fourth factor : a little money. It seems to me that in school, as in life, the same qualities of health, intelligence and character must be exhibited to insure success. If the wealth of children and parents does not enter the picture directly, it nevertheless constitutes an undeniable advantage for the student, since wealthier parents have more time to devote to the supervision of their children's studies, feed them better, provide them with better hygiene, and also collaborate more closely with the school than poor parents. It can therefore be concluded from this that the school environment and the socio-economic environment are much alike ; they are subject to the same influences and those who succeed in adapting to the first also have a good chance of adapting to the second.

This is what seems to me to have been demonstrated by our little study. But I believe one would overshoot the mark if one were to conclude that the school, as it is presently organized with its programs and methods, constitutes a good preparation for life. Such a conclusion is an entirely different matter. The acquisition of an education by those who succeed in life is a proof of intelligence and character ; it is not a proof that the education given them is the best viaticum in the struggle for life. In order to verify the validity of this distinction, let us imagine an elementary school where a thoroughly irrelevant curriculum would be imposed on the children ; they would be taught Hebrew or Chinese, for instance. It is still the most intelligent children, those who later will succeed best, who will obtain their degree in Chinese, but this is not proof that this particular curriculum will be very useful to these French children. One understands, then, that one must analyse this problem in order to see things more clearly. Such a study should consist of asking former students what was most useful to them in the curriculum, what they have judged useless, and what they regret was not included. It should also compare the post-school achievement of students who have been exposed to different types of education. Why has such a study never been conducted in Museums or in the Schools of Behavioral Sciences?

II. The Measurement of Achievement

We are forced at the present time to evaluate students on the basis of the educational program they have been exposed to. We therefore view this teaching and these programs as an end which cannot be argued about, and we must consider as best the student who has been able to assimilate the most knowledge. Let us look especially at the form examinations take, and let us see how the questions are chosen and how they are presented. Many reforms need to be introduced in this area and everyone has had occasion to verify the observations I am going to report. If one studies closely the examination procedures in a school of law or medicine, one is amazed at the great difference in demand made by different teachers giving an identical examination. Some are indulgent — perhaps out of kindness, perhaps out of indifference or skepticism — and they seem to have no other goal than to help the unfortunate candidate who is getting bogged down; they will flunk him only if they can do absolutely nothing else. There are others, however, whose goal seems to be to flunk the candidate; the examination is a real struggle and they stop only when the adversary is down. Still others have formed a personal opinion about a particular topic and want the student to guess the idea or even the word which they have in mind, a thing which would only be possible through some telepathic miracle. The result of all this is that questions asked in identical examinations have such different levels of difficulty that the success of a candidate resembles a lottery. I remember having followed with great interest several examinations in anatomy. Some examiners passed students who were little more than mediocre; other examiners flunked mercilessly much more competent subjects. An examiner's personality, his mood at the time, his heartburns, the presence of a competent colleague who listens to him and judges him, all these factors can affect the manner in which the candidate is interrogated and graded. It is noteworthy that, in general, people who specialize in one field are very strict and demanding with regard to this particular field; an anatomist and a surgeon demand more achievement in anatomy than a chemist or a clinician giving the same exam. A Romanist is more merciless in Roman Law than an economist. I'll also add that the candidate's personal presentation can be an asset or a drawback depending on whether he inspires sympathy or antipathy. Someone confided to me one day that in oral exams a generally objective examiner will not be so, in fact, with a candidate whose face appeals to him.

We attempted to show in our pedagogy laboratory that all these errors and failures are not inevitable and that it is possible to build tests which are measurements of achievement. My associate Mr. Vaney, assigned to the task, worked out a whole series of examinations which permit measuring the level of achievement from age to age of students seven to twelve years old. This method is applicable only at the elementary school level because our laboratory is located in an elementary school and because, up to now, secondary education programs have remained closed to our experimental psychology research. But it would be relatively easy to adapt the method to secondary education, or to any other type of education, since the principle underlying the method would remain the same. This principle can be summed up in the following two propositions:

1. The examination material is not left to chance, to the caprice of inspiration or to the surprises reserved by idea association; it is composed of a system of questions in which the contents do not vary and the level of difficulty is graded.

2. The child's level of achievement is not evaluated *in abstracto* as good, mediocre, bad, according to a subjective scale of values. It is compared to the average achievement level of children of the same age and the same socio-economic background who attend the same schools.

The examination results can be immediately translated, without commentary of any sort, into a rating which means that the particular child's level of achievement is at grade level, at 6 months, 1 year, 2 years above grade, or at 6 months, 1 year, 2 years or more below grade.

This rating system is so effective that, after having used it to measure the level of academic achievement, we extended its use to the measurement of intelligence, muscle strength, physical development, in brief to everything which can be measured in a student.

We do not intend to give in this book the many details which must be known to use the instrument we have just described. It will be sufficient to demonstrate its feasibility by reproducing the very simple table, called an "Achievement Scale," which serves as a base to the procedure (see p. 33). It describes the level of performance which can reasonably be expected from a student, for it has been attained by the average school child of the same age.

The children are examined in three academic areas: reading, spelling, arithmetic. It would be possible, even easy, we believe, to add typical questions on history, geography, science, and to set up composition exercises of different levels of difficulty.

1. *Reading.* In order to characterize reading we felt the need to set up more varied and especially more precise levels than those which would consist of stating that a student reads well, passably or badly. These levels, created for the first time by our collaborator Mr. Vaney, are so well differentiated that, after a little practice, two different observers evaluating the same pupil obtain identical results. Moreover, they

Designed by Mr. Vaney for Use in the Paris Primary Schools.

Child's age	Reading level	Sample arithmetic problems	Spelling	
			Sample sentence	Number of errors
6 to 7	Sub-syllabic or syllabic	You have 19 apples in a basket. If you take 6 of them out, how many apples are left in the basket?	The	16
7 to 8	Hesitating	You have 59 pennies. You give away 8 of them. How many are left?	pretty little	11
8 to 9	Hesitating to fluent	A box contains 604 oranges. 58 oranges are sold. How many are left?	girls are	8
9 to 10	Fluent	7 yards of material are needed to make a dress. How many dresses can be made with 89 yards of material and what will be the length of the left-over material?	studying the plants	6
10 to 11	Fluent to expressive	A worker earns 250 dollars during the month of February which has 28 days. He spends 195 dollars. How much did he save each day?	they gathered yesterday.	4

have the advantage of revealing to us what the exact pattern of development — the psychogenesis — of a learned act is, and this is what we shall explain later. Three main levels were distinguished: syllabic reading, which consists of pausing between each syllable; hesitating reading, characterized by unwarranted stops after each word or group of words; finally, fluent reading, which contains no other stops than the ones required by punctuation and which constitutes a perfectly correct reading performance. After analysing these expressions and thinking about them awhile, we understand that they focus on the intimate reading mechanism. Reading does not consist merely of perceiving written signs and making appropriate articulations as the signs are being perceived; the operation is more complex and demands greater automatism. We do not read aloud what we perceive, but we articulate that which we have just perceived; and while it is being articulated, the following articulation is already being prepared by the next perceiving act. This is what permits uninterrupted reading. In order for two different acts — perception of a word and articulation of another — to take place simultaneously, practice must have rendered these acts easy and it must be possible to perform them with a minimum of attention. It is precisely this practice which is lacking in beginners. They are more or less forced to perceive a first word, then to articulate it, and it is only when the first word is articulated that they perceive the second word and articulate it, and so on. By labeling these different levels of reading "syllabic," "hesitating," or "fluent," one throws light upon the necessary steps involved in the acquisition of this skill and one can identify the precise level of reading ability of a particular student.

Diagnostic requirements made other distinctions necessary, since the above levels of reading are not sufficient to deal with all the different cases encountered and needing to be recorded. With the methods used today, approximately one year is necessary to get a six-year-old child to the correct syllabic stage. Before this time the child knows the alphabet and may even know how to spell, but he does not yet syllabify or, if he does, he makes many errors. As a matter of fact, one finds children who constantly make mistakes when they are at the hesitating or even at the fluent stage of reading. These students — and one finds many of them — have a short attention span or have been poorly taught from the beginning. It is almost impossible to understand what they read aloud. In order to express the idea that a particular child hasn't reached the correct syllabic stage of reading development, we needed a special term. We proposed the expression "sub-syllabic" reading, a very global term which will consequently be appropriate to describe many varied and odd cases characterized by inadequate syllabication.

Also, fluent reading isn't the most perfect form of reading which can be attained. To read aloud is an art. Such masters of this art as

Legouvé have demonstrated the infinity of its nuances. One does not read only, one tells; and when one knows how to tell, one isn't satisfied with pausing in the correct places according to punctuation and meaning, but one modifies one's voice; intonations are given to it which are in relation to the idea and the feeling expressed in the reading material. This is called "expressive" reading and is very superior to "fluent" reading, which, by definition, remains monotonous and indifferent to sentence meaning. We showed in the table that beginning at age ten, children should be able to read expressively, but this is a rule which suffers many exceptions. Although "expression" is an art which can be taught in the same way "fluent reading" is taught, some children learn it more easily than others. Some tend to read expressively even at the hesitant stage of reading; others never reach this point. It is for this reason that we meet people in life whose voice intonations are personal, in tune, capable of nuances, while others speak without intonations or with heavy or faulty ones.

Ordinarily, when we hear a child read expressively, we tend to think of him as intelligent, for we realize that he understands and feels what he reads. However, this can be misleading, for expressiveness is more an artistic quality. It is innate, although it can be acquired. It is more indicative of creative ability than of intelligence, although it is more often found in the intelligent than in the dull individual.

2. *Arithmetic.* Knowledge in arithmetic is evaluated by means of short problems; our table gives only one sample per age. Looking over the problems, one may be tempted to object that they are too succinct, too fragmentary to represent the whole of arithmetic knowledge.

In the first place, one may ask why we always present problems to be solved and never give operations to be worked out? Also, why limit ourselves to subtraction problems for the first two school years? Are not students learning addition and multiplication as well during these years? Later are they not taught about the metric system and fractions? How is it that the table gives no examples of any of these?

Such a rigorous selection was made only after extensive study, and I remember that at first Mr. Vaney had prepared a very long series of problems and operations for each age group. Then it was decided to sacrifice the operations for two reasons: First, they are implied in the problems and would therefore be superfluous; also, operations can be learned and done automatically by students incapable of understanding their meaning and of using them appropriately. I have seen students who compute correctly an enormous eight-figure multiplication but who miss so simple a problem as that referred to in the the table as "the orange crate problem." This is the result of unintelligent teaching, that is, teaching conceived on the basis of a deplorable educational ideal, and we must track down and eliminate this teaching in pure automatism every time we come across it.

This was our first objection; following is the second. Why do we not try to test each student's ability in every area of arithmetic? Why do we not try to evaluate his mastery of addition, multiplication, division, the metric system, fractions? It is because an examination should be short; it should be limited to a small number of tests chosen in such a way that they represent the entire subject matter area. Careful study revealed that operations involving augmentation, like addition and multiplication, are more easily learned and more thoroughly mastered than those involving diminution, like subtraction and division. It is in the performance of the latter operations that the young student is more likely to show signs of slowness, weakness and embarrassment. As soon as a pupil is able to divide correctly, it is useless to study the way he multiplies; there can be little wrong with it since multiplication is implied in the division.

While the child is busy doing his arithmetic work, discreet observation on the part of the teacher reveals interesting little facts. We see from the way the child has put down the problem whether or not he has developed good work habits. Thoughtlessness and lack of attention are revealed in numerous ways. They can be exposed in the omission of carry-over or in errors made in writing down the problem. A particular pupil to whom you dictate the number "604" may write down the number "608." The part played by instruction and that played by intelligence in the working out of problems can be clearly identified. There are children who understand the problem given to them for solution but who don't know how to perform the necessary operations. In the "dress problem," for instance (see table, p. 33), a division is required. They may not know how to divide, but it occurs to them to add the number 7 to itself as often as needed to obtain 89 and then count the number of times they have had to add; they add instead of dividing and it amounts to the same thing. Some other children, however, do not understand the problem but know how to do the operations. Unable to decide which type of operation is needed, they try to guess and choose multiplication; for the "dress problem" they will multiply 7 by 89 and obtain a very large sum, which will not even surprise them. The arithmetic examination, therefore, sometimes gives insight into the pupil's intelligence, his methodology, his power of concentration.

3. *Spelling.* Our examination is concluded with a spelling test, a dictation. We know today that dictation is of no value when it comes to learning to spell but that it is an excellent means of control. Short sentences — as short as possible — have been artfully constructed and made to contain a large number of grammatical hurdles. In prior stud-

ies conducted on thousands of children, the number of errors made by pupils in each age group was determined for each sentence. The average was laboriously calculated. The figures reproduced in our table show the results obtained by the simplest of calculations : Every error involving a rule represents one point ; every error of application, one point also ; no more than two points are ever taken away for any one word. We give a sample of our dictations ; it is meant to be only a sample and this one is a little short. If we want to obtain a true measure of spelling ability, it is wise to give at least three dictations. This is also true for arithmetic problems.

It will be readily understood that once the entire examination has been completed, the results obtained will make it possible to establish the student's performance level. This performance may be at grade level, below or above grade level, one or several years. A nine-year-old's performance may be equivalent to that of an eight-year-old or a ten-year-old child. In the first case he is one year below grade level ; in the second case he is one year above grade level. All this is simple, clear, logical ; and let us take special note of the fact that the results are obtained by means of tests which are not long. The examination takes no more than ten minutes per child. It is a little longer than the ordinary *baccalauréat* examination which, when the number of candidates is large, may be completed in five minutes ; but really, the evaluation of a student's level of achievement made with our procedure appears to me to be more significant.

III. What Service Will the Exact Measurement of Achievement Render?

In my collaborators' hands and in my own, this method of measuring achievement has been found effective. We have used it hundreds of times, either on a whole class for such tests as arithmetic and spelling which can be administered to a group, or on an individual child in the case of the reading test. We needed such an instrument mainly to differentiate normal from abnormal children enlisted in primary schools ; the goal was to identify the retarded subjects and to put them in special classes. We had first tried simply to give a definition of abnormality, thinking this would be sufficient for school principals to identify those of their pupils who were retarded. But our definition was too vague and the use which was made of it surprised us. While one principal claimed he didn't have a single abnormal child in his school, the principal of another school nearby counted fifty of them in his. To do away with all those fantasies, we decided to adopt the definition of abnormality used in Belgium and to establish the following rule : An abnormal child is one who shows a retardation of at least three years in his studies, provided this retardation cannot be explained by frequent absences from school. Because of the rapid use which can be made of it and because of its precision, the procedure which we have just described has been tremendously useful to us in the measurement of educational retardation.

We have used this procedure in so many different circumstances and it was found to be so reliable that we do not hesitate to recommend it to anyone who wishes to know precisely whether or not a child is regular in his educational development and is progressing at a normal pace.

But it must be clear to everyone that its precision is only that included in and tolerated by moral phenomena; educational development cannot be measured exactly in the way size or weight is. A child's ability to concentrate, his memory, his presence of mind are unstable qualities which do not appear to be always in the same state. One day the child may make ten errors in a particular spelling test; the next day he may make twenty errors in an equivalent one. One day he may effortlessly find the solution to a problem he was unable to solve the day before. Are we not also subject, we adults, to these fluctuations, to making these errors? All the more reason to expect them in young people whose psychic organization is still so very unstable. The examination is not meant for — and must not result in — the crystallization of the child at one particular stage. He remains variable as his nature wants him to be. But at least one irrelevant variable is eliminated from the testing situation, that originating from the examiner and his more or less subjective approach to the task of testing.

I think, as Mr. Vaney does, that this same procedure could be used widely in elementary school examinations. These comprehensive examinations which terminate elementary education have the same defects all tests have which are left to the discretion of a judge. They vary in level of difficulty and as a result of trivial incidents which should never enter the picture and which lead to error. In educational journals I have seen problems and dictations which were presented at various sessions of primary school comprehensive exams. The level of difficulty of these exams was not uniform. The selection of the particular dictations and problems was guesswork, and this is a very approximate and defective way of proceeding. If this arbitrary, useless, and even unjust testing is to be stopped, it is necessary to standardize tests by using a procedure similar to the one we have described earlier. And why shouldn't the *baccalauréat* exam — the one called "the scandal of the university" — be subjected to the same standardization procedure? What is good for primary education cannot be bad for secondary education.

There is another possible application I am thinking about.

38

We are very concerned these days about the large number of illiterates found among army recruits. The proportion is thought to be no lower than 6 per cent. It comes as a surprise, since we didn't expect the laws regarding compulsory education to be so widely disregarded. This means they are not seriously sanctioned. There is now an attempt to react to this state of affairs by evaluating exactly the new recruits' level of educational development at the time of recruitment. An examination similar to ours would seem ideal for this purpose. This will be the only way to offer the candidate any guarantee and to make an effective selection. After the selection it would be good to give some consideration to sanction. In our opinion — to mention it in passing — if the length of the illiterates' military service was extended by a few months, the number of illiterate recruits would decrease as if by magic. Should the prolongation of this military service prove too costly for the War Department, it would be easy to decrease the expense involved by granting furloughs and reduction in length of service to reward those recruits who have demonstrated their proficiency as military personnel.

Let's go further. When a little method is introduced into an examination, this examination is changed into a procedure which has acquired a degree of precision; now precision, when allied to accuracy, has infinite and unpredictable consequences which astonish when they occur. What this means is that control is suddenly introduced in domains where little thought had previously been given to it. Do we wish to be given proof of its usefulness? Each day some teacher creates an original method for teaching arithmetic, spelling, languages; if he has some authority and some support — especially political support — he succeeds in having his method assessed publicly. But how is it judged? How are the results evaluated? Always in an approximate way. Its acceptance or rejection depends upon the system of checks and balances provided by the optimism of some and the denigrating tendencies of others. If fashion becomes involved, it acts as a wave which lifts the new method to heaven; but little by little the wave recedes and what was viewed as a marvel is completely forgotten. What has become of the Jacottot method and so many others?

The measurement of educational achievement would give pedagogy the control it needs, the control without which we cannot see clearly, without which we are aware of nothing so that we grant equal recognition to good and bad methods alike. The whole future of pedagogy as a precise and truly useful science depends on the introduction of this reform.

There is another area for possible application. Our contemporaries do not lean heavily toward discipline these days. Professors no longer accept their superiors' remarks with exaggerated deference; they discuss them. They were almost encouraged to do so when new regulations gave the teacher the right to read the comments written by the Inspector on his record. If the teacher disagrees with the evaluation and feels it is unfair, the Inspector will most likely be of a different opinion. How can the truth be established? How can we know who is right? Today, hierarchical superiority can no longer be accepted as an argument which cannot be contested. A teacher's effectiveness is measured, among other things, by his students' progress. The teacher accused of lacking in pedagogic competence can answer: "Look at my students. Measure their achievement and if you find that it is inferior to the average obtained in equivalent classes, then I shall accept your criticisms." The teacher who thus asserts himself is absolutely right; and to encourage him to do so is not to foster lack of discipline.

I had occasion to observe how easy it is to evaluate a teacher's professional competence with the help of this particular method. It occurred to me one day to have a simple sentence dictated to students in the twelve different classes of an elementary school. I took the students' work home with me to correct it and I calculated the percentage of errors for each class. Then I visited the principal.

"Tell me," I said directly, "are you satisfied with all your teachers?"

"Ah!" he exclaimed, raising his arms to heaven. "What a question. I have one who is my despair. For three years I have been asking that he be transferred. But nothing doing. Nobody wants him. It is unfair, for I feel each should take turns and..."

"Isn't this teacher the one in class number 7?"

The principal looked surprised. I had guessed right. The percentage of spelling mistakes in this class was greater than that of class 6, which was a parallel class; it was even greater than that of class 8, which was composed of younger children. This was sufficient information to make a diagnosis. I didn't know this teacher; I had never met him. The undeniable proof was there, written in the children's work. It is all the more important that this diagnosis be made, as the harm caused students by a bad teacher is much more serious than one may think. He is harming not only one child or two but forty or fifty; he is making them lose not just a day or a week but a whole year. They may not only make no progress during that year but also acquire bad habits involving laziness which can be retained over several successive years. This seems unbelievable, yet it is a fact. I made this painful observation by studying a graph which the director of a school made at my request to show the prolonged effect of bad teaching. Thanks to the system of parallel classes, it was possible to trace the influence of bad teachers during several successive years.

Let us summarize. The method which consists of measuring the level of achievement of school children has three main advantages: It reveals each pupil's true level of achievement by making examinations more objective. It permits the evaluation of a teacher's professional competence if that competence is being questioned by a superior. It provides a means of assessing new pedagogic methods which are often introduced into educational practice without prior evaluation. Are these advantages not important ones?

IV

I now suppose it to be a well established fact that a student can be retarded in his educational development. The verification of this fact must be the starting point of a new study. We are not making sterile measurements here or useless descriptions. We want above all to be practical and to be of assistance to the child. It is not sufficient to note that a problem exists; it is necessary, as soon as the problem has been exposed, to look for the remedy. Like medicine, pedagogy implies both a diagnosis and a treatment. The diagnosis has been made; the child must be treated.

In the handling of such a case, group testing is out of place. The time for collective examination is over and individual studies are in order. When it has been established that a child is behind in his educational development, this child must be taken aside and his case must be analysed. We must see how his lack of progress can be explained, for instance, or why he constantly makes the same kind of error. And when an apparent cause has been found, we must look for the most effective way of dealing with it.

It is with this idea in mind that we are going to set up the plan for this book. We must express ourselves very clearly — a moral duty for anyone involved in pedagogy — and the best way to achieve this is to begin by stating our intentions. To help clarify our views, let us suppose that we are in the presence of a child who is constantly last in his class. In a class composed of thirty-five students he is often last and occasionally next to last. Since he never occupies a rank higher than this, he is what is called a "dunce." This book will not be devoted to dunces only. Many other children, even the most intelligent ones, need pedagogic help, as we shall see later in more detail; for however much a student may progress, he can almost always be helped to progress even more after he has been studied closely. The dunce is for us only an example but a typical one.

As soon as we extend our research a little, we realize that the reasons for school failure vary widely from child to child. This makes it necessary to study about a hundred dunces in order to become aware of the many factors which can lead to educational retardation. We list below some of the important areas to be investigated:

1. The child's physical over- or underdevelopment.

2. Some pathological condition such as adenoids, anemia, tuberculosis, neurasthenia, or the beginning of a mental illness, etc.

3. Sensory organs deficiency; more particularly, visual or auditory deficiency.

4. Insufficient intellectual development. The child does not understand; he is lacking in intelligence.

5. Poor memory. The child understands but does not remember.

6. Difficulty in dealing with the aridity of abstract and general ideas; with good ability for practical achievement and manual skills.

7. A temporary disorientation produced by some event in his life; he may have changed schools or teachers, for instance, or he may have been placed in a class unsuited to his needs, or finally, the rapport between the child and the teacher may be poor.

8. Accentuated apathy which, strictly speaking, constitutes laziness. This is inertia, lack of taste or enthusiasm for intellectual work, or insensitiveness to ordinary stimulants to activity.

9. Character instability in various forms.

10. Lack of discipline, that is to say, instability aggravated by feelings of hostility toward the teacher.

11. Finally, let us note the often important influence of the family. It should collaborate with the work of the school, collaborating at one and the same time materially, intellectually and morally. Poor families, especially, often fail to carry out this duty.

The concrete facts which were revealed to us in the course of experimentation can be summarized as follows: When looking for the causes of deficiency in a child, examine his physical condition, the functioning of his sensory organs, his intelligence, his memory, his aptitudes, and his character. These will be the titles of the next chapters.

CHAPTER THREE

The child's body

I. Why It Is Useful to Know about a Child's Physical Development

The problem of the search for causes discussed in the previous chapter leads us to talk first about the children's physiological condition — about their health and their physical development. When a child is unsuccessful in his schoolwork; when he allows other children his age to get ahead of him; when he makes no intellectual effort; when he appears not to understand the lessons; or finally, when, at a certain age, a pronounced change in his personality occurs and he becomes presumptuous, conceited, undisciplined, unbearable, or else sad, taciturn, negligent, a physiological exam must be given to determine if his poor performance could be due to a physical inability to work.

Let us first clarify our thoughts about this idea of "physical incapacity," because this term has often been used to include many very different things, for instance, the state of health and muscular strength. When a person is very muscular we tend to conclude that this person is also healthy. While in general there is a relationship between muscular development and health, it is important to realize that "health" implies a number of physical qualities which are related to neither muscular strength nor corporal development, which are distinct from it theoretically and which can be independent of it practically.

By state of health we shall mean the synthesis of four main qualities:

1. *The absence of morbid predispositions,* such as predisposition to cancer, tuberculosis, to mention only the most dangerous.

2. *The absence of actual ailments, acute or chronic, or the consequences of an earlier chronic ailment.* The only example which needs be given, to expand on this commentary, is that of consequences; let's cite the paralysis in infants which can follow convulsions or the bony deformation which results from scrofulous diathesis.

3. *Tolerance of abuse.* This is the very definition of health. Well-regulated, wise living is not a strain on the organism. Various kinds of indiscretions are a test of its real strength and of its stability. When an

individual eats or drinks too much, when he has to stay up a whole night without any rest, or when he has to take a long, tiresome walk, the way the organism tolerates the extra load and repairs the damage done by it is an indicator of the quality of health. When the organism is not under strain, the degree of health is very difficult to establish even for a physician, since objective signs are lacking in most cases.

4. *Longevity.* Longevity appears to be distinct, to a certain extent, from the qualities described above, and it is generally the consequence of hereditary influence.

As opposed to the state of health, physical strength results from two main categories of factors: *The degree of physical development* (size, weight, and other anatomical measurements) and *the quantity of work an individual is able to produce in a given amount of time.* Here also certain distinctions are desirable. In motility we distinguish skill, speed, grace, and strength. Strength, in turn, must be examined in two ways: first, from the point of view of the maximum amount of strength which can be exerted at a given moment; second, from the point of view of the amount of time the effort can be sustained or shows resistance to fatigue.

Although we have analysed it and have shown the number, the variety, and the complexity of qualities included under the title " physical strength," it is desirable to add that, in practice, it may be useful to look at physical strength as a whole. For in general when children are tall, when their weight is adequate, when they have a vigorous musculature, they are in good health. And the surest, the most expedient way to evaluate the state of health of a group of children is still to measure their physical strength. The procedure would be criticizable if it were applied to a single particular child; it becomes absolutely legitimate when used on a whole group.

When referring to children's physical condition, we shall speak of the presence or absence of strength as vigor or feebleness, respectively.

Let us first talk about the state of health. We shall say only a few words, since this type of study is not part of our domain. We are not involved with medicine here but with psychological pedagogy. The study of an individual's health is the work of the physician not the teacher. However, since the teacher is always present in class and has an opportunity to observe the child over a great period of time, he is in a position to note and to report many things which may have escaped the physician's attention. Research conducted with the collaboration of Inspector Lacabe on the physical and intellectual condition of pupils in the lower fifth of classes has shown that the failure of many children can be explained by poor health. Researchers often sent notes such as the ones following:

This 8-year-old child appears drowsy, dull, in poor physical condition; he was not able to answer a single question; irreproachable from the point of view of discipline, he remains inactive during recess, sad and shy. His height is 4 years below average for his age. He appears sickly, skinny, feeble. His family lives in misery and pays absolutely no attention to his work.

This 10-year-old girl, who is 2 years below grade level, is physically very active... but is very sickly. In 6 months she was absent from school 80 times. Social circle: misery.

When we find a child who is sickly, who has no strength, whose physical development is stunted, who has no desire to play, who is skinny, pale, etc., it is evident that we must adopt a very special attitude toward him. If he is lazy, apathetic, even if he shows signs of insubordination, we must not scold or reprimand him; we especially must not punish him, for he cannot be held responsible for his behavior. We must remind ourselves that the real villain is a poorly nourished or malfunctioning digestive tract, a dilated stomach, or impoverished blood; it is an unbalanced nervous system; it is handicapped breathing resulting from enlarged adenoids; it is a moral crisis precipitated by puberty; it might also be the first symptoms of the serious illness called dementia praecox. While these discomforts of physical origin can be ameliorated to some extent by moral support and reasonable suggestions, such punishment as depriving the child of recess, activity and fresh air, making him copy lines, or increasing his assignments works directly against the goal we seek to attain. Poor digestion or anemia is not cured by punishment.

All the teacher can do is to try gently to spare the child any unnecessary fatigue, to encourage him to get a little exercise, to get him involved in games with some of his milder schoolmates, to have him perform some respiratory exercises, to give him credit for even the least of his efforts and so on. The most important role in this type of case is that of the school physician.

It is a role which up to now has been very restricted; the physician has been made into the "buildings physician" and he becomes interested in the children's health only if they suffer from a contagious disease. Recently public health specialists have proposed that an important extension of school health services be made. They want the physician to follow up each child's physical development and to look after each child's health. Every three or six months he would measure height, weight, chest circumference; he would check vision and audition; he would study the condition of the nervous and digestive systems, of the lungs, of the bony structure, of the skin; and the results of all these measurements and examinations would be noted by him on each child's personal history. This would require a lot of bureaucracy and a very long examination for a physician who, every three months, must examine one at a time the 300 to 600 children of an elementary school! We have shown somewhere else that we could at least save time by holding the teacher responsible for all measurements and for the examination of sensory organs, but this is a detail which is only secondary. What needs to be brought out more especially is the idea physicians have of the usefulness of the medical history to the child. In order for these health services not to be purely fictitious, it would be necessary for the physician's function to be conceived in a way that is different from the way it is currently conceived.

At this time the school physician's role is such that, having examined a sick child or one who is predisposed to illness, he can prescribe no treatment. He is even asked not to give a diagnosis unless the child suffers from a contagious disease. He must be content to advise the family that the child needs medical attention without adding another word. This reserve is imposed by a desire to respect the rights of non-school physicians and to avoid competing seriously with them. Indeed, these physicians would quickly lose all their patients if their school colleagues took care of children free of charge.

This is a beautiful example of professional fraternity, and we would admire it with all our heart if the children's health did not bear the cost of it, an aspect of the question which is too often forgotten. Our opinion is that if physicians depend on patients for a living, it does not follow that patients are made for the physicians. By thus overly restricting the school physician's initiative, we make his function one of little importance. When the sick or sickly child belongs to a well-to-do family, his family in most cases has its own doctor and probably is already aware of the child's condition. The school physician's warning will tell them nothing very new. When, on the contrary, the child comes from a poor family, there is a good chance that the parents have never consulted a doctor. There is a good chance, too, that they will never consult one, desirous as they are of avoiding the expense involved in a visit and in treatment, and even of avoiding the inconvenience of making the visit in the first place. Therefore, it is for the children of poor families, especially, that free medical care should be provided in schools. The children's welfare depends upon it and their welfare is important enough to take precedence over all other considerations.

Up to now we have been concerned about the really serious cases in which children suffer from acute or chronic illnesses; these are exceptional cases. Setting these cases aside, we still need to find out whether or not the physical development of children is progressing at a normal rate. This aspect of the question is not quite as medical and involves pedagogy, as such, more particularly. It also lends itself better to experimentation and to the drawing of precise conclusions, since the physical development of a child is easier to evaluate than the state of

Alfred Binet's house in Samois near Paris

Shortly after the publication of Modern Ideas about Children, Binet took to his bed, exhausted by his long, sustained effort. "I work the way a hen lays eggs," he joked. Although not completely recovered, he attended and actively participated in the monthly meeting of the Sociéte' Libre pour l 'Etude Psychologique de l'Enfant. He was bedfast again the next day, having suffered a cerebro-vascular accident which left him comatose. He died several weeks later, October 18, 1911, 204 Avenue du Maine in Paris. [Death Certificate, Mairie du XIV 'Eme arrondissement.] After funeral services at the Eglise d'Alesia, Alfred Binet was put to rest at the Cimetìere de Montparnasse. He was 54.

his health. Following are reasons a teacher must be concerned about the physical development of his students and the conditions under which this physical examination must be made.

To begin with, a child's age is related to his development. It is necessary to distinguish between two kinds of age : one is chronological age, which is calculated from the time of birth ; the other is anatomical and physiological age, which is derived from height, weight, muscle strength, the development of dentition, the amount of pubic, axillary, facial, body hair, the quality of voice and all the other signs of maturity. Normally, chronological age and physiological age correspond to each other but many exceptions can be found. It is not uncommon to find children who are older or younger than their legal age ; the precocity or the retardation may be as much as two or three years, but rarely more. In case of a discrepancy between the two, how should the child's age be evaluated? It is often necessary to take a student's age into account, for instance, when assigning him to a class, or when having him register for certain examinations with age-limit requirements. It seems natural to take mostly into account the physiological age, for it represents the true, the actual age experienced ; the other is only fiction.

We now pass to another question. It is important to know and to measure the physical strength of an individual in order to determine what physical training he needs, which exercises are appropriate for his body, and how intense the training given can be. Physical education sessions are of various types ; in spite of the general disuse, fashionable today, of gymnastic apparatus work, there still remains a whole series of exercises which do not demand the same amount of effort and do not result in the same amount of fatigue. It is evident that physical exercise must be adapted to the individual's physical strength ; what is good for one may be bad for another. It is ridiculous to subject individuals who differ greatly in physical development to the same amount of muscular work ; this is absurd and dangerous. A certain amount of exertion is salutary for the body, since it helps eliminate wastes and any negative effects are quickly repaired. But when fatigue goes beyond a certain limit, the organism has difficulty in recovering from it ; there is overexertion, exhaustion, intoxication. Consequently, if no consideration is given to a particular individual's physical condition, if both the strong and the weak are included in the same team, we run the risk of assigning exercises which will be insufficient for some, excessive and debilitating for others. What is true for exercise is also true for ordinary games. Properly graded, they have beneficial results. This does not mean, however, that we can praise indiscriminately the programs of certain new schools because they give athletics a large place in the school children's life. Physical overwork is just as undesirable as intellectual overwork.

It is not only gymnastics which must be adapted to the individual's needs but also sports. Today interest in sports is widespread among the young; this interest is one of the most curious characteristics of our time and one of the most fortunate. Bicycling, rowing, football and all those other lawn games we borrowed from the British are very popular. The sickly-looking, bespectacled schoolboy, the bookworm of old times, has almost become a myth. At any rate, he is much less highly thought of, less imitated, less envied. All the physiologists applauded this movement; they saw in it a means of regenerating the race. Patriots were moved; they felt sure this intensive physical exercise would produce better soldiers. In spite of all these arguments in favor of sports, we are beginning to notice that excesses in this type of activity are not, as we naively believed, always conducive to health, but are quite to the contrary.

In colleges and lyceums where sport is the most enthusiastically practiced, the level of academic achievement has come down. We can see in this the application of a rule which can be considered a general one. A certain amount of physical exercise is excellent to maintain health and can also indirectly and very lightly influence intellectual development. But when the desirable amount is exceeded, something occurs in the organism which can be observed in any budget : a spending in one area makes a saving necessary in another. In other words, too much physical exercise is prejudicial to intellectual development. This is a good reason to take a close look at the children who participate in the most tiresome and violent exercises. It is a good reason for teachers and parents, in particular, to evaluate carefully their children's physical strength and allow participation in only those exercises which will not overtax that strength and will not be prejudicial to their schoolwork.

The evaluation of physical strength is also useful when we contemplate sending a child to an "open-air school" or to country or seashore summer camps which aim to tone up anemic children from large cities by providing them with healthy physical activities. The scale and the measuring apparatus could be used before the children leave and after they return. This would permit establishing to what extent the summer camp stay has been beneficial and, as a result, to find out if the formula adopted was better or not as good as another. These measurements are often made today, but they are made with such lack of concern that they appear suspect to us. Those who make them don't know the first thing about the indispensable precautions which must be taken in order to insure the authenticity of the operations. These precautions will be indicated later.

The assessment of physical qualities would also be very useful when children become young adults and leave school to enter into life.

It would give the individual and his parents important information about the professions and trades for which he is best suited. At the same time, the student would learn to avoid taking the wrong course by not choosing occupations which require a physical strength superior to the one he possesses. It can be observed that different trades demand different degrees of physical expenditure. The blue collar worker must be stronger than the white collar worker. The unskilled laborer makes more muscular efforts than the craftsman. And in construction jobs, the working of iron requires stronger individuals than the working of wood. The house painter need not be as robust as the bricklayer. The miner who lives underground must have more endurance than someone who works in the open air. How much hardship, how many disappointments would be avoided if the teacher could discreetly inform each student of his abilities and guide him toward a road which he could follow without peril! There would be fewer failures, fewer discontented, fewer revolutionaries, and, above all, mortality would be lower.

Thus, if we think about this a little, we come to realize with astonishment that a considerable number of problems in education could be solved in the most satisfactory way by a physical examination of students. And our list of these problems is not yet complete. We shall raise two more questions.

The first question concerns the comparative value of two different kinds of gymnastics: the old French gymnastics with gymnastic apparatus work for the exercise of the superior extremities, and Swedish gymnastics. The latter is the more popular today. The discussion has been purely theoretical; there was no experimentation, no attempt to verify its superiority. No one even thought about it, so reluctant are we to thinking, so easily do we succumb to infatuation and fads. It would be a very simple matter to conduct a study on two sufficiently large groups of students and establish which of the two types of gymnastics is the more beneficial to their bodies.

The second question concerns the boarding school system. Is it true that the boarding school "prison," which has saddened the youth of so many men of our generation, is as unhealthy for physical development as it is for the development of the intellect? Again, it is easy to find out by comparing the average corporal development of interns to that of externs. The baleful influence of competitive examinations, of overwork, of the insalubrity of living quarters and dietary errors, all this can be evaluated better by the physical examination of students than by any other means. As long as a group of subjects exposed to a certain type of treatment shows signs of physical deficiency, of sickliness, it is undeniable that the particular treatment is not good. To illustrate: Ten years ago I was conducting this kind of study in teacher colleges. I still remember some of the things I had opportunity to observe. In some schools, I became frightened by the emaciation and the sickly appearance of the students I was weighing. I learned that these young women students were overworked in preparing for a competitive examination which only one in twenty would pass. I also learned that the school buildings were narrow, old, and insalubrious. This was the confirmation and the explanation of what the scale had been telling me.

II. The Relationship between Intelligence and Physical Development

In the preceding pages we have pointed to a certain number of circumstances in which it is advantageous to children, families and society to assess carefully the physical strength of school children. We now want to look at a slightly different question, that of the relationship which exists between a child's intelligence and his physical strength. While examining this problem — which of itself is already of great interest — we shall be led to take into consideration certain social phenomena now occurring which are not receiving much attention and which some day will have an enormous influence on the existence of society.

Let us begin with a very simple question of purely psychological interest.

Is there a relationship of any kind between a pupil's intelligence and his corporal development? Many educators, philosophers and physicians believe that this relationship exists and that it is expressed in vulgar language by the banal aphorism: "mens sana in corpore sano."* But if we review the results of studies involving precise measurements made in various countries, we observe that it is very difficult to establish the truth. For some authors, the most intelligent children in the class are the ones who are the most physically vigorous, and they prove it with figures and statistics. For others, the tail end of classes, the dunces, have the best physical development, and this also is proved with figures and statistics. Still other authors show, in a similar way, that there is no relationship between intelligence and physical development.

But if we carefully analyse all these studies, taking into consideration the procedures used, the reason for the contradictions becomes clear. Such authors as Gilbert,[1] Boas,[2] and West[3] relied on teachers' judgments to evaluate the children's intelligence. They asked teachers to divide their classes into three groups: the most intelligent, the aver-

---

* " A healthy mind in a healthy body. "

age, the least intelligent. Using this method, these authors have found an inverse relationship between physical and intellectual development, and the error is easily understood. In the first place, teachers can make an error in their classification. Second and more important, they tend not to take into account the different ages of the children, and from this omission flow many consequences. I much prefer the method used by the American anthropologist Porter, who, in order to evaluate intelligence, only takes into account the level of achievement and decides that, age being equal, the most intelligent child is the one who is in the most advanced class. With this method, Porter found that the most intelligent children are superior to the others in weight and height.[4]

Wishing to form an opinion of my own about this matter, I proceeded to measure the physical development of about 600 elementary school children. Then, in order to classify them according to intellect, I used two methods concurrently. The first, which we mentioned earlier, could be called subjective; it consists of an evaluation by the teachers. The second method, more scientific, takes two variables into account: the children's age and their level of achievement. Age being equal, the child judged the most intelligent is the one who knows most. Since we know exactly how many years a child, progressing at a normal rate, needs to complete the cycle of study, we can find out for each child whether he is regular, late, or advanced in his intellectual development. It is even possible to know if the delay, or the advance, is one, two, three years, or more. Thus, a ten-year-old child who attends public school will be found in fifth grade if he is regular in his development; if we find him in third grade, it means he is two years below grade; if, however, he is already in sixth grade, he is a year above grade. A similar system can be used in lyceums and colleges, in all institutions which offer a normal course of study. In order to have a very interesting classification, all we need to do is to translate into degrees of intelligence the level of achievement in relation to age. This classification will not be the result of a subjective, and always a little arbitrary, teacher evaluation, but will represent an aggregate of results, the sum of efforts, attention, memory and judgment which school learning involves. It is only natural to judge a child's intelligence from his school success. It is for the same reason that an adult's intelligence is judged from his success in life.

I have employed these two methods concurrently to find out if there is any relationship between a child's intelligence and his physical development. The first method, which uses teachers' evaluations, has given me absolutely nothing. With the level of achievement method, on the other hand, I saw immediately that the relationship looked for becomes very clear and definite. In order to acquire a certainty, however, it was necessary to extend our research considerably and to multiply the studies in various schools. Fortunately my courageous and conscientious collaborators, Dr. Simon and Mr. Vaney, have given me spirited support. We shall not give the details of the operations, which involved weight, height, breadth of shoulders, etc., etc. But we at least want to give a few figures which will make some of the ideas clearer. The following figures were obtained in two boys' schools:

Children with physical development which is :	Children with intellectual development which is :		
	Advanced	Regular	Delayed
Advanced	33 %	36 %	21 %
Regular	45 %	33 %	39 %
Retarded	21 %	39 %	39 %

A short commentary will be sufficient to explain the meaning of these figures. Let us take the first column to the left. It tells us that among the children who are above grade intellectually, there are 33 per cent who are advanced in physical development, 45 per cent who are regular, and 21 per cent who are retarded. This distribution is very interesting. It shows that the children who are above grade intellectually are more numerous among the physically advanced than among the physically retarded; but there are many exceptions, since 21 per cent of the bright children are among the physically retarded.

Thus, the relationship under investigation certainly exists but only becomes apparent when large numbers of subjects are used, and it is contradicted by such a large minority of cases that it can be of no use in individual diagnosis. If a twelve-year-old child has the height, the weight, and the muscular strength of a ten-year-old child, if consequently he is two years retarded in his physical development, nothing can be concluded with regard to his intellectual development. It may be that his intelligence is retarded just like his body; it may also be average; it may even be extraordinarily precocious.

And here we have, for the first time, the occasion to point out a very important distinction to be made between truth as applicable to the average and truth as applicable to the individual case. Certain physical and moral dispositions are only brought out by repeated testing of a large number of individuals; the results of these tests can only lead to conclusions applicable to the group. We shall soon see many examples of this. A very clear one was provided by the study of physical development. Certain other tendencies are interesting in that they lend themselves to individual application; they are the evidence for the presence of a quality which always exists to some degree. Thus the sub-crepitant rale in medicine is not a generic sign but a sure sign of pneumonia, just as in psychology we find many such valuable signs which permit judging and classifying an individual.

Why is it, then, that the physical measurements of a school child do not give us precise information about his intelligence? This lack of relationship is shocking. Doesn't intelligence need an anatomical substratum? Is it not dependent upon a well-formed, well-irrigated, well-fed brain? Is not the brain, in turn, dependent on other organs, the heart, the stomach, the kidneys, and also on the muscular and osseous structures? Is there not a dependent bond between all the various parts of an organism? And consequently, if a schoolboy's physical being is vigorous, should we not find equivalent vigor in his moral being?

Without a doubt these correlations exist but they are not as simple as our imagination conceives them to be; at any rate, they are influenced by a multitude of accessory and elusive factors. Let us give up theory at this point and consider only application. It is evident that, as it applies to the school situation, the tie binding intellectual ability to physical ability is rather loose and that nothing can be concluded about a child's intelligence from corporal anthropometric measurements. The pedagogic diagnosis cannot, at least in the light of what we know now, utilize this anatomic and physiologic data.

However, there are cases in which the physical condition of a child permits us to draw conclusions regarding his mental state. Up to now we have looked at the matter from the point of view of diagnosis. Let us now consider another hypothesis, one which has as much practical importance as the previous one. Let us assume we have positive proof that a child is less intelligent than most of his schoolmates. His understanding is slow and difficult, his memory is poor, his attention span is short. He looks sickly, his height and weight show a retardation of two years, his respiratory capacity of three years and so on. In such a case there is no diagnosis to be made. There is no need to study the child's physical development in order to surmise the intellectual development, since the individual's intellectual status is already as well established as his physical status. The equally impoverished condition of these two aspects of the same individual should not be neglected. It is legitimate to try to see if the two conditions are not arising from the same cause. In order to do that, the help of the school physician will be enlisted. He will examine the child's teeth, his digestive tract, look for adenoid growths, for signs of anemia, for possible heart and lung ailments; and then, after this methodical examination, he will be in a position to know if there is ground for our suspicion. As we have seen, the practice of making physical measurements at school should not be rejected; for if the measurements, as such, taken apart from other data, have little significance for the diagnosis of intelligence, they are very useful when they are confirmed by observations of another kind. Their main advantage is that they attract the educator's attention to a child's questionable state of health, which, without this physical examination, would have gone unnoticed.

The examination and the measurement of children's physical development is interesting not only from the point of view of pedagogy; all these questions, when they are well understood, are seen to have a much broader application and become of really great social significance, since they involve the future of our race and the organization of our society. After having observed that the intellectual underdevelopment of some children is related to their physical underdevelopment, we cannot be content to describe this correlation merely for the sake of its great philosophical interest. It is not sufficient to line up figures. We must know what these figures reveal and we must look at the children who have been measured.

In the school where we are making our anthropomorphic measurements, we searched carefully for the children whose measurements show a retardation of at least two years in development. Dr. Simon, my faithful collaborator, assisted in this task. We had all those retardates brought in front of us. To throw better light upon their intellectual deficiency and to sharpen our observation power, we compared them with school children of the same age whose development was definitely normal. We knew none of the children nor their ages and we tried to guess which of them were the retardates. The children were not undressed; we only looked at each child's head and general appearance. So startling was the living picture displayed before our eyes that on thirty children, half normal and half retarded, who were presented to us one after the other, without our knowing their ages, we made only six classification errors; we were able to identify the retarded in the twenty-four other cases. We were especially guided by their general appearance, body posture, complexion, the shape and expression of facial features. From all this emerged an indefinable impression of physiological misery.

And the saddest and gravest part of all this is that this physiological misery is an expression of social misery, that is, of a much deeper debility which is inherent in the very constitution of our society. Here we are not reporting only the results of our own research. It could, strictly speaking, be charged with not being representative of the population at large. Unfortunately our findings are in complete harmony with those of other authors who have worked in public schools, and these authors are numerous. Let us cite the names of Burggraeve, Niceforo, McDonald, Schuyten, etc. All saw, as we ourselves saw, that a great, a very great proportion of children whose physical development is retarded are children whose parents are poor, even destitute.

In the primary schools it is possible quickly to make a list of the poorest children, since they are usually given special help. They receive this help in two forms: free clothing and free food. It is clear that clothing and food distribution are made by the principal of the school after a discreet investigation of the parents' social condition. We therefore know who the least wealthy parents are and can even establish different levels of poverty and, in a word, social classes. Now, in trying to see how the physically underdeveloped and the intellectually underdeveloped children are distributed in these social classes, we find that the majority of the retarded are in classes where assistance is needed either in the form of clothing or food or both; while the majority of children who are regular in their development, and especially those who are ahead, belong to the least poor classes. Unfortunately this fact has been well demonstrated. A good number of the underdeveloped children who attend our public primary schools are reduced to such condition as a result of deprivations experienced in the family, probably deprivations related to both food and sanitation. And what is graver still is that this decrease in physical vigor is not an individual phenomenon which occurs only in the children and which could be remedied with proper care. No, we are dealing with a hereditary condition which characterizes the poor family; it is not only the child whose physical development is inferior to the average, for the same stunting is found in his father and in his mother. Letters were sent to parents asking them to send us their measurements, the same request going indiscriminately to all parents who had children in the school. The data returned to us — from which, of course, we can only draw global conclusions, since we don't know how careful parents were in their measurement — tend to show that the size of the underprivileged parents is slightly below average, while that of the well-to-do parents remains slightly above average. Of the underprivileged parents 54 per cent were under five feet, while only 47 per cent of well-to-do parents were under that size. The differences are not very large, viewed as absolute values, but they represent a significant trend in one direction.

Thus, using such modest instruments as a scale and a measuring apparatus and making a few calculations which appear very elementary, almost useless, the educator finds himself in the presence of the most alarming social problem of our times. Such problems are not his to solve; they are beyond the scope of school and pedagogy. But he must insistently bring them to the attention of public authorities. Also, to the extent that he plays a role in the distribution of the free food and clothing available, he must see to it that this help is given to the children who need it most. Not only an investigation of the social milieu and of the parents should be carried out, but also careful measurement of the children's physical development should be made in all schools. The results of these controlled measurements should be utilized, since they are a true indicator of the degree of deprivation. Filed in a central office, this information would provide us with a general picture of the school situation and would make it possible to proportion food and clothing allotments according to the number of needy children in each school population. In this way free lunches, for instance, which now are distributed in a more or less haphazard fashion, would be allotted on the basis of information collected in the central office, thus making free food available in greatest amount to the poorest schools. We are not asking for new credits but for a more rational repartition of those we are already being given.

It is by adopting a scientific attitude and by insuring a more rational distribution of the help available that the educator will contribute, in a significant way, to introducing common sense, precision and justice in humanitarian endeavors.

This is what can be said about the way a program of assistance must be managed. But the problem is more involved and the damage greater than we have let the reader suppose. The underprivileged and destitute classes don't show signs of physical degeneration only. Their physical degeneration is accompanied by intellectual and moral degeneration as well. These are not just theoretical views; unfortunately they are facts, undeniable facts. We have observed them not only in Paris but also in provincial towns, and even in rural areas. Everywhere, children of underprivileged and destitute families are less intelligent than the others. This view is supported by the fact that, in general, they are more often retarded in their studies; for instance, their intellectual development at age eleven is that which children from well-to-do families have attained as early as age nine or ten. Also fewer of them pass the elementary school final comprehensive examination. This examination should not be underestimated, for it is a measure of intellectual development. A survey made at my request in a small country school revealed that all the children from well-to-do families had obtained their diploma, while children from poor or destitute families had obtained it only in the infinitely small proportion of one in four. These comments cover intelligence, but this is not all. Moral development is observed to be equally stunted. We shall not talk about the moral nature of young children, for there are few occasions to observe it in school; but we shall look at the parents' moral attitude. Fathers and mothers have important responsibilities toward their children. They must attend to the children's material needs, seeing to it that they are kept clean, adequately fed, and in good health. Parents must teach and impose order, care, dependability. They must attend to intellectual needs, seeing how homework is done and if lessons are well learned. And finally, they must attend to moral needs, setting a good example, providing good advice, giving rewards when deserved, and administering punishment, which is neither weak nor excessive, when deserved. From the triple point of

56

view of material, intellectual and moral care, poor and destitute parents are clearly inferior to well-to-do parents. Mr. Limosin, a rural school teacher who knows many such parents well, has brought me up to date about this matter by means of a careful study. This study can leave no doubt in our minds, so eloquent are the conclusions which can be drawn from it. Moreover, all the principals of Parisian schools who were shown the results of this study assured me without hesitation that their personal experience confirmed those results.

How, then, can we explain this degeneration of the lower classes? If there were only isolated, equivocal cases, we would be tempted to be content with small explanations. We would note, for instance, that a few destitute fathers, who are very busy during the day, come home exhausted at night and have no time to supervise their children's work. Several also are not completely aware, themselves, of the usefulness of education. Other reasons could be set forth, but we do not believe in their generality. The social degradation which we are witnessing is too important to be explained by such unimportant causes, and it appears to us to be the consequences of physical degradation. The various parts of an organism are related to one another; if the physical being is subject to a regression, the mental counterpart must be subject to the same analogous regression. Now, it is as a result of physical degeneration that an individual shows less intelligence, less attention, has less memory, and especially that he thinks less, constantly sacrifices tomorrow to today, satisfies his immediate needs out of all proportion, is readily influenced by the promise of pleasure and by bad example, becoming addicted to alcohol and wasting in a day or two a whole week's salary. The true moral definition of the destitute is not: a human being who lacks money; rather it is: a human being who is incapable of saving. All these mental consequences of physical degeneration are the natural consequences of poor nutrition and hygiene. They are the consequences and at the same time, in an accessory way, the causes. For poor hygiene and poor nutrition are still aggravated by lack of thought and by instability. It is true that the caste system which the 1889 revolution [*sic;* undoubtedly the 1789 revolution] is supposed to have abolished still exists. Castes are no longer recognized or sanctioned by law but, in fact, subsist. They are evident in the physical, intellectual and moral stunting present in the most destitute human beings.

III. The Measurement of Physical Development

After all these general considerations let us talk a little about technique. In the preceding discussions we have shown the importance of evaluating a child's physical condition. Now let us see how this evaluation can be made. Since this is neither a treatise nor a guide, since we are merely attempting to expose a few new ideas which experience has suggested to us, we shall set aside that part of this examination which is not the educator's responsibility and for which he needs to get the help of an intelligent physician. We shall set aside the part which consists of the search for a definite pathological condition such as tuberculosis, scrofula, anemia, epilepsy, etc., including, of course, acute infections. Here we shall talk only about the procedures to be used to study school anthropology.

To begin with, without recourse to any procedure of any kind, the skilled eye detects whether a child is robust or not. A firmly contoured mouth means one thing; flabby, poorly defined and drooping lips mean another thing. Flesh with an outline which is well defined, as if sculpted, is healthier than flabby flesh. Skin color is especially important. It is composed of two basic shades, one red, the other yellow. The value and proportion of each must be such that the face appears tinted no more in one shade than in the other. A white complexion, resulting from the absence of these two colors, or the exaggeration of one of these two colors, represents a deviation from the normal. I shall also draw attention to the fact that body posture conveys an impression of strength or of weakness. At rest, a fatigued individual reveals his condition by two types of attitudes: ligamentous attitudes, in which a position is maintained through the use of ligaments not muscles; or attitudes in which the organism unconsciously seeks a support, leaning against a wall, resting elbows on a table, or reclining against the back of an armchair. The search for support is an obvious sign of physical weakness, for every time we lean against something we experience relief, since the weight supported by the object does not have to be supported by the body. Thus, let us suppose I am seated on a chair and that the chair is resting on a scale. If I rest my two elbows on a table placed in front of the scale, the weight registered will immediately drop, by as much as twenty-two pounds, meaning there is that much less to be supported by the dorso-lumbar muscles.

The instruments used in the measurement of physical development are the measuring apparatus for height; the scale for weight; the caliper for shoulder width; the dynamometer for muscular strength; the spirometer for lung capacity. Altogether five instruments are sufficient, and if we use them correctly we can make extremely useful observations with them.

We shall not take time to describe how to use the measuring apparatus or the scale; these details can be found in any special manual.

We do have a word, in passing, about the procedure for taking chest measurements. We do not advise the use of the graduated ribbon for chest circumference measurement because this method can give rise to errors which are enormous in relation to individual variation and to the annual increase in thoracic perimeter. This fact is easily verified if we try to control our procedure by taking the same measurement on the same chest twice in a row. The magnitude of the discrepancy between the two measurements is surprising.

We propose that another type of thoracic measurement be adopted, namely shoulder width or bi-acromial diameter. It is calculated by measuring the space between the bony landmarks provided by the two acromions. It is important to note that neither the thoracic perimeter nor the bi-acromial diameter gives any idea about respiratory amplitude, but the measurement shows development in width of the body and consequently is a happy complement to the data obtained by the measurement of height.

To these anatomic explorations we generally add a measurement of muscular strength, obtained with the classical dynamometer. This is a metal ellipse which is placed in the hand and pressed between the fingers and the palm of the hand. A meter records the pressure in kilograms and thus measures the maximum strength utilized by the flexing muscles of the forearm.

This is, of course, a very local measurement of muscular strength which tells us nothing about the power of other muscles, such as those of the trunk or legs. Limited as it is, however, the strength of manual pressure as registered on the dynamometer is valuable information and is much more significant than the old clinical method which consisted of telling the patient to "squeeze my hands" and then evaluating approximately the amount of strength spent on the hand squeezing. The main criticism of the dynamometer is that it registers a kind of explosion of strength rather than the continued flow of energy demanded by a sustained test. Of course, this is too bad, for in all life circumstances it is endurance which is needed. Physical strength, like the will and other moral qualities, is revealed more particularly by the continuity of the fight against a lasting obstacle; a short-lived effort, intense though it may be, has much less value. The dynamometer gives less exact information about the amount of strength the whole organism possesses and also about its resistance to fatigue.

In relation to this, I remember some very useful observations I made about ten years ago on a football field, with the collaboration of a team of young people who were relentlessly playing football. I had them squeeze the dynamometer twice: once before the game; then a few hours later when they came to me perspiring, exhausted with fatigue and very weakened. Each time I had them give a series of pressures. What struck me that day was the fact that the first pressures given before and after the game were about equivalent. But the men's facial expressions while pressing the dynamometer were very different. At first, when they were not yet tired, their faces remained calm during the test; after the game, however, the players grunted and their faces became contorted, as if this exaggerated gesticulation was necessary in order to produce the same amount of work as before. Although tired, they produced the same effort as they did when rested, but they produced it in a different way. The same work demanded more effort, and it is here, in this manifestation of a greater effort which had become necessary, that the fatigue produced by the football game was curiously revealed.

When conducting an endurance test, it is recommended that students be asked to press the dynamometer not once but several times. Other instruments have been recommended for measuring the muscular work an individual is capable of producing up to the time of exhaustion — or rather up to the time when extreme fatigue inhibits work, for true exhaustion never occurs. We owe the best known of these instruments, called an ergograph, to the ingenuity of the Italian physiologist Mosso. Though excellent, it is a complicated laboratory instrument which cannot readily be used in the classroom due to its large size, the amount of time necessary to get it to function, and the errors that can result if it is not expertly handled.

I definitely favor the use of the dynamometer for making a quick evaluation of an individual's strength. If there is more time and an in-depth study is needed, an entirely different instrument, the spirometer, should be given preference.

The spirometer is an ensemble of flasks, weights and springs which records an organism's lung capacity, that is, the greatest quantity of air which can be voluntarily expelled from the lungs after a very deep inhalation. Many studies, all in agreement, have demonstrated that lung capacity is the most useful data which can be obtained for the assessment of endurance in the human organism. Adequate breathing is the surest sign not only that an organism is able to furnish a big effort but also that it is able to prolong this effort and consequently to produce a considerable quantity of muscular work. Now, to breathe well is to ventilate our lungs adequately; the quantity of air which we channel through our respiratory organs at each inhalation is a measure of this function. Those who are physically strong are recognized by a little sign which escapes the average person but which physiologists know well. We only need to look at them breathe normally. Their respiratory acts are few but very deep. They breathe slowly, but they breathe deeply. This is also the type of breathing observed in school children who have been subjected to a rational physical training and who are in good form. The physically deficient, on the contrary — those who have not been trained — take rapid and superficial breaths.

In order to conclude about the value of the spirometer, I want to mention still another experiment. Like most studies I talk about, this one was done in a school and the procedure was so simple that anyone can repeat it. Fifteen years ago I conducted comprehensive studies on the physical strength of school children with various collaborators, using all the instruments, all the methods known at the time for the study of either body dimensions or body efficiency of output. We surveyed not only height, weight, chest circumference, muscular strength as registered on the dynamometer, but also work with various ergographs, running speed, length of jump, rope climbing, extinguishing a candle from a distance, reaction time, speed of graphic movements, etc. All the results obtained in each of these tests were scored so that it became easy to rank the students for each trial. Of course the rank obtained by each student varied a little with the type of test; the best runners were not the first in dynamometer work, and those who climbed rope fastest were not the tallest.

We then made a synthetic, global classification in which each test counted for one; it was a classification similar to the one used in high schools for the prize of excellence. We also established which particular test was closest to the general classification and which, therefore, had the greatest representative value; we found it to be, by far, the spirometer test. Thus we demonstrated an important fact over again : the spirometer is the instrument which will give the best idea of an individual's general physical strength. Do you wish to select an individual who is resistant to fatigue and who will be outstanding in an endurance test? Take the one who has the most breath.

Note that the means used to measure physical development fall into two very different categories. The first are anatomic and do not require the participation of the individual. Whether a pupil wants it or not, if we get him to step onto a scale, we obtain his weight and he can do nothing to change that weight. The other measurement procedures are physiological. They suppose an ongoing function and since this function is semi-voluntary, it happens that the measurement which is made of it is related not only to the physiological condition but also to a moral element.

When someone presses the dynamometer, the figure obtained depends on three combined factors :

1. The individual's muscular strength, that is the structure, the volume, and the histological condition of his muscular fibers.

2. His skill and amount of practice. The first time we handle the instrument, we do so awkwardly, not knowing exactly where to place our fingers; little by little and with practice which falls short of fatigue, we obtain readings of increasing value. We may begin with a pressure of 32 kilograms. We press again without hurrying and get a reading of

36; a little rest, a new pressure, and we obtain 40 kilograms. Only a naive person would believe that this increase represents merely an increase in strength due to practice. What has been increased is skill. Let me say, in passing, that this is a very important idea which is too often neglected in evaluating skill and practice.

3. The will. We want, more or less, to press hard. This desire will be stronger if we are interested, excited, moved, than if we are calm, indifferent, apathetic, distracted. To support this view I offer this beautiful example : Have a young man press the dynamometer when he is alone ; then have him press it in the presence of a pretty girl. You can be certain that the reading obtained the second time will be higher. It will be so without the individual's being conscious of having applied greater effort, without his realizing that his strength has increased. In schools I measured this artificial increase in physical strength by having a student climb on a stage and giving him some vigorous encouragement, aloud, in the presence of all his schoolmates. With such encouragement, strength increased by one-sixth, on the average.

The same effect was observed when the spirometer was used. What the instrument registers is a quantity of air which is not entirely controlled by lung capacity. It goes beyond that and includes the effort to inhale and exhale, the skill with which we hold our breath in order to exhale it later, and especially the moral energy which is invested in that effort. Here, again, it is sufficient to have a witness of another sex present during the test to see an appreciable increase in the quantity of air exhaled.

It is undeniable, therefore, that in all the functions which we have just reviewed, the figures obtained represent not only physical strength but also motivation. It would be unrealistic to separate the moral individual from the physical individual. Were we to do so, would such a distinction be useful in any way ? Would it be a legitimate thing to do ? What we are worth physically depends not only on our weight and on our muscles but also on our moral energy. It is our moral energy which commands our muscles, making them contract when they are numbed and sore from fatigue ; it is this energy which sets practical limits to our endurance. These are not fixed, unvarying limits. On the contrary, they vary widely according to the strength of our will, which is like the intense core, the centrum of our personality.

If we are able to go for a very long hike, or if we are able to remain on our bicycle and continue to pedal uphill against the wind, it is not always because we have strong muscles and a large chest and are free from many defects. It is because "we want it that way." Therefore it is right and scientifically sound to include the will among the factors contributing to our physical strength.

Last question : How can we evaluate a school child's physical strength?

At the end of a physical exploration session the examiner is left with a collection of figures which fill his notebook : measurements representing weight, height, width of shoulders, dynamometer pressure readings and so on. What is the meaning of this forbidding looking array of figures, which has so little resemblance to the living reality we have just measured? This is a question we will often ask ourselves, for today the greatest part of our surveys, even the most psychological ones, tend to be expressed as a measurable quantity. After having studied a subject's mental abilities we can say : memory, such a score ; attention, such other score. It is therefore important to realize that, in spite of its apparent great precision, the figure obtained is only a rough one, which can be used only after its meaning has been established and its interpretation made. Since this is a very general problem which we are going to meet over and over again in this book, let us settle it once and for all so that we shall not need to come back to it.

A ten-year-old boy has just been brought to us. The anthropometric measurements having been made, we write down the figures obtained and get the "physical value" of the child. His record reads as follows :

Height	120 cm.
Weight	26 kgs.
Shoulder width	28 cm. 7.
Spirometer	1600 cubic cm.
Dynamometer	17 kgs.

Nothing shows better than these figures that numerical results need to be explained if they are to be understood. This explanation is mainly an evaluation. Informed of a physical fact of some kind, we understand it only if we can interpret it, judge its exact value. We are told Paul is 120 centimeters tall. Given this figure we try to establish if this represents a tall or a small stature and, since this is a child we are talking about, if this child is tall or small for his age. As we see, the interpretation of such a value supposes a point of reference provided by an average to which the individual data are compared. It follows that it is necessary to have at our disposal a list of averages.

Following is a list of averages compiled by my collaborators and me in the course of our numerous studies.

PHYSICAL DEVELOPMENT OF YOUNG BOYS
Paris Elementary Schools. Children 4 Years and Above.

Age	Height in cm.	Weight in kg.	Bi-acrom. Diam. in cm.	Spirom- eter in cm.³	Dynamometer Right Hand	Left Hand
Birth	50	3.250	—	—	—	—
1 yr.	70	9.750	—	—	—	—
3 yrs.	85	12	—	—	—	—
4 yrs.	98	15	21.5	—	—	—
5 yrs.	103	17	23	—	—	—
6 yrs.	108	19	24	—	—	—
7 yrs.	114	20	25.5	935	10.3	9.80
8 yrs.	121	23	27	1050	11.1	10.1
9 yrs.	125.5	26	28	1310	13.8	12.5
10 yrs.	130	28	28.7	1460	14.8	14
11 yrs.	136.5	29.5	29	1600	17.2	15.4
12 yrs.	143	33	30	1800	19.4	16.6
13 yrs.	148	35	31	1950	20.9	19
14 yrs.	154	—	—	—	—	—

But that is not all. This list of averages can be used for only one thing : to determine if, for any given function, our subject is at, above, or below average. This is an important bit of information but a vague one, for we must still find out how much he deviates from the average. The height of the school boy who is used as an example is 120 centimeters, while the average height of children his age is 130 centimeters. Therefore we shall say that he is short for his age ; we shall even add that he is very short. We cannot go much beyond that.

In order to introduce more precision and especially more clarity into the evaluations, I proposed a scoring system which consists of replacing size differences in centimeters by the age difference. Let us take our example again. Our ten-year-old school boy is 120 centimeters tall ; a glance at the table of averages tells us that this is the average for an eight-year-old. Therefore we shall say that with regard to height this child is two years below average, which we put down as " — 2. " This is clear and precise. We immediately see the significance of the retardation. If we apply the scoring system to other measures, we obtain the following :

Height .... — 2.
Weight .... — 1.
Shoulder width .... =
Lung capacity .... + 1.
Dynamometer .... + 1.

Thus we can state that this child is very short. Considering that he is shorter than average, he is relatively heavy and is not a skinny child. The width of his shoulders is normal. His lung capacity is excellent and his muscular strength is very good. This is a very short, strapping child from whom we can demand much. This is what the child is worth physically.

We hope there soon will be schools in which these anthropometric methods will be introduced and regularly applied, since they can be so very useful. They help explain certain deficiencies in attention and intellect. They make it possible to adapt physical fitness programs to the child's physical strength, to make a truly equitable distribution of public assistance, and finally, to establish the comparative value of several gymnastic methods which are now the object of controversy. Also they permit evaluation of " open air schools " and the true benefits derived from summer camps, etc. The criteria for all physical education are the measuring apparatus, the scale, the dynamometer and the spirometer. If this set of criteria is not used, the work done is blind work, that is to say bad work or charlatanism.

FOOTNOTES FOR CHAPTER THREE

1. *Yale Studies,* Vol. II.
2. *Sciences,* New Series, Vol. I, p. 225.
3. *Sciences,* New Series, Vol. IV, p. 156.
4. *Transactions of the Saint-Louis Academy of Science,* Vol. VI, p. 161.

CHAPTER FOUR

Vision and audition

I. Vision

When we become involved in testing vision and audition in school children for the first time, we experience many surprises. To begin with, we assume that all teachers understand the importance of such testing. Since the material presented in class is either of a visual or auditory nature, a good teacher must know whether or not pupils seated at a distance from him are able to see what he is showing them or what he is writing for them on the blackboard. He must also know if these children hear distinctly everything he is explaining to them.

But, in fact, even the most recent pedagogical publications ignore this topic completely. There is not a single page, a single line, mentioning the need to evaluate school children's sensory acuity. If the author of a treatise does show an interest in the subject, it is to tell about the natural history of it, to tell about its development or to report histological information about the shape of nerve cells in the visual cortical sense. All this is very educational, of course, but it is of no help to the teacher either in conducting his class or in identifying deaf or nearsighted students.

We are apt to think, therefore, that the absence of pedagogical treatises dealing with the subject is due to the very natural fact that teachers know how to examine sensory organs and need not be taught how to go about it. This is another error. We visited many schools, both in Paris and in the provinces, and talked with many teachers. They had only the vaguest ideas about this matter. A few were able to tell us about two or three of their pupils who had particularly bad vision, but they deserved no praise for having discovered this themselves; they had been informed of the condition either by the child or by the child's family. Most teachers are not only completely unaware of these problems but also claim they are not competent to deal with them. The teachers who were approached said they felt incapable of determining the sensory acuity of an individual and added that it is not their responsibility, anyway, but the physician's. If we consult physicians about this, they agree with the teachers. They maintain the examination of vision involves the use of complicated apparatus and demands extremely abstruse knowledge in physiology and pathology which only physicians possess. This is not very encouraging but that is not all. I remember that about four years ago I asked some teachers to examine their students' vision. When this became known, the Medical Association immediately showed concern about such usurpation of physicians' privileges. A committee, which was appointed to attend to the matter, lodged a formal complaint with the Superintendent of Schools.

Personally, I have no fixed idea about the matter and don't care whether the examination is made by physicians or teachers. What counts is that it be done. The children's welfare depends upon it. Visual impairment in school children is not rare, by any means. Statistics published in various countries, and notably in Germany, show a surprisingly high incidence rate of poor vision. Various authors have reported the percentage of children with abnormal vision to be 46 % (Mottais), and even as high as 61 % (Cohn). This last figure is to be used with caution. Taken at face value it would mean that abnormal vision is found in the majority of children. The conclusions which can be drawn from all those statistics appear even graver when still other considerations are taken into account. The data tend to show that visual deficiencies increase regularly in proportion to age. Visual problems — near-sightedness in particular — are said to be more common in the 15 to 16 age group than in the 8 to 10 age group. This appears to be well demonstrated by available statistics. Mottais reports the following percentages:

Number of near-sighted in lower grades 0
Number of near-sighted in 8th grade .... 17 %
Number of near-sighted in high school .... 35 %

All the other authors, without exception, have reported a similar trend. The absolute per cent value may vary but the increase in incidence rate with age is observed consistently everywhere. The increase in myopia, in particular, has been strikingly demonstrated. It was hypothesized that the condition develops in school as a result of school activities and that school is therefore responsible for its occurrence.

Other research upholds this view. Statistical studies of myopia compared the incidence of the condition in urban and in rural populations, as well as in different professions requiring various amounts of reading. The results consistently showed that near-sightedness was most prevalent in professions requiring the most reading. It was concluded that the main cause of myopia was an excessive amount of reading activity.

And this is not all. The seriousness of the situation is revealed to us by the study of another aspect of the problem under discussion. It was established that myopia and other visual deficiencies are an obvious cause of retardation in school achievement. This is evident because research shows that, on the one hand, the number of educationally retarded among the visually handicapped is much larger than among normal students; on the other hand, the number of visually handicapped among the educationally retarded is also much larger than among average students. These two facts corroborate each other. For me there is further confirmation in the fact that every time my collaborators and I have made studies of the type described above, they have yielded similar results. I shall mention only two out of all these studies: a survey made at my request in the Bordeaux elementary schools, and a very recent study dealing with the same subject and conducted by Mr. Vaney. This research was done on a very small number of children, but in return the procedure was carefully supervised by a teacher who was well acquainted with each child individually. It cannot be denied that a child with defective vision derives little benefit from visual material presented in class and that all his work suffers as a result.

This is understandable. Educators rely heavily on visual methods of teaching. They show objects or pictures, for instance; they explain a map; they write or draw on the blackboard. All of this teaching of a visual nature is more or less lost on children with visual deficiencies. They do not understand, or they understand poorly, or they form the bad habit of copying from their classmates.

Why don't they complain? Often because they are shy. Sometimes, too, because they are unaware they see poorly or less well than others. Just recently I learned from a young man that he had gone through grade school and to college before discovering he was near-sighted. This seems very strange, yet he himself told me about it and I cannot doubt his word. Sometimes the child hides his visual impairment from his teacher with a kind of unconscious cunningness. A very intelligent professor told me about one of his students who often made serious errors when copying texts written on the blackboard. The teacher was surprised at these errors but didn't hesitate to attribute them to persistent carelessness on the part of the young child. Even though the pupil appeared to be trying hard, the teacher punished him every time. Eventually, having learned to make visual examinations, the teacher discovered that his young pupil was extremely near-sighted and could not read the information written on the blackboard. He tried to interpret or he guessed. While telling me this story the teacher was filled with remorse at the thought of the numerous punishments he had inflicted upon this innocent child. What the child needed obviously was not punishment but a good pair of glasses. [1]

Surely these observations, these statistics, these arguments are impressive enough to motivate us to examine the problem more closely.

Five or six years ago Dr. Simon and I began a study in the Paris elementary schools. Here is what we have established.[2]

Due to the length and to the obscurity of the classrooms, there are many seats from which it is difficult to see clearly the material written on the blackboard. And some children are sufficiently near-sighted to be actually unable to perceive this material when placed in these seats. Now, in general, teachers have not identified the visually impaired children and seat their pupils without giving any thought to the problem. In certain schools, seating arrangements are left to chance; in others, children are placed in alphabetical order; in still others, the seat assigned a child depends on the grade he obtained in the last examination session. The child who ranked first has the honor of sitting in the first seat and the student who ranked last is relegated to the back of the class. It is evident that there is no relationship between these seating arrangements and one which takes poor vision into account. Or rather — I am mistaken — there is an inverse relationship between them. Students who ranked last in the examination stand an excellent chance of being identified as visually impaired.

Convinced of the seriousness of the problem after this research, we set up what we called a "pedagogic examination of vision." We designed an optometric chart, copies of which were made and distributed free of charge by "La société libre pour l'étude de l'enfant" to all teachers in the Paris area and in several other "departements." We shall now explain in detail how a teacher or a parent can measure a child's visual acuity and what practical conclusions can be drawn from this examination.

First, a simplification of the procedure appeared to us to be necessary, and Dr. Simon and I suggested that the visual examination be thought of as consisting of two very distinct parts: a practical test of visual acuity which can be made by any teacher or parent; and a medical test which will be reserved for the ophthalmologist. The practical or pedagogical part is very simple, our aim being merely to establish at precisely which maximum distance a person can read printed letters of a particular size. This is what the measurement of a person's visual acuity consists of. What teacher cannot make this kind of observation on his pupils once he has been cautioned against making certain types of errors? To make this measurement is to carry out the pedagogical part of the examination, and not only teachers but all parents are capable of it.

The medical part of the examination, the one which involves not the teacher but the ophthalmologist, remains to be done. What does it consist of? Once it has been established that the child does not have normal vision, it consists of identifying the cause of the observed visual impairment. The physician will explain that the ophthalmoscopic examination of the child's eyes — or any one of a variety of examinations — has revealed an opacity of the center of the crystalline lens, or a lesion of the fundus of the eye. He will say : "This is a case of myopia," or "This is a case of astigmatism," etc. These are difficult examinations which can only be made by a specialist. They are important procedures, since they determine treatment, but they represent a task which is completely independent from that of the teacher. The latter, I repeat, has only one thing to do : establish who, among his students, has abnormal vision.

This basic principle being understood, let us describe precisely the method which is to be used. It consists of placing a chart composed of letters of different sizes at eye level and in full but diffuse light, against the wall of a covered courtyard. This chart is called an "optometric scale."[3] We suggest that the chart be used outdoors because changes in illumination are not as pronounced there as they are indoors. The examination should be done preferably between 10 A.M. and 2 P.M., and it should not be done on cloudy days.

The optometric scale contains several rows of letters of varying dimensions. These letters do not form meaningful words; this was avoided in order to prevent the examinee from guessing at the letters from the general configuration of a known word. The characters must be perceived one after the other.

What size letter must we be able to read for our vision to be considered "normal"? We have to be able — and the essential part of the method is contained in the following statement — to read correctly 3 letters out of 7 when the printed letters are 0^m007 high, and when we stand 5 meters away from the chart. A very precise rule, shall we say, and, we shall add, a very arbitrary one.

Why tolerate 4 errors in 7 reading attempts? Why the 5 meters distance requirement? Why letters 0^m007 high and not 0^m008 or 0^m006? We shall answer each question in turn. In the first place, it is desirable that a certain formalism be attached to the visual examination so it will not be performed carelessly. If a teacher were permitted to begin the procedure by showing the examinee any one letter on the chart, the examination would no longer be methodical. We would eventually come to asking the child himself to decide if he is far- or near-sighted. The requirements regarding distance and height of letters seem to be even more important and to have a scientific basis. Ophthalmologists have calculated that the retinal image of a letter 0^m007 high, seen at a distance of 5 meters, corresponds to the dimension of the sensitive elements of the retina. It is thought that if two luminous spots are close enough to each other to stimulate a single cone, they do not produce two images but one. In order for two points to be perceived as separate, the distance between them must be equal to the diameter of a cone.[4]

But we realize today that this anatomic localization of the stimulus is of little importance, for perceiving is an act which always requires active participation of the intelligence. The more supple the intelligence, the finer the perception. Sensory acuity is not measured in any absolute way but in relation to its inevitable and necessary interplay with intelligence. [5] In my opinion, the great, the true, the only reason to accept the definition of normal visual acuity given above is not a physiological reason but a social one. In the first place, the number of cases of defective vision discovered with the use of this set of rules is not so large that it represents the majority in society or in a group of children. This makes it possible to give the problem special attention and, when school children are involved, to provide appropriate seating arrangements in the classroom. Secondly, this convention accommodates itself to the limits imposed by the size of the rooms; for children who do not have normal vision, as defined above, are not made to read the blackboard from the back of the class. Finally, if we tolerate a child's making 4 errors in 7 reading attempts, it is because greater stringency would have us recognize too large a number of defective visions. The limit between normal and abnormal is always arbitrary; this limit must be set in the way which best fills the practical needs.

In the case of children 1 to 6 years who do not yet know how to read, we try to establish if they can recognize a 21^{mm} circle, square, or cross from a distance of 7 meters.

All these examinations must be individually administered whenever possible. Cheating will be prevented and children will be given a lot of encouragement without, however, being given any undue help. After the tests have been completed, the subjects whose vision is least normal will be identified and they will be assigned seats as close as possible to the blackboard. We can rest assured that this simple action on our part will render them an immense service.

Moreover, we shall do well to draw the parents' attention to the fact that their children need to be examined by an oculist. It is our duty to inform them of this need in spite of the fact that parents have been known to ignore our warnings most of the time. They simply don't want to be bothered; they especially don't want to spend any money. We shall also see to it that the maps and pictures which decorate the classroom are properly illuminated, that blackboards and maps are free from glare. When using the blackboard, teachers will make legible letters of sufficiently large size. Since they know that 7^{mm} letters can be read from a distance of 5 meters, they can proportion their writing to fit this requirement. We shall also make sure that school books are printed with well-formed letters 1.5^{mm} high and that 2.5^{mm} interspaces are left between lines. All these precautions seem overly meticulous, but they are so useful!

I don't think further pleading is needed to demonstrate the advantages of performing visual examinations on school children. But I want to take this opportunity to digress a little and talk about mental tests. These tests are rapid experiments designed to help us assess children's mental abilities. There are people who, for several reasons, like to make fun of the testing method. The American philosopher William James feels that tests are not interesting enough and that the child is therefore not motivated to do his best.

> No elementary measurement, capable of being performed in a laboratory, can throw any light on the actual efficiency of the subject; for the vital thing about him, his emotional and moral energy and doggedness, can be measured by no single experiment, and becomes known only by the total results in the long run.[6]

In relation to this he gives an extraordinarily touching example, that of the blind naturalist Huber, who, passionately interested in bees and ants, was able to observe them better through other people's eyes than these people could through their own. And James ends with a beautiful defense of the power of the will:

> If you wish to be rich, you will be rich; if you wish to be learned, you will be learned; if you wish to be good, you will be good. Only you must, then, really wish these things, and wish them with exclusiveness, and not wish, at the same time, a hundred other incompatible things just as strongly.[7]

His remarks are correct and his conclusion is sound. But does this mode of reasoning decrease in the least the value of mental tests? I don't believe so, for the examination of vision is really a mental test. It is an experiment of the type made in the laboratory; it is short, precise, partial. We could write the list of James' and a few other writers' objections alongside it. It could be said, in particular, that it fails to arouse students' interest. The latter will never try as hard to read the meaningless letters shown on an optometric chart as they will try to read from afar the enticing poster announcing a circus. But should we conclude that, for this reason, measuring students' visual acuity is useless? I am very sure no one will conclude this, and I challenge all critics of the test method to get themselves out of this predicament.

Since I am going to use mental tests often in the course of these studies — after having carefully selected them, of course — I shall now tell how to judge them. It is necessary to make a distinction, since there are tests of results and tests of analysis. The first are excellent; the second must always be used with caution. To place someone in a situation which is familiar to him, to make him work, then to let the evaluation of his performance be the results of the experiment, is to use the first kind of test. For example, if we wish to know whether or not a child has normal vision, we have him read letters of a definite size from a certain distance. If we wish to know about his memory, we give him something to learn in a given amount of time and eliminate possible sources of distraction. If we wish to know about his ability to draw, we have him draw without assistance and assess his work by using an exact method of evaluation. These are tests of the child's performance; we are concerned with the results not with the means. Now, if after having studied the memory of a pupil we attempt to analyse the nature of his pictures, if after having had him draw we try to see how much visualization he has, our point of view has changed. Instead of a synthesis, we are making an analysis; instead of looking for a result, we are looking for a process. This is more daring, and on this particular point we are in agreement with James. Whatever the lacunae of a mind may be, they can be compensated for by other faculties sustained by an iron will. An individual can be a draftsman without being able to visualize. We shall even go so far as to maintain, without paradox, that an individual's talent is often made up as much of his shortcomings as of his abilities. And people who, in the presence of a great talent, have attempted to analyse it have had the same surprise a chemist would have if he put a human being in a crucible and, after having heated it, finds only a few ashes. Let us not forget what happened to those who wanted to analyse Zola's talent. His attention span was carefully measured, as was his memory, his ideation, his reasoning. And in the residue of all these analyses, neither his lyricism, nor his work power, nor his absence of taste were found, nothing of what characterized his powerful literary personality.

II. Audition

It is as important for teachers to know about the condition of their students' audition as it is for them to know about the condition of their students' vision. It is a fact that a good part of teaching is carried out through the use of speech, and what good is speech if it is not understood or if it is incompletely understood? The teacher's task is twofold: First, he must be careful about his own way of speaking. He must not speak too fast; his voice must have sufficient intensity; his words must be articulated clearly, for clarity of articulation contributes more to being understood than loudness of voice. Finally, it is necessary to learn to direct the voice outward and not inward; we must, as music teachers say, project our voice.

Secondly, the teacher must identify those of his students whose hearing is impaired. It is not a matter of identifying children afflicted with total deafness, those who do not look back even when they are called loudly from behind. We feel a teacher will rarely have to make the very simple experiment which we report and recommend in passing. Total or severe deafness is rare, and where it exists, the parents already know about the condition. Most often deafness is partial and the child is hard of hearing. This partial deafness may be unilateral, involving a single ear. It may be transitory, the result of rhinitis or due to enlarged adenoids. The audition of a child affected with this last condition is often impaired. Be that as it may, children with abnormal audition, like children with abnormal vision, must not be relegated to the back of the class. Rather, they must be seated in the first row as close as possible to the lectern.

We know today that if these precautions are not taken, deaf children are greatly handicapped. Precise statistics have shown that partial deafness, what may be called school deafness, is a constant cause of educational retardation. Moreover, it has been observed that the degree of educational retardation is proportional to the degree of deafness; for instance, pupils who don't hear a whisper at a distance of 1 meter show a greater and more frequent retardation than those who hear it at a distance of 3 to 4 meters. And really, this relationship seems so natural that there is little reason to doubt its existence.

Statistics also show that the number of cases of deafness identified in school are extremely numerous. Some authors claim that out of three persons picked at random, at least one is found to have abnormal audition. School studies conducted in Germany report the percentage of abnormal auditions discovered to be around 25 per cent. In France, even more eloquent statistics were published recently. The percentage of partial deafness identified in studies supposedly conducted on student teachers was said to be no less than 75 per cent. These findings are really frightening. Were they true, the deaf would be in the majority and it would become abnormal to have normal audition. We have encountered this type of statistics in relation to visual deficiencies and have already said what we thought of them. The figure quoted appears to us to be exaggerated and biased; such statistics are given by specialists who, consciously or unconsciously, want to increase, inordinately, the prestige of their field of endeavor. For a psychiatrist there are only mental cases; for a specialist of audition there are only deaf people. It is in the rules. Let us not protest, let us just smile. Another reason to be skeptical is that all the data published about auditory deficiencies depend logically on the adopted standard, on the chosen definition of "deafness." If, for instance, we decide that for audition to be considered normal it must pick up a whisper from a distance of 100 meters, all of humanity will be classified as deaf. If we are satisfied, however, with a whisper being heard from a distance of 50 centimeters, almost no one will be placed in that category. It is necessary to remember that the definition of normality is purely a matter of convenience or convention. It is not a physiological or a medical measurement. By this we mean that the limits must be set in such a way that the individuals classified as deaf are those for whom the auditory impairment represents a handicap. In a school, for instance, children who while sitting at the back of the class can't make out what the teacher is saying should be considered partially deaf.

In practice, then, how can a teacher identify this particular kind of deafness? Don't count on the children to be much help to him. The child is a small passive being who is not used to complaining about his sensory impairments. If he can't see what is written on the board, if he can't hear the sentence the teacher has just dictated, he does not protest. He gets by as well as he can with the help of his memory, his imagination, or with the help of his classmates. The teacher himself must therefore make an examination of audition. But how?

It is a controversial question to which we can give no very clear answer. Auditory acuity is not measured as satisfactorily as visual acuity. To measure auditory acuity would require a source of auditory stimulation which would ideally have the two following qualities:

1. It would be comparable to the human voice. The way in which a child perceives his teacher's voice will reveal whether this child is deaf, hard of hearing, or normal, and it is this only which it is important to know.

2. Stimulus intensity should remain constant, for no measurement is possible with a stimulus which varies in intensity from day to day or from one moment to the other.

Now, the stimuli we have had to use so far have never had the two essential qualities we have just described. The watch has only one of them, namely, unvarying intensity. Speech also has only one, that of being a spoken word, consequently that of being the particular sound we are interested in perceiving. A few details will show what we mean.

We used the watch method extensively in one school. The blind-folded child was asked to listen for the "tic-toc" of the watch and instructed to give an answer every time we asked the question: "Do you hear it?" The watch was sometimes brought close, sometimes moved away; a graduated line drawn on the floor permitted us to assess our distance from the child for each trial. We made no noise so as to give no indication of the direction of our movement. In order to do away with the error introduced by certain subjects who think they hear when they really don't, we had the child respond from time to time when the watch was hidden in our pocket so that the sound of it was completely muffled. These examinations are difficult. They require almost absolute silence and take approximately three minutes per child. The differences in auditory acuity noted from one child to another are important. Some perceive the sound of the watch at a distance of 6 meters and even farther; others don't perceive it at a distance of 25 centimeters. I would find it difficult to calculate a valid average from such divergent results. It was recently proposed to consider as normal an audition which picks up the sound of a watch at a distance of 2 meters. Let us accept this figure as an approximate one without attaching too much importance to it.

The big shortcoming of this kind of audition examination is that its precision corresponds to nothing which can be utilized. What good does it do to know that a child perceives such pitch of the tuning fork, such tic-toc of a watch, such sound of a siren from a long distance? These particular sounds are not the ones he needs to respond to in class, and if he were a little deaf to them it would be of no serious consequence. But if he is deaf to the sound of the teacher's voice, he will not profit from the teaching and he will be wasting his time in school. What would be desirable would be finding a simple sound of measurable intensity with an audition parallel to the audition of speech. The examination would bear upon this simple sound and a conclusion could be drawn about the effectiveness of speech perception. Unfortunately the sound of a watch does not have this quality. A child can hear speech poorly and the sound of a watch well and vice versa.

We became convinced of this after making two different studies. The first one was based on the manner in which children heard the watch; the second was based on the way in which the same subjects heard the spoken word from a distance. In order to make this last classification, we rounded up 17 students in a covered courtyard; their teacher pronounced 40 words 10 meters away from them. The children wrote down everything they heard and the ranks obtained were function of the number of errors they made. Now, in comparing the results of the watch experiment with the results of the voice experiment, we observed there was practically no correlation between them.

We shall not conclude that the watch method must be rejected. It may be useful in cases of marked deafness. As for the teacher's voice, it is difficult to think of it as a standard. The human voice is a physiological function characterized by extraordinary instability. None of its elements are constant, neither its intensity nor its pitch, nor articulation. No two persons pronounce in the same way or with the same loudness or pitch or timber, and an individual's speech pattern varies from one moment to another without his being aware of it. We had occasion to observe this ourselves. The professor who had been asked to pronounce 40 words in the courtyard repeated the experiment a few minutes later in front of another group of students and little did he realize that the second time around he shouted less. In general, therefore, using speech as a stimulus to measure audition is quite incorrect. It is like measuring different lengths with a rubber yardstick which is stretched to different degrees.

So what can we conclude? We conclude, first, that audition of the spoken word cannot be measured with satisfactory precision using the overly simple procedures available to us in a school. It would be necessary to have recourse to either record players or to the perfected audiometers which now exist but which are expensive, complicated and bulky. Our second conclusion is that, everything considered, even an imprecise measurement is better than no measurement at all. Our criticisms of the watch method and the speech method do not strip them of all value. If we use them we shall probably make errors, but if we don't use them we run the risk of making bigger errors. The teacher should, therefore, not ignore them completely. A dictation including words and figures painstakingly articulated in a carefully controlled voice of average intensity could tell the teacher which of his pupils are hard of hearing. The procedure is quicker than that involving the watch method, since it only requires correcting the children's work, and we doubt that it is less precise.

FOOTNOTES FOR CHAPTER FOUR

1. Jourde,"An Indispensable Experience," *Bulletin de la Société de l'Enfant,* N° 31 (1906).

2. For technical details, see *Année Psychologique,* XII, p. 233.

3. A variety of these charts is available. The one that we use can be obtained at cost from "La Société Libre pour l'Etude de l'Enfant."

4. E. Javal, *The Physiology of Reading and Writing* (Paris: Alcan, 1905).

5. I have shown somewhere else that it is impossible to measure sensory acuity scientifically. See *Année Psychologique,* IX (1903), 247.

6. W. James, *Talk to Teachers,* 1899, p. 135.

7. *Ibid.,* p. 137.

CHAPTER FIVE

Intelligence : its measurement and its education

I. The Different Kinds of Cases in which
the Question of Intelligence is Raised

If you are truly and deeply interested in a child, no question you can ask about him is more interesting, more important for his present education, more distressing to the heart of a father or mother than the following: "Is this child intelligent or not?" When the subject is a successful student, gets good grades on his homework, ranks high on tests, there is little doubt that he is, for his actions are a good indicator of intelligence. The same is true of adults. To evaluate their worth — intelligence and character-wise — look at their social contribution. But often a child does not succeed in his studies, does not profit from the school program, and is among the last students in the class. We observe that in this case education has failed. Who or what is responsible for this failure? An answer to this question is what we must establish, in as objective a manner as possible and with the sincere hope that the explanation we find will contain a remedy.

We already saw in Chapter Two that the state of health and the physical development of a child who does poor work must be carefully assessed. We shall not repeat these physiological explanations of inadequate intellectual work here. Let us assume that we are in the presence of a child whose health is satisfactory, whose physical development is normal, and whose sensory organs are not appreciably impaired. He is placed in a class with schoolmates of the same age group and therefore receives the education ordinarily given children his age. Finally, we assume that his school attendance is regular; the number of absences from school found in his record is not much higher than average (twenty absences a year are considered an average number).

If we are consulted about a case of this type, the little pedagogical problem which has to be solved takes the form of a dilemma. We must choose between two main explanations: either the child is a good worker or he is not a good worker. Either the child makes commendable efforts to understand, remember, do his homework, but does not succeed because of a lack of intelligence; or he is sufficiently well endowed to profit from education but is unwilling to make an effort, does not apply himself, is lazy. It is clear that the teacher and the parent must incriminate either the child's intelligence or his character, as the case may be. In this chapter we shall assume we know, beyond any doubt, that the child applies himself, that his failure is due to intellectual deficiency, and we shall study this intellectual deficiency. Many teachers and parents seem to feel that when they have stated that a child is lacking in intelligence, they have said everything there is to be said and any further inquiry into the matter would be a waste of time. This is much too succinct a judgment. If we limit ourselves to this explanation we shall get nowhere. What a vast array of problems still to be solved! First, how great is the observed intellectual deficiency? Is it large or small? If it is serious, is it so serious that the teacher can do no more than despair? Then, is the intellectual deficiency real, or is it a condition that appears to be a deficiency, or is it magnified, exaggerated by exceptional circumstances? And also, what does it consist of exactly? What particular function, what kind of work puts it most in evidence? Finally, what are its causes? And are these causes of such a nature that they can be modified? It is absolutely necessary to look into these various questions, to study the points they bring forth, to elucidate them.

We believe it is desirable to begin our exposition by listing the different kinds of cases which are found in school practice and in which defective intelligence can rightly be suspected in a child. Our listings of these cases will not be exhaustive, but enough will be said to confront our readers with the true complexity of things and to give them an impression of reality. Let's first take the case of a school boy who at present appears disoriented. He has just come from a rural school and now finds himself in school in a large city where his schoolmates have different ideas, different habits, and use a different language. The teaching methods differ from the ones he is used to and he finds them confusing. The teacher is like a stranger to him, appearing very aloof, and since there are many students, the teacher cannot give anyone any special attention. This kind of abrupt change in environment is very distressing to the child, especially if he is still very young and is therefore unskilled at adjusting to new situations. We often hear it said that a change in schools — even when the two schools are in the same town — produces a slackening in the performance of the transplanted school child over a period of several months. There is all the more reason for this to happen when the change made is from the country to the city. What must be done in a case like this? How can we judge a child who does not know his lessons well, who answers questions incorrectly in class and especially who appears not to understand what is being explained to him? An evaluation of his intelligence may be very useful.

We have supposed that the transplantation was made between schools of equal standing or quality. But it often happens that a child has come from a school where the instruction has been inadequate and the teaching methods defective. As we commonly say, he was given a poor start. If we have him read, we can observe the bad habits he has already formed. His reading may have a singing quality to it, or he may read haltingly. Again, he may read fairly fluently but he either murders, mercilessly and without scruples, all the difficult words he comes across or he does not hesitate to omit them. What is true for reading is true for other subjects in the curriculum and especially for arithmetic. There are school children who can perform the four types of operations perfectly but who are completely unable to use them correctly in the solution of problems. They use multiplication where division is needed. For instance, they will conclude that a merchant has more goods after a sale than before, or they will obtain other fantastic results which it will not occur to them to question. They were taught to compute, not to reason. We all know schools where education degenerates into routine and students only pay attention to form. The penmanship and the brackets in their workbooks are irreproachable, but the substance, the essential part of their work is filled with nonsense. Everything is superficial; the teacher enriches their memory but does nothing to develop their judgment, their spontaneity, in short their intelligence. Everything is taught in the way catechism is, that is in question and answer form, and if someone words a question in a manner which is unfamiliar, the child remains silent. He waits, before answering, for question A — which is in his book — to be asked, and right away he remembers answer B. In relation to this, William James tells an amusing story. "A friend of ours who was visiting a school was invited to ask a question about geography from a class of young pupils. Looking at the manual, she said : 'Suppose you dig a well about one hundred meters deep. Would the temperature at the bottom of the well be higher or lower than at the top ?' Since everyone was silent, the teacher said : 'I am sure they know but maybe you are not asking the question in the right way. Let me show you,' and taking the book, he asked, 'In what state is the interior of the earth found ?' Half the class answered immediately : 'The interior of the earth is in the state of igneous fusion.'" It is a good example of automatic teaching.

But there is a better example. I once met a young woman who had just come out of a boarding school where she had spent about ten years. She not only knew nothing about life and had the bewildered look of someone coming out of jail, but she also had received no intellectual training of any kind during her boarding school experience. She read poorly, her spelling was fanciful, she was not even able to perform a multiplication, and she knew nothing about history or geography. Even her sewing left much to be desired. What she almost knew were the Scriptures and a large quantity of prayers and canticles she had been taught in Latin, which she recited without understanding them. This was not merely a case of wasted education. It meant further that such intellectual faculties as reasoning and judgment had not been developed in the student. She had been turned into a gullible, superstitious, fearful human being who gave stupid answers to questions in spite of the fact that she was not lacking in natural intelligence.

In this connection, I shall take the liberty to digress a little. I appear to have condemned automatic education, while many good authors we know have maintained that automatism must be the aim of instruction. Even Dr. LeBon said so in the following words : "Education is the art of making the conscious pass into the unconscious."

Actually I believe the statement is very sound. It seems to me that the ideal for a mathematician is to be able to multiply and to carry over without thinking about it, to use the multiplication table without hesitation. In the same way, a physician knows his profession well if, when examining a patient, he makes the right diagnosis quite automatically, without effort and without difficulty. But the sound statement which I quoted above would cease to be sound if it were carried too far; for instance, if we were to conclude that the whole organism must be turned into an automaton, made unconscious by education. Automatism is good only if it remains partial, only if it bears on certain aspects of the work to be done so that these become easily, accurately and quickly completed, thus enabling the individual to utilize the energy saved for developing adequately his critical judgment and his initiative. The unconscious must be used to bring relief to the conscious, to give it full play.

It also frequently happens that after giving a child a more or less cursory examination, the principal assigns him to a class which is too advanced for his level of development. Much damage is done to the student in this way and the year's work is likely to be wasted. In the lower grades, normally composed of pupils ranging in age from six to eight years, we sometimes find children who are five years old or younger. It is not surprising that these tiny tots cannot profit from programs which are not designed for them and that they remain at the bottom of the class. Let's take the case of young Ernest, for instance, who started first grade on the first of October. He only became five years old on the fourteenth of the month and has been placed one year above grade level because his parents, who value instruction and education, wish him to get an early start. The little man is in good health, his physical development is satisfactory, even a little superior to the average for his age; his height is that of a child one year older and his weight that of a child two years older. His vision and audition are good. But the teacher complains that this pupil pays little attention in class and that his intelligence is not sufficiently active for him to be able to follow. It is a fact that the rank he occupies is not good; on the average he is forty-ninth in a class of fifty. The only valid remedy in this case would be to send the child back to kindergarten.

Young Emile's case is similar to that of Ernest but a slight difference between the two must be noted. Emile is a year older. At age six he is in the same class as Ernest and is therefore at grade level. Let us add that as far as his eyes, ears, physical development, and state of health are concerned, he is normal. And his parents pay attention to him in the way parents of most very young children generally do. In spite of all these good reasons for succeeding, he ranks forty-fourth in a group of fifty students and this is not due to lack of diligence but to a slight delay in the awakening of his intelligence. His mind is still a little sluggish. The teacher, a far-seeing pedagogue who has studied him, says : "He is one of those first-graders about whom we say, ' He is not with us.'" These children are neither lazy nor inattentive, but they often need several months to see, grasp and learn what is being taught them. Then they make rapid progress and follow the class well.

Here is another case of placement error, only this time it is an older child, who can consequently be studied more closely. Raoul is ten and a half years old and is in the sixth grade, where children normally enter beginning at age eleven. He is a fairly intelligent child and his family follows his school progress with interest. Up to now his school attendance has been regular. He went through kindergarten, then through first and second grades in the normal fashion. He then skipped third grade and went directly into the fourth. His audition and vision are normal. He is a healthy, even a vigorous looking child. His weight and height are right for his age. During recess his attitude is a normal one ; he is cheerful, alert, active, never violent. But in class his behavior leaves much to be desired. He pays only moderate attention to lessons and has become even more inattentive during the second semester than during the first. He therefore tends to get behind. His lessons are poorly learned and his homework is neglected. As a result he ranks thirtieth in a class of thirty-two, which is sad for him. His teacher, who is not lacking in pedagogic insight, has not scolded or punished him. He has understood exactly what was happening. "A slight advance on his age group," the teacher explains, "put the child in a situation where he has to deal with rather arid subject matter. Abstractions are grasped with difficulty and they demand painful and premature efforts on his part. At the present time he seems to be suffering from a kind of mental fatigue from which he escapes through diversions." This is a normal, quite classical case. Let us learn to recognize it so we will know how to handle it. Raoul must not be rebuffed or allowed to become discouraged. We must wait and remind ourselves that for this student the present year is an incubation year. What he does not now understand, he will understand better next year and, given a chance to repeat the class, he will give excellent results.

This type of case is common. It is important to understand that intellectual development is not a regularly increasing process. The normal learning curve has plateaus. From time to time a point is reached at which a child makes no apparent progress. He is resting, as it were. Physical growth may be taking place in its turn at this time; we don't exactly know. Teachers and parents must be conscious of the fact that these latent periods do occur and that there is no need to worry about them. The data recently reported by Mr. Bocquillon will convince them of this.

This data shows that out of thirty-nine lazy children who made up the last fifth of a class, thirty-one improved their performance the following year and obtained honorable ranks. Thirty-one cases out of thirty-nine is more than a simple majority; it represents four-fifths of the group.

By way of contrast, we shall now describe a case which, on first examination, resembles from all points of view the one we have described above. This student, like the one above, is not able to assimilate the material presented in class. He is twenty-ninth in a class of thirty-two pupils and is therefore Raoul's neighbor. But his problem is more serious and his future is already compromised.

For Ramond, who is in the same class as Raoul, is not ten and a half years old but a good thirteen years old and is therefore three years below grade. His previous training may have been defective, for he attended a Congregationist school where, as a rule, little thought is given to the development of judgment. His audition and vision are normal. There is nothing to say about his physical development, which appears to be normal too. He plays with animation, almost with violence. His parents, who are fairly well off, are very interested in his work and even have him tutored after school. He is very assiduous, rarely absent from school. In class his behavior is correct; he is very docile. He studies his lessons well but he memorizes words more than he understands meaning, and his written work, although lacking in substance, is fairly good as to form. The teacher, who has studied him carefully and who has even tutored him on occasion, has become aware that Ramond is mentally retarded. His deficiency is characterized by a slowness of conception, a difficulty with self-expression, an absolute loathing for abstractions, a manifest inability to grasp general ideas. "All of the child's knowledge," adds the teacher, "rests upon memory and even this memory responds only slowly to his needs. His loathing for intellectual work is the inevitable consequence of what preceded. Tutoring produced only insignificant change. It proves that an insoluble problem exists, a natural deficiency." We do not subscribe, of course, to this pessimistic opinion and we find it hard to believe that improvement is impossible. But the point here is that there is an imperative need for a teacher to differentiate between these two types of cases — that of Raoul and that of Ramond. Ramond is in danger of becoming a true social failure. How can we make the distinction? It is especially important to take the age difference into account. In general, the student who will probably not progress eventually is relatively old; by that we mean that he is at least two, sometimes three years below grade. His place would be in a special class where, with customized teaching which we shall describe later, these retarded can be helped to make significant progress. The example of the retarded child I have just given is not a very clear one. It is that of a borderline case. A clearer example follows and is of particular interest because the subject is still very young. Armand is in first or second grade. He is eight years old and is therefore from one to two years below grade. The poor child is skinny and sickly. He is physically underdeveloped, his height being four years below normal for his age and his weight three years below normal. His vision and audition are defective and, to complete this sad picture, let us add that his family is destitute and takes absolutely no interest in his school work. A physically deficient subject is recognized by these signs. Armand is also intellectually deficient. In class he is drowsy, lifeless, dull. No question he was ever asked was ever answered. Given letters to copy, he distorts them and reproduces endlessly a sign of his invention which in no way resembles the original. But he is not unruly and never needs admonishing. During recess he is passive and inert, sitting motionless on a bench and watching the other children's games without becoming interested in them. He is sad and shy. If we invite him to play with the others, he obeys but soon gives up the game and goes back to sit down. The teacher concluded, with reason, that this child is both physically and intellectually retarded. We gave this example to complete the series, but it is evident that this manifest case of retardation ceases to be interesting to us. Such a child is not a problem from the point of view of diagnosis, for even the maid will identify him as being abnormal.

Now we see the case of another type of student who does not profit from the school program for a truly paradoxical reason: he is too intelligent. We sometimes meet brilliant children whose intellectual development is very superior to that of children their own age. They are not the last ones to find this out. In class a minimum of effort gets them the best grade. Their vanity is kindled, their work is whimsical. They learn their lessons at the last minute and readily become insubordinate. They do homework which was not assigned to them just to attract attention. During study periods they prevent other students from working. They are resented and punished but they are always forgiven come examination time. Classes for the gifted should be created. These classes would be as useful, if not more so, than classes for the normal child, for the elite's contribution — and not the effort of the average — determines the progress of humanity. It is therefore in the interest of society that the elite everywhere receive the culture they need. A child of superior intelligence is an asset not to be wasted.

And now let's come back to those who do not understand and who display a lack of intelligence. This category of children includes two types of individuals and it is very important to distinguish between them. Some have a general, global deficiency of intellectual faculties. They have no aptitudes of any kind; they are equally untalented in all areas of education. Some others, better endowed, have a few partial abilities. Most often they are resistant to general ideas and abstractions but their hands are skilled. They have good grades in drawing and especially in workshop activities; some are even superior in manual skills. The tool interests them more than the pen, and there is no great harm in that if they later become good workers. While the school teacher thinks of them as lacking in intelligence, the workshop foreman thinks well of them and appreciates them. We see how necessary it is to differentiate between these two types of cases: the child with aptitude for manual work and the child with no aptitude at all.

One large category of children, who should be called "pseudo-retardates," are those who are betrayed by their appearance. They have a certain handicap, it is true, but this handicap, of itself not very important, is so detrimental to them that they are often taken for imbeciles. It is well known that fluent speech argues in favor of the one who possesses it. But take the case of a child who stutters or one who, without having a real articulation problem, has difficulty in finding his words. People readily become impatient about his speech insufficiency and judge him poorly. Then there is the child who is slow in speaking or in thinking. It is ordinarily believed, and with reason, that readiness of mind and liveliness of facial expression are signs of intelligence. But there are slow individuals who make us wait a long time for an answer, either because they are thoughtful, because they have doubts, or simply because they are slow in everything. It is rare for them not to be underestimated. I recently was examining a young child whom a teacher had ranked among the last in the class on the basis of his intelligence. I took the time to interrogate him at length with a method which I will describe later, and I was forced to recognize that he was being done an injustice and did not deserve the bad opinion people had of him. It is true that it is rare to meet such an unlively child. He was slow to talk, slow to write, slow to walk, slow to do anything. I had him make dots on a piece of paper during ten seconds. In spite of many trials he never succeeded in making more than thirty-five dots, while his schoolmates of the same age made sixty. This child was only slow and a little somnolent. There are others who are affected in other ways. Take the case of the emotionally disturbed child, for instance. The presence of his schoolmates or the least glance from the teacher may unleash in him a violent storm of emotion which confuses him, disorganizes him, renders him incapable of thinking about anything. He is not led to violent or unreasonable acts by emotion, he does not become impulsive; on the contrary, he is paralyzed by emotion. No comparison is more suitable for him than that of a mad compass. Every examiner is familiar with this type of individual whom fear stupefies. I was told recently about one of these children. Raised at home with his sisters, he never went out alone. He was taken to school by a maid, coddled and spoiled by his mother, and subjected to all sorts of influences which increased his edginess. He was even made to learn piano. In class he was so thoroughly disturbed by the least incident that he only gave stupid answers to questions. We have just described the main types of circumstances in which it is necessary to make a diagnosis about intelligence in school. We gave only illustrations, and by listing those we do not wish to set limits to an extremely vast question. It is almost at each instant that we need to know if a child is intelligent and this investigation is of prime importance.

II. The Measurement of Intelligence

Let us see now which procedures should be used in the diagnosis of a child's intelligence.

In actual fact and when dealing with extreme and clear-cut cases, an observing teacher can sometimes get an accurate idea about his student's mental ability.

I do not think it is necessary to dwell a long time on the small empirical means used daily for this purpose. We take into account quickness of mind, clarity and soundness of answers, and a thousand other signs which are often very useful and which can render great service. However, teachers sometimes find the task difficult and sometimes, too, commit undeniable errors, a few of which I have had occasion to witness. The same thing can be said about parents. If they are intelligent and well-informed, parents will know admirably well how to evaluate their children's intelligence, but most often they lack standards of comparison. They have a tendency to view behaviors as being exceptional which are ordinary manifestations of normal intelligence. Moreover they are extremely optimistic. They are easily impressed by the young child's clever words. These words, sometimes charming and sometimes also only echoes, often — too often — express only one thing: out-of-place frankness and lack of judgment. Parents, even more than teachers, need to be taught how to evaluate children's intelligence.

Are physicians more skillful?

I know how much we owe physicians. I know what a great service they do us by showing us that many intellectual disturbances which occur in children have a physical origin. But how would they know if a child has precisely the intelligence of his age? No special kind of study has prepared them for this task, and tact and common sense do not take the place of specialized study. How, through what kind of reasoning, indeed, can we guess the age at which a young child knows how many fingers he has, or distinguishes between morning and afternoon, or names the main colors correctly, or knows how to give change? It is absolutely impossible. While talking to a student it is easy to establish whether he is slow or quick, talkative or taciturn. In this way we get a general idea which is not without value, especially in extreme cases; in those cases which are so clear — let us just say it — that everybody agrees about them. But in order to know if a child has normal intelligence for his age, or if he is retarded or advanced and how much, it is necessary to have a precise and really scientific instrument.

Can psychology give us this instrument? The profession cannot be at fault if it has not done so up to now, for the question of the measurement of intelligence has not ceased to be the order of the day for twenty or thirty years. Numerous are the program-makers, the armchair technicians who have thought out experiments designed to reveal and to measure people's mental capacities. What suggestion has not been offered? Rebuses to be guessed, sentences to be completed, illegible writing to be made out, a complicated thought to be understood, a machine to be disassembled and assembled, a hidden mechanism to be imagined, a drawing to be criticized, an absurdity to be uncovered, a series of abstract words to be explained, etc. A much simpler test was also proposed once: It would have consisted in knocking as fast as possible on the corner of a table. From the number of knocks given in five seconds, the child would have been judged intelligent or not.

Suppose that we first sort out these different tests, some of which are perhaps lacking in clarity and precision. If we retained the best of them and if we applied it rigorously and consistently to a whole series of school children of equal intelligence, would this simple test permit us to uncover their intellectual differences?

Experimentation has already given the answer to this question, which I shall show by analysing briefly all the conclusions to be drawn from a single test. The test which I am taking as an example was suggested and used by Biervliet, our distinguished colleague from Ghent University. A visual test, it consists of measuring visual acuity under certain well-defined conditions.

To begin with, out of three hundred university students who had gone through his class, Biervliet selected ten whom he judged the most intelligent, on the basis of his personal experience with them and their subsequent success in their studies and in their profession. With the same precautions, he chose ten other students whom he considered the least intelligent of all, for inverse reasons. The selection he made, therefore, was fairly severe; he retained one subject in thirty. He then carefully measured the vision of each of these students, seeking to establish the greatest distance from which, given a certain lighting condition, the student could read a small text attached to a wall. This maximum distance gives a figure which represents a measure of visual acuity. A subject who reads the text from a distance of ten meters is, as far as visual acuity is concerned, superior to one who reads the same text from a distance of eight meters, for instance. There is nothing new up to this point. This is the classical method. The ingenuity of the procedure resides in the following fact: the measurement of the maximum distance from which the readings were made was done not just once but several times in succession, with texts of the same typographic size but having different meanings. The maximum distance from which reading was successful was jotted down each time. Suppose the series of measurements were as follows:

First trial = ten meters
Second trial = eleven meters
Third trial = nine meters
Fourth trial = eight meters
Fifth trial = twelve meters, etc.

The variation between the measurements could be easily obtained by calculating the average of all the distances, then by calculating the average of each distance in relation to that average. In the example given, the average distance would be ten meters, and the variation 1^m2. An interesting and somewhat unexpected finding was that the performance of the subjects in the most intelligent group did not differ much from the performance of the subjects in the least intelligent group, as far as the maximum reading distance was concerned. Only this first group average variation of the maximum distance differed significantly. Thus the maximum reading distance was 5^m902 for the most intelligent group and 6^m427 for the least intelligent group. The latter, therefore, had a slightly superior vision, since they could read the same text from a greater distance. But the average of their variations was different: 0^m116 for the most intelligent group; 0^m393 for the least intelligent group. Here the difference is much greater, the relationship of these two figures being one to four. From this we shall conclude, if we can be permitted to generalize from this little experiment, that the most intelligent students are not differentiated from the others as much by the power of their vision in relation to distance as by the reliability of this vision. There is less variation in their performance from one trial to another. If they read the text from a distance of six meters on the first trial, they will only vary about 0^m10 in subsequent trials; the less intelligent group's variation will be much greater. Now, since these variations depend on attention and since a small variation is the result of greater attention, we shall conclude from this, reasonably enough, that the superiority of the intelligent subjects manifests itself more particularly in a greater power of attention. We have reported Biervliet's experiment in its entirety — interpreting it in our own way — because it is typical. It makes it unnecessary for us to describe an infinite number of other experiments which were conceived on the same model and which led to exactly the same conclusion. [1]

Let us take good note of this conclusion and carefully evaluate its practical worth. Any test which brings people's intelligence into play and which involves a level of difficulty appropriate to the individual's intellectual level is sufficient to reveal an intellectual difference having the value of an average. If we have divided the subjects into two groups, one composed of the most intelligent, the other of the least intelligent, the little psychological experiment will almost certainly permit differentiating the first group from the second. A psychological experiment would not even be necessary for that. The same differentiation would be effected by measuring the volume of students' heads. It could also be effected, I am sure, by asking children the most elementary questions, such as, "How old are you?" or "How is the weather?" or simply by watching them open a door. If it is very easy to differentiate one group from another, it is not nearly so easy to differentiate one individual from another. Were the Biervliet experiment to be repeated on twenty subjects of unequal intelligence who had not previously been divided into two categories, the results would not make it possible to identify the most intelligent subjects.

Thinking about this problem, we became convinced that the short-comings of the mental test method reside in two main facts. On one hand, the method is fragmentary, bearing only on one or two faculties and not on the faculties as a whole. Thus the Biervliet test measures attention mainly, almost exclusively. On the other hand, an individual's mental faculties are unequal and independent. Poor memory may be associated with good judgment, and someone who demonstrates a remarkable retention power in a memory test can be a remarkable fool. We have seen examples of this. The scope of our mental tests is always limited. Each of these tests is suitable for the analysis of a single faculty and cannot expose the totality of an intelligence. Now, it is mainly this totality which determines the value of an individual. We are a cluster of tendencies, and it is the combined effect of all these tendencies which manifests itself in our actions and makes our life what it is. It is this totality, therefore, which is important to evaluate.

Dr. Simons and I have recently proposed a synthetic theory of the functioning of the mind, which it will surely be useful to summarize here. This theory shows clearly that the mind is a unit in spite of the multiplicity of its faculties and that it has an essential function to which all others are subordinated. After we have become acquainted with this theory, we shall better understand the conditions a test must fill if it is going to expose the totality of an intelligence. [2]

In our opinion, intelligence, viewed independently of the phenomena of sensitivity, emotion and will, is, above all, a faculty directed toward the external world and striving to reconstruct that world by means of the small fragments of it which we perceive. What we perceive of the world is element A, and the very complicated work of our intelligence consists in soldering to this first element a second element, element B. All knowledge is therefore essentially an addition, a continuation, a synthesis. The addition may be done automatically, as when we perceive a small figure in the distance and say, "There is our friend over there on the road." On the contrary, the addition may be effected after a conscious search; for instance, when a physician who has studied at length a patient's symptoms concludes, "It is a ruptured blood vessel; he is going to die," or when a mathematician who has labored over a problem for a long time states, "X is worth so much." Now let us not forget that a number of faculties are already working on these additions to element A; namely, comprehension, memory, imagination, judgment and especially speech. Let us retain only what is essential, and since all this leads to the invention of an element B, let us call the whole process an invention which takes place after a comprehension. All we have to do is draw a line and our schema is complete. The work described cannot be done haphazardly, without our knowing what the matter is all about, without adapting a certain position from which we do not deviate. We must therefore take and maintain a definite direction. Similarly, the work cannot be completed successfully if the ideas which are generated in the process are not evaluated as they occur and rejected if they are found to be unsuitable to the goal that is being pursued. Censorship must therefore be exercised. Comprehension, invention, direction and censorship — this is the essence of intelligence. We can consequently already conclude from the preceding that these four primordial functions will have to be studied by our method and will therefore fall under the scope of special tests.

But since the task consists, more particularly, in measuring a child's intelligence — an intelligence in evolution — let us ask ourselves in what ways this intelligence can differ from that of an adult. Let us avoid putting ourselves off with fine words. Let us not say that a child's intelligence differs from that of an adult in degree and not in nature. Rather let us try, with as much precision as possible, to grasp the essential difference which exists between the child and us. All that follows is written with an eight- or nine-year-old school boy in mind. It will be understood that the younger the child is, the greater the reported difference will be, and the older he is, the smaller the difference will be.

There are many intellectual differences between a child and an adult. Some of them can be ignored here for they are without importance. For instance, a child has less experience than an adult; he knows less, has fewer ideas, knows fewer words. Let us note also that he has different goals, different interests, different concerns. The sexual instinct is not as strong in him as in the adult, for example. And all this has many practical implications. Thus, because of his lack of experience and knowledge, he cannot be given the free direction of his life. But these do not represent differences in the psychological organization of intelligence and we need not be concerned about them. Should these differences not exist, the youngster would nonetheless retain the intelligence of a child. To characterize this intelligence, let us go back to our schema, which includes direction, comprehension, invention and censorship.

The young child displays a lack of direction in everything he undertakes. He is heedless and inconsistent. He is apt to forget what he was engaged in doing, to become disgusted with his occupations, or to become distracted by a fantasy, a caprice, an idea which crosses his mind. In a conversation or in telling a story, he skips and hops from one subject to another in response to idea association. Observe his lack of direction as he goes to school. He does not go straight to the goal, as an adult would, but zigzags along, forever stopping or making unnecessary detours to view some spectacle which interests him, distracting him from his goal and attracting him to the opposite sidewalk. When absorbed by some occupation, he loses sight of others and often needs to be told, "Pay attention."

His comprehension is superficial. There is no doubt that he perceives exterior objects, their shape, their color, the noise they produce, almost as exactly as an adult does and that his sensory acuity is very good. He can therefore judge and compare simple sensations, colors, weights, lengths with an accuracy which surprises us. But if perception must go beyond simple sensations and become true comprehension, then the child's perception shows signs of weakness. It has been said of the child that he is a good observer. This is an illusion. He may be struck by a detail which we adults will not have noticed, but he will not see a whole, a panorama of things, and especially is he incapable of distinguishing between the essential and the accessory. If we have him tell about an event which he has witnessed, we observe that he has had only a superficial view of it and that the setting rather than the hidden meaning impressed him. As a matter of fact, an interpretation in depth is impossible for the child because this requires language, and he is still at the sensory intelligence stage. The verbal intelligence stage begins later and consequently he does not understand many words which are very clear to us or he attaches the wrong meaning to them. And if we make a careful study of the language he uses, we see how "sensory" he

92

remains; he uses very few adjectives, some substantives, and many verbs, proving that he is mainly sensitive to words expressing action. Rarely used are conjuctions (for, because, if, when), those small words which are perhaps the noblest part of language, the most logical, since they express the subtle relationships between ideas. He uses concrete words mainly, abstract words much less often. All this points to the same thing: a comprehension which is of a sensory nature and which remains superficial. [3]

His power of invention is equally limited. First, it is more the product of imagination than of reasoning, more sensory than verbal. And secondly, it is superficial, it does not evolve, it is undifferentiated. We have two very clear examples of this. If we ask a child what he thinks of some objects he knows and to define them for us, immediately his thought develops in the utilitarian sense. He defines each thing according to the use made of it and this use is viewed in the most limited, the most banal form. "What is a knife? — It is for cutting; a horse? — it is for pulling a cart; a table? — it is to eat on; a mother? — is for preparing meals; bread? — is to eat; a snail? — is for crushing." Similarly, he explains that we work to avoid being punished or to be rewarded. His mentality also comes through very candidly on another occasion when we have him describe pictures. Looking at a picture which depicts misery, for instance, showing poor people collapsed on a bench, the five- or six-year-old child will say: "It is a man. Here is a woman. There is a tree." A child from eight to ten, trying to describe what he sees, will say: "The man is sitting on a bench. There is a woman near him." Adult intelligence is needed to see beyond the picture, to understand its meaning and say finally: "They are people without shelter, destitute people, people who are suffering." Now let us take careful note of what these answers tell us about the child's mentality. They prove to us that his inventive power is still poorly differentiated. The very young child interprets the picture by means of vague, banal imagery which fits all kinds of pictures equally well and which consequently is suitable for none. To say that the picture shows a man or a woman is to make a banal observation. We are being more specific when we describe the position people are in, the way they behave, the occupation they are engaged in. Specialization is still greater when the child goes beyond description and interprets the meanings of the picture. Enumeration, description, interpretation, these are three stages of the evolution of thought. This evolution consists of passing from vagueness to precision, from the general to the specific; the young child is in the process of making this transition.

The power of censorship is as limited in him as are the other powers. He is uncritical about what he says or does. His mind is as awkward as his hands. He is remarkable in his ability to put himself off with fine words and not to perceive that he does not understand. The "why's?" with which his curiosity badgers us are not very embarrassing, for he will be naively satisfied with the most absurd "because." He is not very successful in differentiating between what he imagines or wishes and what he has really seen, and this confusion explains many of his lies. Finally, everyone knows about his extreme suggestibility, which lasts until about age fourteen. It is of a complicated nature, for it is attributable to his character as much as to the immaturity of his intelligence. At any rate, this suggestibility is still another proof of his lack of censorship.

With the kind of mentality we have just described, the child resembles an adult imbecile, intelligence-wise. And if we had enough space we would list a whole series of questions, problems and difficulties to which the adult imbecile and the normal child respond in exactly the same way. The resemblance is due to the same lack of censorship and direction, the same superficial comprehension, the same undifferentiated invention. However, we have a strong feeling that this resemblance is not and cannot be complete between two beings who are preparing for such a different future. The development of the adult imbecile has been completed; the child is only at the very beginning of his. And precisely because he is in the process of development, the child possesses a certain number of very interesting qualities which, though not mentioned in the preceding schemata, are very characteristic of his condition. First is his power of memory. The child's memory is quick and durable because this quality is necessary for his entire eventual evolution. A mind without plasticity would be incapable of being transformed. Compared to any adult, the child has a better memory. He may not learn faster, but he retains what he has perceived longer. Another important characteristic of the child is the extra store of energy which he continually needs to spend, rendering him restless and noisy and making him so resistant to the discipline of silence which we want to impose upon him at school. "Be still!" is the warning we are forced to repeat endlessly to him, often followed by "Pay attention!" The third, final characteristic is the child's ceaseless experimenting with all sorts of things to become familiar with external objects or to exercise his faculties. As a baby he takes objects, manipulates them, strikes them, sucks them, and later he spends hours involved in play. The child is essentially someone who plays. In its deepest sense, play is a preparation for adult life, an amusing rehearsal before the real performance. All beings in the process of development are distinguished and characterized by their involvement in play. We hardly need to add that the adult imbecile does not play.

This special mentality of the child is what we shall attempt to evaluate by means of a series of tests.

There is nothing like necessity to generate new ideas. We undoubtedly would have retained the status quo, using fragmentary tests, if a matter of truly social interest, three years ago, had not made it mandatory for us to measure intelligence by the psychological method. It had been decided to try to organize some special classes for abnormal children. Before these children could be educated, they had to be selected. How could this be done?

We have already said that teachers' ratings of children's intelligence need to be controlled and that a student's educational retardation does not mean much when his school attendance has been poor or when records of his school experiences are lacking, which so frequently happens in Paris. What could be done? Each day some new child was brought to us about whom none of the indispensable information was available. Neither the parents nor the teacher nor the child's past school experience could be of any help to us. We were truly left to our own devices. The child was here in our office, alone with us, and after fifteen to thirty minutes of questioning we had to come up with a precise judgment about him, a redoubtable judgment, we felt, for his whole future was at stake.

It was under these circumstances that our devoted collaborator Dr. Simon and I formulated a plan for measuring intelligence which we called "a metric scale of intelligence." This instrument was slowly constructed on the basis of studies made in elementary and nursery schools, on children ranging in age from three to sixteen. Studies were also then made in hospitals, in children's homes, on idiots, imbeciles and morons, and finally, in all types of environments, even in the army, on literate and illiterate subjects. After hundreds of verifications and modifications, my carefully considered and definite opinion is not that the method is perfect, but that it is the type of method which needed to be used. And if, after us, others perfect it — as we certainly hope — they will only perfect it by using our own procedures and by drawing upon our experience.

The main plan in this method is as follows. Imagine a large number of tests, both short and precise, presenting an increasing level of difficulty. Try these tests on a large number of children of different ages and note the results. Identify the tests which are successful for a given age and that younger children, even if only a year younger, are unable on the average to complete. Build a metric scale of intelligence which permits establishing if a particular individual's development is normal for his age, retarded or advanced, and also permits evaluating the number of months or years of retardation or advance in development.

The following table contains a list of our tests. A short commentary will be sufficient to explain it. Those who might wish more ample details, especially with regard to practical application, are asked to consult our previous works. [4]

A Metric Scale of Intelligence

Five months	Eye movement control.
Nine months	Pay attention to sound. Seize an object after visual perception.
One year	Distinguish foods.
Two years	Walk. Go on a small errand. Ask to go to the bathroom.
Three years	Show own nose, eye, mouth. Repeat two digits. Enumerate the persons and objects in a picture. Give own last name. Repeat six syllables.
Four years	Tell his sex. Name a key, a knife, a penny. Repeat three digits. Compare two lines and indicate which is the longer.
Five years	Compare two boxes of different weight and indicate the heavier. Copy a square. Repeat a ten-syllable sentence. Count four pennies. Put together a puzzle composed of two parts.
Six years	Distinguish the right hand from the left ear. Repeat a sixteen-syllable sentence. Make an esthetic comparison. Define familiar objects and their use. Go on three errands. Tell own age. Distinguish morning and evening.
Seven years	Identify missing parts on faces. Give the number of fingers. Copy a written sentence. Copy a diamond. Describe a picture. Count thirteen pennies. Name four coins.
Eight years	Read an assignment and remember two things from reading. Count three pennies and three nickels, then give total. Name four colors. Count backward from twenty to zero. Compare two objects from memory. Write under dictation.
Nine years	Give the complete date of the day. Name the days of the week. Define better than through usage. Read an assignment, retain six things from readings. Give back change on twenty cents. Put five boxes in order according to weight.
Ten years	Enumerate months of the year. Recognize the different kinds of coins. Compare two sentences in which three given words are used. Answer eight questions involving intelligence.

Twelve years	Criticize absurd sentences. Include three words in a sentence. Find more than sixty words in three minutes. Give definitions of abstract words. Reconstruct disconnected sentences.
Fifteen years	Repeat seven figures. Find three rhymes for a given word. Repeat a twenty-six-syllable sentence. Interpret a picture. Resolve a psychological problem.

The first tests were made in nurseries beside the cribs, and we worked with bells, cookies and candy. The first awakening of intelligence is revealed in following an object with the eyes, for instance a lighted match which is being displayed. Then comes the response to sound; when we ring a bell behind the baby's head, he turns around. The child seizes an object which is presented to him as early as nine months of age. A little later he knows how to distinguish between a piece of wood and a piece of chocolate, and he carries the latter, in preference, to his mouth. The first spontaneous words come between eighteen and twenty-four months. It is at two, and even a little sooner, that walking without help begins and that language is sufficiently well understood for the child to be able to carry out an elementary task, such as going to fetch a ball. At age three the nursery school experience begins. In this setting we had to exercise great caution, not only to avoid frightening the tiny tots but also to get them to talk to us. Mutism is the usual form of shyness in young children, and besides being shy, some of them already show signs of stubbornness. There were a few who absolutely refused to open their mouths in front of us. This was not because they were mute, however, for the teacher told us that on occasion they could be quite talkative. The nursery school experiments are simple enough. The first ones consist of having digits or words repeated. We give the child three digits, for instance, "Two-eight-seven," and he must repeat them exactly. When told to, he shows the most apparent parts of his face, or he begins naming the very familiar objects presented to him. This is already more complicated, for speech development supposes that we understand other people's speech and that we can find the words necessary to express our own thoughts; now this second event occurs later than the first. We also ask these very young children to give their family name and to answer the following question correctly: "Are you a little boy or a little girl?" The last language exercise is done with pictures, which have the great advantage of always interesting children. At this age youngsters are still at the enumeration stage, and while running a finger over the picture, they say, "A man, a woman, a baby," and so on. Nursery school tests also contain some research on sensory intelligence. We ask the children to decide which of two lines is the longer or which of two boxes is heavier, and when we have succeeded in getting their attention, we are surprised at the soundness of their judgment.

For ages six to twelve years, the experiments were conducted in elementary schools and it is there that we worked the longest. We did not encounter any difficulties. As early as age seven the child is well adapted and well disciplined. We found no case of cumbersome shyness, no child ever refused to answer us, and none appeared uncomfortable after a few minutes of conversation with us. What we did have to watch for in some of these subjects, however, was their pride. When dealing with a twelve-year-old who already considers himself a man, it is well not to ask overly simple questions which could make him feel that he is being made fun of. These studies of school children took quite a bit of time, the examination of the younger children lasting approximately twenty minutes, that of the older ones from thirty to forty-five minutes.

The tests these young children are subjected to are numerous and investigate all the intellectual faculties : sensory intelligence, as well as language which begins playing an important role in the child's psychological life; the exercise of attention, and what we called direction, comprehension, invention and censorship, in performing the tasks included in the tests. We shall give only a few examples.

There is a whole series of questions about practical life which a normal child should be able to answer; for instance, " How old are you?"... " Is this morning or afternoon?"... " Show me your right hand! Your left ear!"... " How many fingers do you have on your right hand? On both your hands?"... " What is the date today (day, date, month, year)?"... " What are the days of the week?"... " What are the months of the year?" If we consult the table to determine at what age a child can answer these very elementary questions, we are surprised to find out it is only by age nine that the complete date is known, by age ten that it becomes possible to recite the list of months without errors. Besides these questions about practical life, our table contains questions which bear more directly on school knowledge. Thus several exercises involve arithmetic. At age five a child already can count up to four pennies, but it is only at age seven that he can count up to thirteen pennies and at age eight that he can count a sum of nine cents composed of mixed coins. At this age he is also expected to know how to count backward from twenty to zero. From a nine-year-old child we can demand much more. We can ask him to give back change on twenty-five cents. An amusing little game introduces this test. We pretend the child is a merchant. We buy a four-cent item from him, pay him with a quarter, then ask him for the change. This problem represents a much greater level of difficulty than the test for seven- and eight-year-olds. This proves to us that mathematical ability begins to develop rapidly starting at age nine. If we refer back to the Achievement Scale (Chapter Two, page 33), and if we study the sequence of tests presented to the students, we observe the difference between the problem for age eight, a simple subtraction, and the problem for age nine, which includes a division with a remainder. Thus in two different ways we reach the same conclusion: progress in math begins at nine. Another glance at this same Achievement Scale shows that progress in reading begins much sooner, around six or seven, and that progress in spelling takes place about the same time.

Reading is represented in our series of problems, but it is in a form which presents a greater level of difficulty than a normal reading test. We have the student read a news item and after he has read it, we require that he tell us about it in his own words. We have shown earlier that the reading act must attain a certain automatism before reading can become fluent. When at age nine this automatism is sufficiently developed to make it possible for attention to dwell freely upon meaning, we require that six different facts or memories be retained from our news item. When this is achieved, it is proof that the child reads not only with his eyes but also with his intelligence.

Finally, there is a whole series of tests which have nothing to do with either school knowledge or practical life — at least for the most part — and which depend almost exclusively on natural and bare intelligence. And we could say without much exaggeration that any child, whatever his age, could succeed in these tests if he had the necessary intelligence. For instance, to repeat five digits demands a small effort of attention. To perform three tasks which are requested at the same time requires consistency in the pursuit of a goal, a good direction. Mothers know well that a child of a certain age should be given only one order at a time, for he would forget the others. Direction is even more necessary in a curious ordination test which consists of arranging five boxes in order of decreasing weight. To place the boxes in the correct order it is necessary not only to perceive the differences in weight, which are large enough, but also to keep in mind the idea of order and to complete the placement without becoming distracted, which is more difficult. This is a good test of what we call direction.

Comprehension is also tested in several problems. For instance, when shown the faces of two women, the child must indicate which is the more beautiful; or he is asked to compare two objects from memory; or he has to tell the difference between glass and wood, between a butterfly and a fly, between paper and cardboard. Finally, he is asked complicated questions, the meaning of which he must perceive before he can give an answer; for example: " Before taking a position in a matter of importance, what must we do?" or " Why do we forgive a bad action committed in anger sooner than a bad action committed without anger ? " or " Why must we judge a person after his acts rather than after his words ? "

Invention will be tested with exercises in which the child puts a little of himself, adding to what has been given to him. To answer a question like the ones we have just transcribed supposes both comprehension and invention. So does defining objects or describing pictures. Invention is more difficult in an exercise which consists of composing a meaningful sentence in which three given words are contained. [Those given by Binet are " Paris, " " fortune, " and " creek. "]

Finally, let us say that the evaluation of censorship is done all throughout the examination by observing the subject's general attitude and the way he goes about executing the work. But there are special problems which are designed to expose deficient censorship. These are represented by sentences to be criticized. The subject is told ahead of time that a sentence which contains an absurdity is going to be read to him and his task is to identify the absurdity.

Here are a few of these sentences : " An unfortunate bicycle rider smashed his head and died instantly ; he was taken to the hospital and it is feared he may not recover. " " A railroad accident took place yesterday. It was not a serious one ; only forty-eight people died. " " I have three brothers : Peter, Ernest and I. " " Yesterday the body of an unfortunate young woman cut in eight pieces was found on the fortifications. It is believed she killed herself. "

For age thirteen and above we leave elementary school. The remainder of the tests are divided into two categories : one which is suitable for subjects fifteen years of age, and the other suitable for adults. This last part of our research was conducted on young men and women employed in business or industry. Clerks, sales people, accountants, mechanics, then seamstresses, laundresses and milliners were examined. With these adults it was necessary to take more precautions than with the children : to be more attentive, to give more explanations about the results, and especially to use infinite tact in the handling of errors, excusing them to the best of our ability so as to avoid wounding people's pride. But in general this is not an insurmountable difficulty, and it is easy enough to conceal from the examinees the fact that the test is an evaluation of their judgment. When they fail, for instance when they cannot show by their explanations that they have understood the slightly ambiguous text which has been read to them, we tell them : " You have forgotten... It is difficult to remember everything, and you may not have a great memory. " They hasten to accuse their memory and their honor is safe.

Finally, our last examinations were conducted on soldiers who were convalescing at the Val-de-Grace Hospital in Paris and who no longer showed signs of pathology. An army physician had invited us to make these examinations. This was in response to a letter we had sent the War Ministry suggesting that a procedure for identifying mentally retarded recruits, now used in Germany, be adopted in France. While interrogating some fifteen soldiers in the course of testing, we had occasion to collect a few truly inept answers. These inept answers had been heard before by officers who were curious about their men's education and had often provided humor, sad humor, in many newspapers. For our part, we admit that illiterate or poorly educated soldiers are very numerous. However, when we make this type of examination, it is important to be conscious of a possible source of error which lowers the performance level of the examinees enormously: the shyness of men in the presence of their chiefs. We were struck by this fact during our experiments. We stood like military judges in a large room with austere walls decorated with a panoply of swords. Among the soldiers brought to us were several who, in spite of our friendly welcome, remained pale, had a shivering voice and convulsive motions of the face and hands. These emotional individuals gave us some fantastic answers. We became aware, at the time, that the presence in the room of several high-ranking officers who had been interested in our work had a disastrous effect on the soldiers' intellectual functioning and that after the officers departed, the soldiers' responses became generally better. We conclude, therefore, that many soldiers' answers which provide amusement in the newspapers are due to an intellectual functioning temporarily hampered by emotion.

Let us extract from our notes an important bit of information. Although our Achievement Scale was designed to measure children's intelligence more particularly, it also made it possible for us to find out the average limit of the intelligence of adults, when these adults are normal and members of the working class. From the standpoint of abstract comprehension, they do not perform beyond the twelve-year level. Two tests, one composed of problems related to intelligence and the other composed of problems related to judgment (we have given examples of both), constitute the touchstone of normal intelligence in the working class individual.

While applying our method of investigation in the schools we obtained the following results, which showed the way in which intelligence is distributed in groups of individuals. We found that out of a total of 203 school children, 103 were regular, the level of their mental development was exactly the one considered normal for their age; 44 were above normal and 56 were below normal.

Let us add a detail. We spoke of children who were ahead, of others who were behind. But how much ahead or behind were they? The great majority of exceptional children only deviated from the normal by one year. Only 12 out of 203 (approximately 6 per cent) were two years behind, and among children judged by teachers to be normal, we found none whose retardation was greater than two years. On the other hand, we found only 2 who were two years ahead.

We might add that every time a teacher came to see us, after we had completed our study, to bring to our attention the fact that a particular child appeared to him to be gifted, we found this pupil had performed well on our tests. He was either a year ahead or he was normal; he was never retarded. One other significant detail: whenever we have had to examine children who were suspected of retardation and who were judged so, not for vague or trifling reasons but because their school performance was at least three years below grade without this being justified by irregular school attendance, intellectual retardation was always revealed by our Achievement Scale. The following information was extracted from my notes and was obtained on a group of thirteen children brought to my pedagogic laboratory in 1908. These children were suspected of mental retardation. Intellectual retardation of from one to five years was found in all of them, as the following data show:

One year	= 4 children
Two years	= 2 children
Two and a half years	= 1 child
Three years	= 2 children
Three and a half years	= 2 children
Four years	= 1 child
Five years	= 1 child

Let us note, in passing, that the intellectual retardation found is important and much greater, on the average, than the maximum intellectual retardation found in normal subjects. I personally believe that any intellectual retardation equal to two years constitutes serious presumptive evidence for mental retardation.

Just what does the measurement of intelligence consist of? As in relation to instruction and physical development, the word "measurement" is not used here in its mathematical sense: it does not indicate the number of times a quantity is contained in another. For us the idea of measurement is closer to the idea of hierarchical classification. The more intelligent of two children is the one whose performance is better on a certain kind of test. Moreover, taking into consideration the averages obtained in the testing of children of various ages, the measurement is established as a function of mental development. And for intelligence, as for instruction or for physical development, we measure it in terms of the retardation or advance a given child has in relation to other children his age.

This represents a complete method of evaluation which we believe to be new. We do not have the time to discuss the main philosophical consequences of this method, but one of these consequences must be underlined: by convention, an average child of a given age is considered more intelligent than a younger child, and, in other words, a precocious child has an intelligence superior to that of the average child his own age.

Clearly this instrument cannot be put in just anybody's hands. Its use demands tact, judgment, a knowledge of errors to be avoided, and especially a clear understanding of the effect of suggestion. Also there is nothing automatic about it. It cannot be compared to a railroad station scale on which you only need to step to obtain a printed record of your weight. It is not a tactical method, and we warn the physician under pressure who might be tempted to have nurses administer the test that he would be in for a disappointment. The results of our examination are worthless if taken at face value. They need to be interpreted.

We realize, when we state that an interpretation is necessary, that we seem to open the door to arbitrariness and to deprive our method of all precision, but this is only an appearance. Our intelligence test will always be very superior to the one a professor tries to give during the ten-minute *baccalauréat* oral examination because ours has several definite advantages: 1) it is conducted according to a pre-set, unvarying plan; 2) it takes age into account; 3) responses are evaluated in relation to a norm and this norm is statistically derived. If we state that, in spite of all these precautions, the method needs to be used intelligently, we do not feel that making this reservation about the method decreases its value.

The microscope and the graphic method are tools which are admirably precise. But how much intelligence, circumspection, erudition and art are implicated in their use? Think for a moment about the value of observations made with the microscope by an ignoramus stuffed with an imbecile. We have seen examples of this and it made us shudder.

We must give up the idea that an evaluation procedure can become sufficiently precise to be put into anyone's hands. Any scientific procedure is only an instrument which must be guided by an intelligent hand. We have studied more than three hundred subjects with this newly forged tool. With each examination our attention has been awakened, surprised, charmed by the observations we had occasion to make, on the side, about the manner of answering, the manner of understanding, the mischievousness of some, the obtuseness of others, and the thousand and one peculiarities which made it so that we had under our eyes a most arresting spectacle: an intelligence in activity.

The few persons to whom we have, very rarely, accorded permission to witness one of our examinations have understood this too, and they have spontaneously told us what a massive impression they received and how each child's intelligence stood out, as it were, even when they had known the child for a long time. It is this massive impression which we must know how to obtain, interpret and attribute a just value to.

Moreover, the verification of the level of functioning is interesting only if it is accompanied by an interpretation of the causes which are responsible for the level of functioning. Thus it is important to ask oneself each time what the influence of the family and social environment has been. A child from a good family who often converses with his parents has a more alert mind than another who is left to himself. He has a richer vocabulary and, especially, more ideas about all sorts of things. Our tests provide a reference applicable mainly to the Paris primary school population. Take children from rich families and you can be absolutely sure they will answer better, on the average, and will be one or two years ahead of the primary school child. Take children from rural areas and they probably will not answer as well. Take Belgian children from the parts of the country where both French and Walloon are spoken; the children from the Walloon proletariat will answer even less well, especially in tests involving language. Our colleague Professor Rouma, at Charleroi Teachers' College, brought our attention to these surprising inequalities in intelligence which were revealed by our tests and which depended on the social environment.

On the other hand, the examination of the level of functioning does not tell us if the child who is behind is in a phase of intellectual rest which will be of short or long duration. It does not tell us either if this intellectual obtuseness is due to enlarged adenoids. All this research is done at the time of the examination. It is important and it demands the finest and the nimblest mind. We are far from automatism!

If we give our tests to hundreds of children, we become aware of a fact which is important for the psychology of intelligence : it is impossible to find a single subtest which, when it is passed, assures that all preceding tests have been passed and all more advanced tests failed. For instance, let us take the test of picture interpretation, which is easily passed at age eleven. There are younger children, however, who pass it, and there are older children who fail it because they still *describe* the picture. Each child has his own individuality. A particular child is successful on test A and fails test B. How are the individual differences observed in experimental test results explained? We don't know exactly but we can suppose, with much apparent reason, that the mental faculties involved in the different tests are themselves different and unevenly developed in different children. If a particular child has a better memory than another, we shall find it natural that he performs better than the other child on a test involving simple repetition. If he has greater aptitude for drawing, he will show greater ability in comparing

104

the lengths of various lines. Another reason can be given. All our tests pre-suppose an effort of attention, but the strength of attention fluctuates constantly, especially in the young. Now it is intense, a minute later it is weak. And an examinee who is temporarily distracted, disturbed, or bored during a trial may fail the test. The soundness of this last reason cannot be doubted. We are so convinced of this that we feel it is unrealistic and absurd to attempt to judge a child's intelligence from the results of a very small number of tests.

III. The Education of Intelligence

After the evil comes the remedy. After identifying all types of intellectual defects, let us pass on to their treatment. We shall suppose, in order to lay bare the problem, that one of our students has definitely been found to suffer from a distressing inability to understand what is going on in class. His judgment and his imagination are equally poor and, if he is not mentally deficient, he at least is considerably retarded in his educational development. What shall we do with him? What can we do for him?

If we don't do anything, if we don't intervene actively and effectively, he will continue to waste his time and, realizing the fruitlessness of his efforts, he will become discouraged. This is a serious matter for the student, and since this case is not exceptional, children with defective comprehension being legion, we can say that it is a serious matter for all of us, for society. The child who, while in school, loses the taste for work runs the risk of not acquiring it again after he leaves school.

I have often observed, to my regret, that a widespread prejudice exists with regard to the educability of intelligence. The familiar proverb, "When one is stupid, it is for a long time," seems to be accepted indiscriminately by teachers with a stunted critical judgment. These teachers lose interest in students with low intelligence. Their lack of sympathy and respect is illustrated by their unrestrained comments in the presence of the children: "This child will never achieve anything... He is poorly endowed... He is not intelligent at all." I have heard such rash statements too often. They are repeated daily in primary schools, nor are secondary schools exempt from the charge. I remember that during my examination for the *baccalauréat,* Examiner Martha became infuriated by one of my answers (as a result of a confusion of words, I had given to a Greek philosopher a name belonging to one of the personages from La Bruyère's *Characteres*) and declared that I would never have a philosophical mind. "Never!" What a strong word! A few modern philosophers seem to lend their moral support to these deplorable verdicts when they assert that an individual's intelligence is a fixed quantity, a quantity which cannot be increased. We must protest and react against this brutal pessimism. We shall attempt to prove that it is without foundation.

Had I been forced to treat of this subject five or six years ago, I would have had few means of argumentation. I would have shown that instruction and education often go hand in hand and become confounded; that to be exposed to sound ideas improves behavior; that example, imitation, and emulation broaden horizons. I would have given examples of people I know who acquired a critical mind and freedom in discussion only through the help of others. Young people have become less naive, more resourceful, more active after a trip abroad or military service. Intelligent women whom I know would have continued to hold to the most narrow religious practices without someone's suggestion, a man's most often, which opened their eyes. Then, after having run out of examples, observations and even anecdotes of this type, I believe I would have relied mainly on the findings of experimental psychology. This science is a little dry, but it becomes eloquent for someone who knows how to interpret the figures it provides. It shows us, without a doubt, that all there is in us in the way of thought and function is capable of being developed. Every time someone has taken the trouble methodically to practice a task which has measurable effects, the changes in performance measures resulting from practice were seen to inscribe themselves in a characteristic curve which deserves the name "progress curve." If one learns to use a typewriter, the number of words written per hour increases. In the case of one particular subject, the number of words typed passed from 300 to 1,100 per hour after fifty-six days of practice, in which the student worked only one hour a day.[5] When another practiced daily crossing out certain letters in a text, performance speed increased so that after 250 trials distributed over two years, the amount of work which originally required six minutes only required three minutes.[6]

This improvement is general. Up to now no reliable experiment has ever contradicted these findings, while thousands have upheld them. Of course this improvement is not infinite and we cannot believe either that its extent and rate are indeterminate. It is an improvement which, on the whole, is regulated by a law of remarkable fixity. It is important at first and later levels off little by little. Late in practice it becomes insignificant, and there comes a time when, in spite of the greatest effort, it becomes practically equal to zero. At this time the subject has reached his limit of skill. That he has a limit is undeniable; it varies according to the individual, and for each individual according to the function studied. Sometimes several years are needed for peak performance to be reached and, further, this peak performance may be maintained during several years of nonpractice. Bourdon saw it maintained for as long as seven years. Now if we consider that intelligence is not a single function, indivisible and of a particular essence, but rather that it is formed by the chorus of all the little functions of discrimination, observation, retention, etc., the plasticity and extensibility of which have been determined, it will appear undeniable that the same law governs the whole and its parts, and that consequently anyone's intelligence is susceptible to being developed. With practice, training, and above all, method, we manage to increase our attention, our memory, our judgment and literally to become more intelligent than we were before. Improvement goes on in this way until the time when we reach our limit. And I would also add that what is important for intelligent behavior is not so much the strength of our faculties as the manner in which they are used, that is to say the " art " of intelligence, and this art necessarily becomes more refined with practice.

This is about the most scientific idea I could have found in order to encourage teachers to educate the intelligence of their less gifted pupils. And of course, with such consideration in mind, one comes to accept as highly probable the idea that intelligence can be developed. But it is still only a probability and we would very much like to have a certainty.

The recent creation of classes for the retarded, about which I speak so often with pleasure because I have learned so much in them, gave us the proof, the certainty that we needed. Here we present no debatable argument but tangible facts. Children who are admitted in these classes are not only educationally but also intellectually retarded, for to be three years below grade level, to know at twelve only what children in general know at nine, a pupil must be deficient in attention or in comprehension. The most severe tests guard the door to the special classes. Only proven retardates are admitted to them, those whose school attendance has been regular. It might have been supposed that these children would gain nothing from the special program and that these new classes would be a bluff added to so many others.

It might have been supposed, too, that since there is no special pedagogy, properly speaking, and that pedagogy is the same for all, the very best teacher could do no more for these retardates than is ordinarily done for normal students. This is exactly the objection which was raised at the beginning by teachers for the retarded. They told me, " If there are new original methods, show them to us. " We were forced to tell them that there were no such methods and that they must do in these classes as they do in the regular ones. This answer discouraged them. Then, to our surprise and joy, we discovered that all these early fears were useless. After a year we re-examined all these retarded pupils, one after the other. We knew what their school performance was like when they first were admitted to the class because we had saved their old workbooks. We evaluated their new performance and

·

noted their progress. This progress was already evident in their general appearance. They had a more open attitude, their countenance was more alert, more attentive, and they dressed more carefully. But these are only appearances and appearances may be misleading. What convinced us was that in dictations which were rigorously equivalent, they made fewer mistakes. Also they put more expression into their reading, and difficult words were less distorted. Finally, in arithmetic, an area in which they were so weak at first, they had made enormous progress. Some problems which they failed pitifully the year before were now easily solved. Charmed with these results but still distrusting myself and my immediate collaborators, I wished to subject our work to some kind of control. I asked the school principal to evaluate the children's progress in his own way every six months. His estimates and measurements confirmed ours. Progress was definitely clear, undeniable and even important. Is a figure required? Let us admit that at the time they entered the special class all the children's school performance was three years below grade level. Retested after a year in the class, they were found to be only two years below grade. What does this mean? Let us do a little analysis so we can fully understand the situation. Had these children remained in the regular class where they so joyously wasted their time, their retardation would have increased; it would have become equal to about three and a half years. Had they performed like normal students during that year they would have advanced exactly one year, but they would not have caught up any of the lost time and their retardation would have remained equal to three years as it was in the beginning. Their retardation has decreased because they profited from the class more than normal children do. If their retardation is now two years instead of three, it is because they were able to complete two years' work in one.

We can anticipate an objection. Someone will say: "What you have increased in this case, what you measure with this precise method, is not the child's intelligence but his educational level. You show well enough it is possible to teach ignorant children rapidly; you do not show that their intelligence has increased." I beg your pardon. These children were not merely ignorant. Each had a mental defect — weakness of attention, poor comprehension or another type of deficiency. And it was this deficiency which hindered their progress in ordinary classes and with ordinary methods. Now instruction is being assimilated. This is a fact. Also new habits of work, attention, and self-control have been acquired. This is another fact, and this second fact is even more important than the first. What exactly is the part played by instruction and what is the part played by intelligence in these final results? It would be extremely difficult to know this and it may be useless even to try, for an individual's contributions, his social usefulness, his marketing value depend on both these factors. These children's minds are like a piece of fallow land which an experienced agronomist has cultivated. Result : instead of weeds we now have a crop. It is in this practical sense, the only one accessible to us, that we say these children's intelligence can be increased. We have increased what constitutes the intelligence of a student, his capacity to learn and to assimilate instruction.

In the face of such encouraging results, our hopes and our ambitions grow. We are happy to have concerned ourselves with the retarded for such a long time. When we became interested in these unfortunate children, along with so many other people of good will, we were moved first by a feeling of pity ; also by a desire to protect the social interest, to try to decrease the number of those human beings who will later be useless and who could possibly become harmful. But especially, we fervently hoped that the study of the deficient would profit the normal in the same way that, in a different domain, the study of the mentally ill contributes to the understanding of the psychology of the normal individual. We were not mistaken. Methods which are useful in the education of the deficient would, with slight modification, render normal children the greatest service. One of the best teachers of special classes I have known, Mr. Roguet, told me with a gleam in his eyes : " What would I not have accomplished in the past with my students, intelligent children, if I had treated them as I have treated these. "

How then, by what process did we manage to hold all these weak and wandering attentions, to force open all these closed intelligences ? We shall now attend to this explanation for, as everyone understands, it is one of capital importance. But it must not be thought that we have any new principles of education to offer. To understand the reason for the effectiveness of the special classes it will be sufficient to observe that we were able — partly deliberately and partly by chance — to avoid a few of the most dangerous errors of present-day pedagogy. What we are going to say about it will seem so simple, so commonplace, that a little time and thought may be necessary in order to grasp its full significance.

The educators' first concern was to adjust their teaching to the child's level of understanding. They spoke in such a way that they were always understood. If many of the retarded pupils did not profit from the regular program, it was partly because of a weakness of attention, but mainly because the lessons went over their heads. Regular lessons were too complicated, too abstract for these students, involving too much basic knowledge which the children did not have. Let us suppose, for a moment, that we are listening to a geometry lesson and that the hundredth theorem is being explained. If we had no prior knowledge about the first ninety-nine theorems, we would not be able to understand, had we the mind of a Pascal. This gives an idea of the state of confusion the mind of a retarded student may be in when he tries to understand a lesson which is way beyond him.

By keeping a child in a class which is too advanced for him, we disregard the greatest principle of pedagogy: proceed from the easy to the difficult. The violation of this principle is universal; it gives rise to the most deplorable errors on the part of teachers who are very intelligent but who know nothing about pedagogy. For this cannot be overemphasized: today, ignorance of pedagogy reaches fantastic proportions. I constantly see children struggling with assignments which are too difficult for them. But the teacher consoles himself easily with the quite gratuitous assumption that "This will at least make him work." I recently saw a young girl who, for her first task in modeling, was made to copy a bust which had a complicated movement. "You will have trouble," her professor said to her, "but you will learn a lot." Why not have a novice attend a lecture in differential calculus? It would be exactly the same type of error. A little challenge is a good thing; it is stimulating to the student. But too much difficulty discourages and disgusts him. It makes him lose precious time. More importantly, it causes him to form bad work habits because he is forced to try inaccurate solutions which he cannot correct since he cannot judge their incorrectness. Under these conditions we become resigned to the fact that we do not understand, and we work blindly, that is to say very badly. What results is a disorganization of the intelligence, while the precise goal of education is to organize. I have seen over-zealous parents make the same error. They were annoyed because their young child showed fear and they wanted to cure him of this shameful shortcoming. They were right to want to cure him, but they went about it the wrong way. The right method consists of going from the easy to the difficult. The child must first be made to experience very slight fears which he will be able to overcome, for — this is the task — he must learn self-control. Then as the child's power to control his fears increases, the intensity of the fears he is exposed to can also be increased, but very slowly and very cautiously. This way success is almost always assured at the end of the training period. But if we want to act abruptly, brutally, without adapting the fear experience to the child's strength, we do him more harm than good. If we expose him to a painful, atrocious fear which he is unable to dominate, what we create in him is mental disturbance, disequilibrium. We teach him not to react and to be afraid. One of my friends who was excessively shy as a child had a physician father, who, in order to teach him to be brave, took him to the morgue. He showed him a corpse and had him touch it. The child was traumatized and signs of the shock still persist today. Ten years later in Paris he could not enter the amphitheater and gave up the study of medicine. As we see, this case is another example of a failure to recognize the elementary principle of method and prudence.

Now we understand why deficient children who were admitted to the special classes profited so much from the program. An observant teacher was present who, having only about fifteen students, could get to know each of them individually. This teacher watched each child carefully, making sure the lesson had been understood. If it was not, the same lesson was presented over again instead of introducing new concepts. A small effort was demanded from each pupil, but this effort was proportional to his ability and it actually had to be made. Few things were taught, but these few things, which were always elementary, were well learned, well understood, well assimilated. Ask from each child only what he is really capable of doing. What could be simpler? What could be fairer?

So much for the program of things to be taught. Now the teaching method needs to be defined. On this last point, too, our special classes have taught us much. Faced with pupils who could neither listen, nor see, nor stand still, we decided that our first job was not to teach them the things which seemed to us the most useful to them, but to teach them how to learn. This is why, with the help of Mr. Belot and all our other collaborators, we designed what we called "mental orthopedics exercises." This expression is eloquent and it has made a hit. Its meaning is clear. Just as physical orthopedics correct a curvature of the thoracic spine, mental orthopedics straighten, cultivate, fortify such mental abilities as attention, memory, perception, judgment, the will. We do not try to teach the child new concepts; we strive to increase the efficiency of his mental faculties.

We began by teaching the students to remain motionless. It was agreed that every day and in every class the teacher would invite his pupils to assume a pose, like that of a statue, and to retain this pose a few seconds at first, then a whole minute. They were to take this position instantly, at a first signal from the teacher, and to resume their activities just as abruptly at the teacher's second signal. The first time we did this nothing was accomplished. The whole class was shaken with uncontrollable laughter. Then, little by little, the children quieted down. The exercise had lost its novelty and they had grown accustomed to it. Pride became involved. Each tried to outdo the other in the length of time he could maintain the position. I saw boisterous, disobedient babblers who were the despair of their teacher start making a serious effort to cooperate and putting all their pride in remaining motionless. They were therefore capable of paying attention, of exercising will power and self-control. This activity, which we call "playing statue," was so appreciated by the children that they asked for it. Encouraged by these first results, we began our dynamometer exercises. Each child in his turn squeezed the grips of the instrument, listened to the pressure reading and recorded it on his workbook. The dynamometer gave rise to general emulation. We used it once a week during a whole year and the children never tired of it. They were all the more enthusiastic because the teacher was careful to record the progress made at each session on a large piece of paper attached to the wall. Nothing was so interesting as to watch the curve go up gradually from week to week, showing that the motor capacity and especially the will power and the self-control of the whole class were being educated and were growing. Then exercises involving speed were introduced. In one exercise the subject, using a pen on a piece of paper, made the largest number of dots possible in ten seconds. The practice is excellent for the lethargic pupil. The basic idea in all these exercises is to compel the child to put forth an intense effort and to incite general emulation. This was achieved by recommending that teachers give warm words of encouragement and especially feedback. Individual grades as well as averages were posted regularly in the classroom.

I shall also list, in the category of actions, the exercises developing motor skills. They were of various kinds. We began by transporting jars full of water, which had to be carried from one table to another without spilling the least bit of water into the saucer. This was very difficult, for the distance was great and the jars were filled to the brim. Then complicated exercises involving corks were devised. "What has all this to do with school?" someone will ask. And some uninformed father who only sends his son to school to learn spelling and arithmetic might be very surprised to discover that we have the child play statue on certain days and play with corks on others! Let us be serious and, beneath the surface of the task which must often be made to appear interesting, fun, even comical, let us see the reality: these games are nothing other than exercises for training the will. They are unpretentious lessons which are proportionate to the child's ability and which truly force the will into activity. For will power is needed to maintain a fixed position, a steady gaze, and the hand extended for a long time without shaking. Without it we would give up standing still at the least sensation of fatigue and at the least feeling of boredom. In the same way, exerting rigorous pressure on the grips of the dynamometer is painful. The more we press, the more the palm of the hand hurts, but also the harder we press, the higher the registered reading is. The same idea is valid for all the exercises we have listed. To give lessons in will power, to teach children to make an effort, to put up with a little physical suffering, to experience the pleasure of self-mastery, is teaching which is well worth as much as a lesson in history or in arithmetic.

We were doing too well to stop. Chance had made us discover a new method. We sought to extend it, to perfect it, and we worked out a general mental orthopedics program covering all the mental faculties. Remembering some ancient feats Robert Houdin talked about, we wanted our students to learn to perceive quickly a large number of objects at a glance. To train them to do this we showed them large boards on which several objects or pictures had been glued. After a very short exposure time during which the student was to look at, study, gather in his mind all the items, the board was hidden. The subject then had to write down from memory the name of everything he had seen. In keeping with Mr. Vaney's always precise recommendations, we designed a set of such boards, each displaying an increasing number of objects. Then we wished to teach the children to observe; we trained them to answer questions about what they had seen in the street, on the playground or in class. Next came memory exercises consisting of the quick repetition of words, digits or sentences, which increased in numbers each time. And finally, exercises involving imagination, invention, analysis, judgment... But let's move on. Little by little we put together a complete program of mental orthopedics, which included different exercises for each school day. These exercises are done regularly in our special classes. The results are recorded with the greatest care, and we find that children trained in this way make unexpected progress when we compare their latest performance with that of the first sessions. For example, in a class of retarded children, the trained students perceived nine objects in five seconds and managed to write down the names of these objects from memory. Not all the subjects accomplished this but about two-thirds of them did. Is it not surprising? Picture the difficulty to yourself. Nine objects picked at random are fastened to a board. The child looks at the board for five seconds, goes back to his seat and writes down the names of these nine objects from memory. He does not forget a single one and does not make any substitutions.

The adult who sees this is very surprised! I remember that when a new law involving the retarded was about to be voted on, several congressmen came to visit our classes. They observed the children's performance and some of them, puzzled, asked to try the experiment themselves. They were not nearly as successful as our young retarded students. You can imagine the surprise, the laughter, the colleagues' raillery and other comments. To be a congressman and to show oneself inferior to a retarded child! In reality, despite the piquancy of the adventure, everything can be explained. The congressmen did not take the intensive training our children had undergone into account.

Everyone agrees these exercises are excellent. Bearing not on just one simple faculty but on a whole group of them, the exercises facilitate discipline, teach children to look at the blackboard better, listen better, remember better, judge better. They bring pride into play and they incite emulation, perseverance, a desire to succeed and all the positive feelings which accompany action. Above all, they teach the child to will, to will more intensely. The will is truly the key to all education, and consequently moral development takes place at the same time intellectual development does. But this still is not all. I believe that as we study with some perseverance these simple exercises devised to give a little tone to retarded children, we shall come to realize that the method which inspired the exercises is not a special method geared to a few inattentive, deficient, aboulic subjects but that it is a method which is suitable for all normal subjects as well. I would even go farther and say that it is the only way to teach. But this statement needs to be explained fully to rule out any possible misunderstandings.

Defying the most objective critics, old university methods retain their supreme power. They have been repeatedly condemned for continuing to use verbal instruction in which the professor lectures and students passively listen. The lesson thus conceived has two shortcomings: 1) It only impresses the student's verbal function. It does not bring him in contact with real life situations but just gives him words. 2) Moreover it only exercises his memory. His role is a passive one. He does not exercise judgment, does not think about or discover anything, does not produce; he only needs to retain. The ideal for him is to be able to recite without error, to make his memory work, to know what is in the text and to repeat it cleverly on examination day. That day he is judged by the effect his words produce, by the glibness of his tongue, by appearances. The result of this deplorable practice is, in the first place, a lack of curiosity about everything which is not in a book. There is a tendency to search for truth only in books, to believe that original research is done by flipping through the pages of a book. There is an exaggerated respect for written opinions and indifference to the lessons of the external world about which we know nothing. There is a naive belief in the omnipotence of simple formulae, a lowering of the meaning of life, a difficulty in adapting to contemporary existence, and above all, a routine mind which is sadly out of place at a time when society evolves with infernal speed.

I recently conducted a study on the evolution of philosophical instruction in high schools and colleges. In connection with this study, several of my correspondents made interesting comments about the mentality of philosophy students. They have, I was told, an innate taste for discussion, and for discussion not of facts but of dialectic. What motivates them is a desire for an eloquence contest, for the pleasure of defending any opinion whatever with purely theoretical arguments and without being fundamentally concerned about truth. Is it not absolutely certain that a taste for empty dialectic, hair splitting, and abuse of arguments and ideas is promoted *a priori* by this verbalism which the university tries its best to propagate? After they have become university students, young people retain the habits they have acquired in high school. Given a choice between a one-hour lecture and a one-hour session of practical work, most students definitely prefer to sit in class. If at the end of a lecture we call for those who wish to learn how to operate some apparatus or to study a demonstration, we embarrass them. The majority, having jotted down their little notes, only wish to leave. If we insist, we see them disappear the way by-standers do before the bowl of the juggler who is taking up a collection. It is hard to get even the most intelligent of them to understand that what is heard in a class is found in a book in an even better form, while the laboratory demonstration can never be replaced.

What, then, do we demand in the way of reform, and how should we conduct the war on verbalism?

We shall not, of course, go so far as to forbid the teacher to use speech, but we feel his words must not be the core, the gist of the lesson. They must be only an accompaniment, a guide, a teaching aid. The student's mind must be put directly in contact with nature or with schemata, pictures reproducing nature, or rather with both nature and schemata at the same time. Speech should only intervene to comment on the sensory impression made. Above all, the students must be active. Teaching is bad if it leaves the student inactive and inert. Instruction must be a chain of intelligent reflexes, starting from the teacher, involving the student and coming back to the teacher. Instruction must be a stimulus prompting the student to respond and creating in him a reasonable amount of activity, for he only knows what he has done, what he has performed. Philosophically speaking, all intellectual life consists of acts of adaptation. And instruction consists of making a child perform acts of adaptation, easy ones at first, then more and more complex and perfect ones. This is why object lessons, field trips, manual tasks and laboratory exercises are so popular today. They answer the need for student activity. Walk into a classroom. If you see all the children motionless, listening effortlessly to a fidgety teacher engaged in a long-winded discourse, or if you see these children copying, writing the course the teacher is dictating to them, tell yourself that it is bad pedagogy. I would prefer to see a class where children are not as quiet, where children are more noisy but are busy performing the most modest task, provided it is a task in which they make a personal effort, which is their own production, and which demands a little thought, judgment and taste.

This brings us back to our mental orthopedics exercises, for they are a clear-cut, striking example of this new pedagogy, which makes the child an active individual instead of reducing his role to that of a listener. Our plans and methods are only an illustration, and of course this illustration is very specially conceived for children of a certain age, of a certain intellectual development, from a certain culture. In its technical detail it is appropriate only to them, but the principle of the method appears to me to be recommendable.

An objection is going to be made. Without a doubt, it will be said, these are excellent methods for training a child's mind at home or even in class. Instead of explaining ideas to him, it is better to have him discover them. Instead of giving him orders, it is better to let him act spontaneously and intervene only to verify. It is excellent practice to let him acquire the habit of judging for himself the book he is reading, the conversation in which he participates, the current event everyone is talking about. It is excellent for him to learn to speak, tell stories, explain what he saw, defend clearly, logically, and methodically the opinions he holds. Also it is better for him to practice making decisions, to orient himself while traveling, to plan his day, to imagine, to invent, to function on his own, and to experience both the merit and the responsibility involved in free action. All this, it will be said, is excellent in extra-curricular life provided, of course, that education — limited under these conditions to a role of check and control — remains effective in the rectification of errors. But, someone will ask, can this method in which it is the child who is active and the teacher who is passive, this general education method, can it be applied to instruction? When the child has perfected his attention, his will, his judgment, he will still have to learn the subjects included in the school program. He will still have to assimilate grammar, arithmetic, geometry, and everything else. In order to acquire this knowledge is it not necessary to have recourse to memory and do we not find ourselves confronted again with the fact that memory is the basis of instruction?

I do not believe this is true. And those who have grasped the deeper meaning of the mental orthopedics exercises will understand without any difficulty that such exercises can make it possible to assimilate any kind of knowledge. This is so because any knowledge is summarized into an action which this very knowledge enables one to execute. Consequently it is possible to learn through action, as stated in a favorite formula of American educators, "Learning by doing." To know grammar does not consist of repeating a rule but of being able to express one's thoughts in a sentence which is correct, clear and logical. To know multiplication does not consist of being able to repeat the definition of this operation but of combining any multiplicand and any multiplier and giving the correct product. It is therefore always possible to replace the formula by the exercise, or rather to begin with the exercise and to wait until the practice of it has resulted in training and the formation of a habit. Then the rule, the formula, the definition, the generalization can be introduced.

The general plan of an instruction conceived in this way, according to an active method, was set up long ago by some great philosophers.

Useful suggestions can be found in Rousseau's work, more systematic ideas in Spencer, [7] and a complete plan, methodical in its execution, was laid out by Froebel for nursery school children. In our times all this has been told and retold, perfected for practice by the most competent people. In France these are Belot for language, Queniou for drawing, Laisant for the sciences, and LeBon for living languages and all subjects in general.* In America there are Dewey, Stanley Hall and many pedagogues. We only need to repeat after them : Teach written language by assigning plenty of narratives, plenty of reading, plenty of compositions. Dull grammar lessons, instead of being presented first and being allowed to act as obstacles, will be presented last and will then help to make students thoroughly conscious of the rules which already have been learned through usage. Teach arithmetic by giving problems to be solved, geometry by having things constructed, the metric system by having measurements made, physics by having small rudimentary apparatus built and operated. Teach esthetics by showing reproductions of masterpieces and of mediocre works side by side and having the differences discovered, explained, felt. Teach art by encouraging free drawing and by putting off to a later date the study of the laws of perspective. Teach the living languages by imposing the habit of speaking them, and by facilitating the understanding of them.

There are enormous advantages to following this course. Instead of first introducing the general idea, which is incomprehensible and empty for those who do not know its contents, we always begin with the concrete experience, the special fact — for an exercise is always special. In so doing we follow the easiest, the most normal course, the one which goes from the particular to the general. Moreover, by getting the child to act, we intensify his interest in his work. We expose him to the valuable stimulus represented by the warm feelings which accompany action and reward successful efforts. This stimulus will be all the more powerful as we take more exactly into consideration his natural activities and his special aptitudes. Before attending school all, or almost all, children like to sing, draw, tell stories, invent, manipulate objects, move them about, modify them, use them in constructions. By grafting education and instruction on these natural activities, we take advantage of the impetus already given by nature. Nature furnishes the activities ; the teacher only intervenes to guide them. It is from this double point of view that the active method proves superior, and

---

* In Footnote 7 Binet refers the reader to Gustave LeBon's *Psychologie de l'education,* in which LeBon describes fully and clearly all the new teaching methods. Binet adds the comment : "I hope I will be able to try these methods in a Paris elementary school or in a private school. I am convinced, from the little I have already seen, that the results would be marvelous. I know that since these experiments have already been conducted in America on millions of individuals, it may appear useless to repeat them. But the study of these methods remains empirical as long as controlled experiments have not been made. A study is not scientific until controlled experiments have been done. Thus while we welcome with immense satisfaction what has been achieved in America — and what has been admirably described by Buyse in his recent book (*Méthodes Américaines d'education,* Charleroi, 1908) — we feel we cannot dispense with repeating these experiments on a small scale in a French school, with a view to scientific control and to the adaptation of the method to the needs of our own population, our own tradition, our own mores."

we can say that it reproduces the fundamental law of evolution. Through it the child's mind is made to follow the same paths the soul of humanity has followed.

FOOTNOTES FOR CHAPTER FIVE

1. Works of Meumann, Ebbinghaus, Gilbert, Scripture, Seashore, and especially Ziehen, etc.

2. For details, see Binet and Simons, "L'Intelligence des imbeciles," *Année Psychologique,* XV, p. 1, and a new theory of dementia, *ibid.* Foreign works related to this same question are those of Acht, Watt, Bühler, Marbe, Messer, Dürr, etc. See the Larguier report in *Année Psychologique,* XIII, p. 497.

3. Tracy, *American Journal of Psychology,* VI, n° 1.

4. See notably *Année Psychologique,* XIV (1908), 1, for a complete exposé of the method.

5. E.J. Swift, "Memory of Skillful Movements," *Psychological Bulletin,* June, 1906.

6. Bourdon, "Recherches sur l'habitude," *Année Psychologique,* XVIII (1902), 327. For a comprehensive study, see Thorndike, *Educational Psychology,* p. 80.

7. Herbert Spencer, *De l'education,* pp. 98, 123. See also Gustave LeBon's *Psychologie de l'education.*

CHAPTER SIX

Memory

I. The Relationship of Memory to Intelligence and Age

La Rochefoucauld once said that we often complain about our memory but never about our judgment. The distinction is right. It is as if memory was not a part of our personality. To have a bad memory is not a dishonor and to say that someone has a great memory is not necessarily to pay him much of a compliment. It is a fact that having a good memory makes it possible to simulate a host of qualities which we do not possess; wisdom, for instance — all we need do is repeat, at the appropriate moment, something we have heard while listening to others. Furthermore, the adversaries of present-day teaching methods are openly critical of the role these methods assign to memory. They feel, with good reason, that intensive cultivation of memory is made to the detriment of judgment and spontaneity. Finally, according to a widespread presumption, memory is a faculty which is independent of intelligence; so much so, in fact, that it is viewed as the sign of a mediocre mind. Some people maintain, for instance, that students who have the best memory are among the least intelligent, and extreme examples are given of imbeciles who couldn't even learn to read yet who could recite by heart series of dates and complicated chronologies which had been taught them. It was concluded from this that the greater the memory, the smaller the judgment.

Although all the criticisms and preconceived ideas are partially true, they should not be allowed to make us forget the fact that memory is at the base of all instruction. To learn is to exercise our retentive power; it is to acquire memories. Whoever has little memory learns almost nothing or learns poorly. We could even go so far as to say that no progress is possible for a mind which is incapable of retaining what it has perceived or conceived. Certainly memory is one of the most powerful mental faculties, and if we try to see how it is distributed in humanity, we shall see that it is distributed proportionally to intelligence.

It may be difficult to understand this if we have studied only average individuals whose abilities vary only over a small range, but if we study such accomplished subjects as a Leibnitz or a Goethe, we see that these admirable minds were also endowed with encyclopedic intelligence. Nothing of what was happening in their time was foreign to them. They made great syntheses. They had to know and to retain much and therefore they had to possess a great memory. Their memory facilitated their work better than a huge library could. To use a book we must be able not only to open it at the right page but also to know the place where the needed information can be found. In this way memory is like a big, animated, intelligent book which opens itself at the right page. Let us be more precise. Memory furnishes an abundance of material on which our mind works. The more abundant the material is, the more work increases, the more judgment has an opportunity to be exercised, the more critical judgment is refined by comparisons, and the richer the imagination becomes. Memory may not increase the depth of intelligence but it gives it richness, bulk, quantity, as if multiplying the products of intelligence.

While studying a case in which great precision was possible, I had opportunity to observe the relationship which exists between intelligence and memory. This was on the occasion of a short incursion into the curious and picturesque world of chess players, some of whom have the admirable ability to play several games without looking at the chessboard. With the board far from them, they order a move which another person makes for them, and each time this person also informs the player of the opponent's move. Several players were even able to play correctly without seeing and to win four, five, six, and even more games in competition with seeing but less talented adversaries.

This blind chess play implies a great ability for strategic representation. In order to play the game and win, it is absolutely necessary to visualize, with accuracy and precision at all times during the competition, the chessboard and its squares as well as the complicated position of the pieces in relation to one another. Memory is therefore definitely involved. Now it is very remarkable that this blind-play virtuosity is not observed in mediocre fourth- or fifth-rate players, in those who are referred to as the duffers. On the contrary, it is found in almost all first-rate players because of the sole fact that they have exercised chessboard strategic intelligence to the utmost. Not all these masters have achieved the same blind-play proficiency, but all can play with their back to the chessboard. This may be the case in which the bond which unites the mental faculties of memory and strategic ability is seen most clearly.

Is it the same with school children? Some of our studies conducted in schools have clearly shown that it is. I visited several Paris elementary schools and I had children of the same age but of a different intellectual level learn a poem. We know, and I say it again in two

120

words, how easy it is, quickly and effortlessly, to identify the most intelligent and the least intelligent children in a school population. All we need do is to look at the child's school achievement in relation to his age. Those who at age ten are already in the seventh grade are more intelligent than their schoolmates of the same age who are in the fifth grade, and the latter are superior to those who are detained in the third grade.

I therefore had all the ten-year-olds in a school learn the same poem. The poem which had been selected could be easily understood by all. It had been dittoed and each student received a copy. All the children studied it simultaneously in a low voice and were given ten minutes to complete the task. At the end of the ten minutes the copies were picked up and each child was asked to write from memory everything he had retained. By calculating the average of verses and half verses remembered by children of different ability levels, it became very easy to establish that ten-year-old children who are in the seventh grade learn faster than ten-year-olds who are in the fifth grade, and ten-year-olds who are in the fifth grade learn faster than those who are in the third grade. Age being equal, seventh grade children remembered twice as much prose and verses as their fifth grade schoolmates in the same amount of time.[1] This rehabilitates memory; perhaps not memory in general, basic memory, but rather the memory of ideas and of comprehension. We shall come back to this question in a moment.

The preceding considerations have a counterpart. While it is desirable to have a good memory, it is undesirable to have too much. And we have too much, not in an absolute way, this would make no sense, but when our memory is greater than the intelligence we possess or when it is so super-abundant that it is impossible to make intelligent use of it.

To make a comparison, we could say that memory is like farm land. Intelligence is the capital invested in the tilling. If memory is too great in comparison to intelligence, it is like being the owner of a very vast estate but lacking the funds necessary to cultivate it.

I believe that it is precisely when memory is out of proportion to intelligence that we say it is useless. I have seen very clear examples of this uselessness in imbeciles. Let's say, first, that we commit an error, or that we suggest an error, when we talk about the great memory of imbeciles. This is not a general rule but rather a very rare exception. Dr. Simon and I have studied hundreds of deficients and imbeciles in our primary schools and in mental hospitals, and we have observed that most often, almost always, their memory is far from being developed to an unusual degree. On the contrary, low intelligence is usually associated with a small amount of memory; this is the rule.

Thus, in a memory test involving a moderately detailed story which is simple and easy to understand, we find that a retarded individual's recollections are fewer, more reduced, more fragmentary than those of a person of normal intelligence. In response to the verbal presentation of a list of digits to be repeated, he will repeat one or two of them when a normal person will repeat six under the same conditions. But although exceptions are rare, they are sometimes found. We remember a tall and strong eighteen-year-old girl with a big nose and flourishing health who was an imbecile and who was endowed with a remarkable memory. If we presented a list of digits or words to her, she repeated them exactly from memory. She could repeat as many as ten digits, and this is more than we could do ourselves. She therefore had a better memory than we had, perhaps also better voluntary attention, but she could not utilize her faculties. In spite of her great memory, she had been unable to learn anything, even to learn to read.

Many years ago, in my Sorbonne laboratory, I studied two now famous calculator prodigies, Inaudi and Diamanti. They both had an extraordinary memory for numbers. More recently I saw a young girl, the sister of one of the men mentioned above, whose memory for numbers is as outstanding as that of her brother.

All these individuals could learn a considerable quantity of meaningless numbers. Inaudi was able to repeat about fifty digits after a single hearing. Diamanti learned about one hundred digits in a half-hour study and so did his sister. What is surprising about this is that we fail to see what use can be made of such a great memory. It is a gift which is of little interest in life, a gift which has no practical application. There is no point in keeping so many figures in our minds, since it is simpler, surer and less tiresome to jot them down on a piece of paper. Had these calculators had a mathematical ability proportionate to their memory, had they been a Cauchy or a Poincaré, then their memory would have been an advantage. It would have given them an immense combining power. But our three subjects were rather mediocre calculators. They did not contribute anything to mathematics and they understood nothing about transcendent problems. Their powerful memory was of such little consequence for them that the only use they could make of it was to display it in variety shows. This is the proof that it was a kind of monstrosity.

A disproportionate memory has another inconvenience. It promotes cheating and encourages laziness. To make a personal effort to arrive at a conclusion on one's own is always a little painful. We are more inclined to endorse the view of our newspaper. If we write a book, we use a large number of quotations. Confronted with difficult life circumstances, we wait for other people's judgments and we adopt them. This is stupid and dangerous, for mental faculties atrophy when they aren't exercised. The less we exercise our judgment, the less judgment we have. A lazy student who has a good memory will foolishly prefer to learn word for word a text which he does not understand rather than look for the meaning of it, a task which would require very little effort.

I have observed the consequences of an overly great memory in a young Southerner who really has very little intelligence. His parents were able to get him into a liberal profession only because of his memory. This young man is truly exceptional. He is like a walking telephone book. He has used this marvellous faculty to hide his incurable mental deficiency from everyone. His professors, of course, never became aware of anything. In high school the whole geometry course remained an enigma to him, a foreign language, as did the algebra course. But since he had to pass the *baccalauréat* examination, he had the courage to learn by heart a complete algebra course, as well as the geometry course, including the properties of the sphere. One day, in a mood for confidences, he explained to me how he proceeded. To remember the proof of a theorem, he didn't need to learn the whole thing and repeat it like a phonograph, for there were parts which he vaguely understood, but he always had to work out the proofs with the same letters on the diagrams. If he had been obliged to change the letters on the diagrams, he would have been lost. He passed the *baccalauréat* examination. Later, having renounced the study of medicine for reasons which I don't remember, he undertook the study of law. The practice of law is the career of the idle and the undecided, of all those who don't know what they want and who have never been guided. He succeeded brilliantly and passed all his examinations. This may appear quite natural, since law does not require as much as mathematics in the way of comprehension. However, I found out while examining him that for law also his memory was a powerful asset. What he has learned is the text of the law, the main commentaries, the distinctions, the controversial questions with the symmetry of opposed systems and their different arguments. All this involves memory and his memory has imperturbable strength. In this area he can not be defeated. He is one who remembers all the items of the civil code and their numbers. In order to expose his intellectual deficiency it is necessary to muzzle his memory and ask him questions which require not only knowledge but also critical judgment. During the examination, the professor should have asked him to discuss particular cases. In this type of situation, the candidate is forced to use reasoning in order to determine which article of law is to be applied, in order to grasp the essentials of a situation, and in order to choose among opposed interests. I have observed many times that the discussion of special cases throws him off completely. But his law professors didn't realize this. They made the same error the *baccalauréat* examiners and the high school teachers had made. Now this young man has just become a lawyer. He has entered a liberal profession. He will not plead, I suppose, for speech is indiscreet and can expose shallow-mindedness. I am more apt to think that he will get a seat in the magistrature. Is this not unfortunate? It would have been infinitely better, in his interest and in ours, to have guided him toward more modest occupations in which he could have contributed something.

The result of all this is that our conclusion about the usefulness of a great memory has many nuances. It is not proper to disparage memory. It is not proper to think too much of it either. Its merit depends on the use we make of memory. Like Aesop's tongue, it can serve for the better or for the worse. Or, to look at things more philosophically, it is to be hoped that memory will develop in relation to intelligence and will be proportioned to it.

When does memory attain its greatest power? The educator must undeniably wait for a function to reach peak efficiency before imposing the maximum amount of work upon it. Now according to prevailing opinion, children have a much better memory than adults; and according to numerous experiments which have been conducted in laboratories, the adult consistently displays the best memory. In the same way, if we conduct an experiment involving memory on several children, we discover that the older child has the best memory, and this leads to the same conclusion. Let's take the example of an apparently very simple experiment which consists of identifying a line of a certain length among other lines of different length after having looked at it a short time. We found that children six to eight years old make 73 % errors; children nine to eleven years old make 69 % errors; and older children, eleven to thirteen years of age, make 50 % errors. [2]

How can the contradiction between popular belief and the findings of scientific research be explained? It stems from many existing but unrecognized sources of error. Nothing is simple in this domain and measuring memory isn't an easy thing. Those who believe it is haven't tried it or have done so uncritically. Let us suppose I am with a ten-year-old child and am trying, in competition with him, to learn a ten-line poem. Which one of us will learn the lesson better and faster? It is possible that I will. But this does not prove that my memory is superior to that of my young emulator, for by awarding myself the victory I am overlooking two very important factors: the duration of retention of the material and the adjuvants of memory which an adult is more adept at using than a child. In fact, it is possible that ten days from now the child will remember the poem better than I. Moreover, if he was less successful than I at the time, it is because he didn't have the aids to help his memory that I had to help mine. Only those who have gone to the trouble of performing experiments know how difficult it is

124

to study an isolated mental function. Any memory exercise performed voluntarily brings into play many other faculties. It at least involves attention and some comprehension and, depending on the case and on the task, it will be sometimes memory, sometimes attention, and sometimes comprehension which will be called upon to play the greatest role. If the task consists of memorizing meaningless words, or digits, or sentences written in an unknown language, and if we must retain all this after a very short study time, it is especially attention which is involved. If what we want to remember is composed of meaningful sentences, even if the meaning is easily understood, it is necessary to begin by understanding in order to retain these sentences. That is to say, we must begin by assimilating what we learn to what we already know; here the power of intelligence comes very much into play. This is the reason why the most intelligent children *appear* to have a greater memory than their less fortunate schoolmates. For this reason, also, older children appear superior to younger children. In order to expose memory, and memory alone, we must set things up in such a way that neither a great amount of attention nor a great amount of comprehension is needed to complete the task. This could involve retaining unrelated words or, better still, remembering an interesting story and remembering it a long time. This is the touchstone of memory.

In accordance with this distinction, we shall see that younger children do not repeat a series of digits as well as older children. This is because they have less voluntary attention. Also they do not learn something by heart as well or as fast, since their comprehension is less developed. On the other hand, they remember a series of words as well, especially if the series is long and cannot be repeated by the sound. This can be demonstrated in many ways. The American psychologist Kirkpatrick had groups of children reproduce words which had been read or heard. The older children repeated the largest numbers of words, about two more, but if the children were tested for retention three days later, an equalization was observed. [3] Another method, the recognition method, was helpful to me. I had a teacher read aloud in each class a list of one hundred disconnected meaningful words. The children's task was to reproduce in writing all the words they remembered. The number of words retained was not found to vary much with age. Children eight to thirteen years of age presented lists of average length as follows (starting with the youngest): 15, 11, 14, 14, 18, and 16 words. Hardly any increase in retention was observed as a function of age. Then the children were presented the same words again, mixed with other words which had not been read to them the first time. For this recognition test the young children's performance remained as good as that of the older children. In children eight to thirteen years of age the average list of recognized words was 64, 58, 63, 50, 61, 57 out of 100. There is no evidence of progress. We have to conclude from this, since the results are equivalent, that memory not only does not increase between eight and thirteen, but that it actually decreases. If it remained stationary, the older children, being so superior from the point of view of attention and judgment, would certainly get greater yields from this mental faculty. Let's conclude, therefore, that since memory reaches its peak efficiency in childhood, it is important to cultivate it during childhood, to profit from its plasticity, to stamp upon it the important, the critical impressions which will be needed later in life.

II. Measurement of Memory in School Children

All educators know that memory is a gift which nature hasn't distributed equitably and in equal quantities to all individuals. Some of them have great difficulty in learning and remembering, either because they originally had a defective memory or because a prior illness affected their faculties. Others learn fast, easily, almost effortlessly, as if playing. There are children who remember a lesson for a long time and with tenacity. There are others who need to review often so as not to forget completely what they have been taught. For many very important and serious reasons a teacher should try to evaluate his students' memory as exactly as possible. The first reason is a moral one. When a child does not know his lesson, he is ordinarily given a bad grade or a punishment. This is done almost automatically, without thinking. Yet it would be only elementary justice to find out if the young delinquent has truly failed to apply himself to his work, for if punishing laziness is legitimate, punishing poor memory is not. The fact that a child is unable to recite his lesson proves nothing. It is only a reality, a result, and this result needs to be explained. Is it the child's fault that he doesn't know his lesson? How long did he study? How much effort has he invested in the task? What could conceivably have interfered? This is what we don't know. A child who has poor memory and who is given bad grades because of it is being done an injustice. Punishing his memory is also discouraging him, even demoralizing him. The thing to do would be to study him closely, evaluate the extent of the memory deficiency, and show satisfaction at his least efforts. And this is not even saying enough. A truly benevolent teacher will also try to give the child advice; he will suggest exercises for training and strengthening memory. I would also like to see educators proportion assignments to their students' ability in the area. Ordinarily the number of lines to be learned is set for the whole class, without distinction, according to some rigid rule which does not take individual differences into account. Those whom nature has endowed with a poor memory suffer a lot from this. They are forever worried about a lesson which is not known and about the impending punishment. A judge friend of mine told me that his lack of memory, which none of his professors had noticed, had been the nightmare of his high school years. To treat all children in the same way is truly to act in a manner which is anti-hygiene and anti-education. Here, for instance, is the case of two students, Gend and Bar, both twelve years old and in the same class. Their memory is so different that during the time one takes to learn sixty-one verses of a poem, in an experiment which I shall describe later, the other cannot learn a single one of them. Is it not ridiculous to give these two students assignments of the same length? It is a little bit like imposing the same dietary regimen on two children, one who has an ostrich stomach and one who is dyspeptic.

Putting too much of a burden on a defective memory can only have an unfortunate effect. It results in confused, poorly connected memories which cannot be utilized. Would it not be preferable for the child, for his instruction and the development of his intelligence, if we took his poor memory into account and had him learn little but well? Of course, an experienced teacher will not come right out and announce that such and such a student must learn fifty verses and such other student must learn ten verses. He would be suspected of being unfair, and the experience would come as a shock to children who have a false sense of equality. But with a little tact and skill we shall get the child with a poor memory to understand that even the slightest effort on his part will be taken into account and that if he knows four verses out of twelve well, we shall be satisfied.

It is evident, therefore, that a teacher interested in the psychology of individual differences will find profitable the measurement of his students' memory, or at least the memory of some of his students. But teachers who are reading this will undoubtedly make many objections, the most common, and one I have often heard, being that measuring memory is impossible. Since we have just finished showing that it is possible to measure even intelligence, we don't feel that answering this very theoretical objection would be of great utility. Whoever is able to complete a very complex task is able to complete a simpler one. Another objection which we have heard is that making accurate measurement takes a lot of time. Classes are large and the program is heavy. If teachers conduct psychological experiments during class time, what is going to happen to grammar and arithmetic lessons? When school is over leisure time begins, but the teacher needs rest or he may have to do some tutoring; consequently he does not feel much like devoting time to experiments. We shall answer this second objection very quickly by showing that it is possible to measure children's memory collectively during class time and that the required experiment is not nearly as long or painful as it appears to be. It will not take more than an hour even if it is repeated three times.

We have several excellent methods for the measurement of memory. We shall list only three:

1. One procedure consists of having the child learn some material during a pre-determined amount of time. Afterwards the student is asked to reproduce what he has learned during the study session. It is worth noting that this procedure involves the "voluntary recall" of retained material. The student recalls what he has learned, and it is on the basis of the power of recall that memory is evaluated.

2. We owe the second procedure to Ebbinghaus, whose name should always be cited when experimentation on memory is being discussed.[4] Ebbinghaus has shown that previously learned material which has been forgotten sometimes leaves a trace in the memory. The proof of this is that less time is needed to relearn this material than was needed to learn it the first time. The difference between the original learning time and relearning gives the method its name: the "Saving Method." This method is used to investigate and measure memory.

3. The last procedure involves the "recognition of material." For instance, one hundred disconnected words are read publicly in the class. After having heard these words, students generally can only reproduce from ten to twenty of them from memory. But if the original words are presented again in a list containing new words, words which had not been read before, they are easily recognized. It has been said that the power of recognition is double the power of recall. This is still an understatement.

For the pedagogic measurement of memory we shall use the voluntary recall method because it is the most complete of all and because it is the one most used in life.

For instance, since what we are attempting to do is to find out how much effort a child has to make in order to learn his lesson, it seems logical to make the experiment with a lesson he will be given to learn. From a purely psychological point of view, this experiment could be criticized. As soon as a task involves the word for word learning of material, and material to which the student is more or less indifferent, it is not only memory which is involved but also attention. Attention enables the child to resist boredom and distractions of all sorts, to struggle against difficulties. For every difficult test, whether this test has to do with memory, imagination, observation, or anything else, attention plays such a considerable role that the results depend as much on this faculty as on the others. And this statement is valid for all laboratory experiments. If we absolutely wanted to eliminate attention as a variable, it would be necessary to tell the children an extremely fascinating story which they would listen to effortlessly. Then we would have them repeat the story without demanding that they repeat it word for word. In brief, we would arouse their interest and make attention unnecessary. Only memory would be involved. Is such an analysis necessary in this case? Not at all, and doing it would be an error, since what we are concerned about here is evaluating school learning ability, that is to say, the kind of memory which could be called "scholastic memory." Now this memory involves material which is generally not very enticing to the school child and which only becomes assimilated, thanks to attention.

The material we present for study will therefore be a fable, a piece of poetry or of prose. Anything ambiguous or which could prove to be above the child's level of comprehension will be avoided. The learning time will be pre-established and the child will be informed about it when he is given instructions of the kind which follow:

> Here is a reading assignment which you will learn by heart during 10 minutes. You will have to repeat it word for word. Learn as much of it as possible but above all learn accurately. After 10 minutes the book will be taken away from you and you will be expected to write down from memory what you remember.

We repeat these instructions two or three times in order thoroughly to impress the child's mind. We add a few words to incite emulation, and the signal to begin is given. The experiment is conducted under discreet supervision and without anything further being said aloud. This test can be administered collectively to thirty or more students. If this is the case, however, it is necessary to prepare everything with the utmost care. A very strict discipline will be imposed upon the class; measures will be taken to prevent cheating and to prevent silence from being broken by an untimely visitor or by a student's inopportune question.

The memory test we have just described cannot give dependable results if it is administered only once. Under this condition it may be a good indicator of a group trend but it will be of no value in individual diagnosis. The results from a single test do not give a true picture of the child's ability because, like all other mental faculties, memory is extremely variable. Being in the wrong frame of mind or becoming distracted or misunderstanding instructions will result in a test performance which is very inferior to what the subject is capable of. For instance, there are students who, when asked to learn a piece by heart, become impressed with the competitive aspect of the task and try to retain the largest possible amount of the material. What happens to them is this: they have learned the whole piece superficially and they are unable to reproduce a single correct line from memory. If they have in reality retained something, what they can show of it is equal to zero. These students will have to be given the test over some other day after they have received a few extra instructions. The results of a memory test only mean something if the test has been administered a minimum of three times.

To illustrate what precedes with a precise example, I had children in a Paris eighth grade class learn verses during ten minutes. In keeping with the rules I have described, the students were to reproduce in writing and from memory what they recalled immediately after the ten-minute study session had elapsed. After they were finished, the papers were picked up without a word. The experiment was repeated eight days, thirteen days, and seventeen days later with different poems. The poems used were : Stop, " La lune " (" The Moon ") ; Viennet, " La chute d'un gland " (" The Fall of an Acorn ") ; Jauffret, " Les deux savetiers " (" The Two Cobblers ") ; De Lachambeaudie, " L'enfant et les bottes de son père " (" The Child and His Father's Boots "). We had made sure none of the children were familiar with any of these works. Each child was given a book which contained the poems. Once the experiment was completed, the number of verses correctly reproduced by each pupil was computed. The average number of verses learned was small because the children had learned the poetry as if it had been prose and most of the verses were incorrect. It made us think that these students had never been taught how to keep time, and if this is so, it is unfortunate. Why let them remain foreign to what constitutes part of the beauty of a verse ? It is all the more unfortunate, since the concept of rhyme can be of great help to memory. But let us go on. A first glance at the children's work shows that individual differences in memory are enormous. One of the students was able to reproduce the extraordinarily high number of fifty-four verses from memory. Several others reproduced only ten and another was only able to remember four.

Let us repeat the experiment eight days later. It is conducted on the same subjects, who are asked to reproduce from memory the four poems they had learned for the earlier session. To rule out the possibility of inadvertent forgetting, they are reminded of the titles of the poems. This second trial is less superficial than the preceding one. It gives more information about the natural strength of memory, for when we learn, it is normally to remember and not just to reproduce or repeat the material we have learned immediately after we have learned it. There are bad memories which have no retention power. This second trial, like the first, shows us that individual differences are considerable. The maximum number of verses learned and retained is sixty-one ; the minimum is zero.

After having computed the data and classified our students according to the memory strength they have just demonstrated, we call the teacher in charge of the class. He is a very intelligent and a very conscientious man with a precise and methodical mind. We ask for his

130

classification of the students without showing him ours. This request puzzles him. He knows that if he uses the grades on his notebook as a guide, he will be confounding two factors : memory and diligence. It is a fact that each grade is based on these two factors in variable proportions. Having thought the matter over, the teacher decides it is preferable to classify the students on the basis of what he can surmise about their memory. He divides them into three groups and shows us his classification. The strength of the student's memory — whether it is good, average, or weak — determines the group he is assigned to. What is this classification worth? We are going to find out. I reproduce it on the following page, in three columns along with relevant information. In column (3) we give the average recitation grade the student has received from his teacher during the month which has just ended. In column (1) is found the total of correct verses reproduced immediately after the study of the four poems. And in column (2) is the total of correct verses reproduced after eight days.

If we compute the average recitation grade for each group of students, we find that these averages are approximately equivalent : 8 for the first group; 7 for the second one; 7.6 for the third one. The teacher did not, therefore, utilize his recitation grades in order to form his groups. He did not do so for several reasons. These grades often represent encouragement given to the students whose memory is poor, and this is excellent; this is a very wise idea on the part of the teacher. Some of these grades were assigned for tasks in which the part played by memory is unclear. Was the teacher right when he opted for a different type of classification? Yes, certainly; his three groups are, on the whole, those we would have formed with our memory experiment. The average number of verses remembered immediately after the study session is 29 for the first group, 21 for the second group, and 19 for the third group. In the reproduction test eight days later, the number of verses remembered is 15 for the first group, 11 for the second group, and 7 for the third group. We see, therefore, that we are in agreement with the teacher and that he did not commit an error. Students in his first group retained more than students in his second group. As to the students in the third group, they retained less than the others. This is the proof that we are dealing with a professor who is a good observer and who has evaluated his students' ability correctly.

Results from a Collective Memory Experiment in the 8th Grade of a Paris Primary School.

Names of Pupils	Number of verses reproduced		Average of Recitation Notes Given by the Professor	
	After Study (1)	8 days Later (2)	(3)	
Brui	43	24	9	Students
Alt	25	7	9	whose
Bar	37	28	9	memory
Qui	18	9	8.5	is judged
Gro	30	9	8	good by
Gren	26	13	7	the
Laver	26	3	9	professor
Piqu	33	15	8	
Leber	31	32	7	
Averages	29	15.5	8	
Pasq	15	4	7	
Bon	9	6	6	Judged
Bar	54	61	8	
Ga	27	7	8	average
Jar	19	1	7	
Ric	6	0	6	by
Bertr. A.	13	12	8	
Vu Paul	20	11	6	professor
Chap	31	7	7	
Averages	21	11	7	
Gend	4	0	7	
Via Paul	32	25	8	Judged
Wari	28	18	9	
Desail	11	1	8	weak
Meye	23	1	6	
Vova	27	2	9	by
Lero	10	5	6	
Monid	19	4	8	professor
Averages	19	7	7.6	

But good observers though we may be, we are not infallible, especially when the only thing we have to guide us is an impression. If we examine our results closely, we are forced to note cases in which the teacher's opinion appears to us to be unfounded. In our opinion he was in error for seven children out of twenty-six; that is for one-quarter of his students. Thus he placed in the good memory group two children, named Alt and Qui, who in reality have a mediocre memory, and a third child, named Laver, whose memory is quite bad. It is probable that Laver is a very industrious student who manages to supplement his defective memory with hard work, for his recitation grades are excellent; in fact, there are none better, his average grade being 9 out of a possible 10. Another teacher error consisted of placing in the average memory group three other students, named Pasq, Jar, and Ric, whose memory is extremely weak and who also must work very hard. And finally, making the inverse type of error, the teacher believed he recognized average and weak memories in children who in reality have excellent ones. Included in the weak memory group were Via Paul, who retained 25 verses after eight days, and Wari, who retained 18 after the same lapse of time, performances which are much more brilliant than those of the children included in the good memory group. But the most extraordinary error was that concerning young Bar. Although he has remarkably powerful retention power, having reproduced 54 verses immediately after the study session and 61 verses eight days later, he was placed in the average memory group. I questioned the teacher about this remarkable case and was told that Bar is a fairly young, scatter-brained child who is endowed with a good memory. But this was only an afterthought. The teacher had assigned Bar to the average memory group because he believed him to have an average memory. An error was evident in this case.

I am convinced all these errors will be avoided in the future if we take pains to measure the student's memory with the same care we measure his visual acuity. The time spent on these tests is not wasted time and the benefits the teacher derives from them are considerable. He will learn to proportion assignments to his students' ability. He will learn not to punish a student for carelessness when his problem is difficulty in retention. In this way he will avoid being cruelly unfair to a poor child who is trying hard but who has a weak memory. The total edification process will thus be oriented in the direction of truth. And this is something.

III. The Perversions of Memory

For a recollection to be useful it must have many qualities but none of these qualities is more important than reliability. We need not ignore a recollection which is incomplete provided we are conscious of the fact that it is incomplete and provided we don't have a tendency to make involuntary substitutions for the forgotten parts. Forgetting is always regrettable, but when we are aware that it has been done we can often make amends, or, if this is not possible, we can be cautious and can stand on our guard. But think about all the unfortunate consequences which can result from being convinced of a fact which we think we remember but which we really imagine! Suppose we read the following news item to some children : " Day before last the police arrested an individual on Pigalle Street because he was disturbing the peace. He was taken to the police station, etc., etc. "

The children, who have carefully listened to the story, are asked to reproduce it from memory. Most of the reports are commonplace and are characterized by childish language and by the omission of some insignificant details. But among the reproductions will be found some which contain extraneous information. According to one of the students, for instance, the arrest was made in front of 20 Pigalle Street, although the material which was read made no mention of a number. Another report stated that the arrested person was very well dressed, a detail which was not included in the story.

Let us give another example. Assume we show each of several children in his turn a cardboard on which five or six small pictures have been pasted. The cardboard is exposed to the child's view for twenty seconds. Immediately afterward, this child is questioned about what he has seen. A good many of the students describe the pictures accurately and most of their errors are either omissions or form and color alterations. The label, which was rectangular with the corners cut off, is described as being oval. The green stamp is said to be red. These are the early forms invention takes. They are frequently encountered and mainly involve colors, numbers and dimensions; much more rarely they involve the individuality of things. It even happens from time to time that a child will, without being aware that he has done so, perceive an object which was never there. Say, for instance, the cardboard had three pictures on it; the child will claim he saw a fourth one. If we ask him to describe it, he does so. One child may describe a photograph, another a dial, yet these resemble nothing either of them has been shown and we don't know how these objects came to their mind.

Here is a last example which an amusing rumor experiment provided us with. A child is told a story which he must repeat word for word and without modifying it to another child. The second child tells it to a third and so on. All these stories are told under the supervision of the teacher, who encourages precision and accuracy and prevents the experiment from degenerating into a joke, as happens in parlor games when each person consciously adds little details to make people laugh. This would render the experiment useless. On the contrary, each subject must make a serious effort to echo the story faithfully, without adding or omitting anything. Modifications are interesting mainly when they are made involuntarily and unconsciously. I tried this experiment in a primary school. The director was assisting me. The children came into his office one at a time and everything took place with the greatest seriousness. As soon as he had finished telling his story, each student went into the next room. He wrote down the story he had just told so we could keep track of it. By comparing the different versions to the original, we saw that children often reproduce exactly what they have been told but that they sometimes also amplify or dramatize. Most often it is the meaning, something like the direction of the story, which is exaggerated; if, for instance, it is a story about an accident, we can be sure the number of dead will increase from mouth to mouth.

We see that the results of these studies, which on first examination appear to be more in the realm of games, have serious practical implications for the evaluation of testimonies. They show that memory often is contaminated by an imagination which has not been sufficiently bridled by judgment. The witness's good faith may be absolute. He asserts and he believes he is asserting only what he is sure of, what he really has seen. But, without his knowledge, his memory has been invaded by his imagination as by a parasite plant. What he believes he remembers is actually his own creation and, what is also very odd, this creation of his has all the characteristics of a true recollection. Nothing distinguishes it from such a recollection, neither the precision of its details, nor its plausibility, nor the firmness of the belief which accompanies it. We stated above that if we examine several pictures pasted to a cardboard during a definite exposure time, we may make an erroneous report about the color of one of the pictures when we attempt to recall it. On the cardboard was a green stamp; we recall it as red. This is a precise and natural detail which is asserted with the same zest as if the stamp we saw were red when it is actually green. We also told a story about a scuffle which took place on Pigalle Street, and a student added, "in front of number 20." This is not a vague, hazy, ordinary detail; it is a definite number. And a lawyer who would wish to plead the child's veracity would say, according to the usual formula: "Here is a detail one does not invent!" In reality the imagination is extremely fecund in "details which we don't invent."

These experiments were repeated many times in Germany. * They became the object of extensive and thorough studies and a new science issued from them, called today the " science of testimony. " The following proposition, which is of considerable importance, was proven to be true an infinite number of times : There is no such thing as an absolutely and totally true testimony. If we have an adult testify in a complicated case, a picture description, for instance, or a report about a story, about a conversation or about an event which took place in his presence ; if further we take the precaution of having the witness swear under oath that what he reports is true, we find that if he is sincere, he never gives a testimony which is completely false, containing only details which are false, nor does he give testimony which is completely true from beginning to end either. Testimonies are always a mixture of truths and errors, and though the error part can be very weak in many cases, it practically never is down to zero. Approximately 25 per cent of the statements made under oath by all witnesses who were tested were found to be false.

We see, therefore, how careful we must be even when listening to testimony given by a trustworthy, intelligent and competent person. No part of it can be accepted as an article of faith. We see, too, that it would be dangerous to declare a witness untrustworthy and to accuse him of lack of sincerity or of having an unreliable memory because part of his testimony contained an obvious error. This proves nothing about the remainder of it, error being a constant element in any testimony. What these observations teach us, on the whole, is that human testimony must be neither overestimated nor underestimated. It never constitutes an absolute proof but rather a moral presumption, the value of which must be controlled with proofs of another kind.

We saw that great prudence must be exercised when we attempt to evaluate adult testimony. When child testimony is involved, even greater caution is required. That children are prone to conscious and unconscious lying is a well-known fact. This is due to the interplay of a large number of causes, some of which, of an impulsive nature, are not effectively held in check by others of an inhibitive nature. What leads the child to lie is the power of his imagination, the profusion of mental images, naive vanity, and the desire to attract attention. It is also the weakness of anything that could contribute to quieting down this imagination : the weakness of attention, the errors in judgment, ignorance

---

* In a book about suggestibility, in which I had described for the first time experimental studies about the values of testimony, I stated that these experiments were so important that some day a science of testimony would certainly be created. These experiments were, in fact, repeated in Germany. They were extensively developed and gave rise to a very rich literature. They are usually referred to as the "Stern Method," after the name of the man who made the studies the second time. A complete exposé of the question, written by myself, then by Claparède and by Larguier can be found in Année Psychologique (see Vol. XI, p. 128 ; XII, pp. 157, 275).

about many things such as the meaning of words and the meaning of things, lack of morality, lack of respect for truth, and, above all, this great, this enormous suggestibility and docility which are signs of an underdeveloped character. Combine these various influences and you have the child's lie. It is characterized by the improbability of the story, by the assurance the child puts into his lies, by the stubbornness with which he fights against evidence when he feels he is being contradicted.

If these facts were of interest to general psychology only, we would not have dwelled upon them here. But really, the tendency to invent, to embellish, to confound some facts and to make some others up completely is much stronger in some individuals than in others. There are children who, on the whole, are truthful. They are good observers, serious, calm, methodical, and we can believe what they say to a certain extent and with only a discreet check. Some others, however — and they are not the least intelligent — have so much imagination and are so emotional that they are always dangerous witnesses. It has been said that women make more errors than men while giving more copious reports. And what is true of women is always also a little true of children. At any rate, it is the students who make the largest number of errors who must have the largest share of the teacher's attention. The parents' confidences, sometimes a school incident, will bring them to our attention. The inventions their homework and their lessons contain betray them too. We shall also be able to identify these types of unconscious liars by asking them for information concerning things they can only know very little about. When asked a question, the answer to which he does not know, the child must get used to answering, "I don't know." The teacher, for his part, must be very careful not to elicit a false answer through suggestion. The child who answers with inexact precision, even when he does not know, must be watched. The teacher will render him a big service by putting him on guard against himself. This is the kind of service which can have a salutary influence on a whole existence, for it is educating judgment, and, after the education of the will, I don't know of a more beautiful endeavor.

I suggest, therefore, that a very sound proposal made by Claparède be adopted. It would institute observation lessons in the upper grades of elementary schools and in high schools. A program of observations to be made would be carefully prepared, and after the children have completed these observations, they would be asked to give either a written or a verbal report about what they have observed. Or they would be made to answer precise questions which the teacher would ask in an examination similar to that given by an examining magistrate. I think that if a teacher had two opposite qualities which are called imagination and common sense, he would know how to give his new type of assignment an interesting twist. He could readily demonstrate how easy it is to make a mistake, even at a time when we feel most confident we are not making one. This would represent excellent training in the exercise of prudence and critical judgment for many children who, in general, are quick to make extravagant assertions. It would also show that it is possible for a genuinely sincere person to make an error, and that consequently a lie or a bias need not be seen behind every mistake.

The teacher would also show that although a striking relationship seems to exist between a strong conviction and the truth of an assertion, it does not necessarily follow that this relationship exists. It is possible to be ardently convinced and nonetheless to be completely mistaken. Whoever asserts with impressive authority what he has seen and heard can be just as much in error as someone who is cautious and hesitates. This has more to do with personality than with truth. If we analyse things a little farther when cases susceptible of being analysed present themselves, it would be easy to demonstrate to the students that if we sometimes make errors in our observations, the majority of errors occur later, during the kind of maceration the fact undergoes in memory. It is during the act of memorization that perception becomes distorted and that unconscious conjectures are added to complete an incomplete observation. The teacher's lesson would become even more instructive if, in some cases, he intervened directly with all his authority to question students about their observations. He could quickly write some of those insidious questions which are such formidable suggestion machines. With a little skill he could have a docile child say that he has seen what it was not possible to see. He could cause endless errors and illusions. The dilemma, especially when the two questions which compose it are false, produces remarkable results. To ask under which of two conditions an event took place, to ask if a particular object is big or small, red or blue, is almost to force the child to opt for one of the alternatives he is presented with. Since the two alternatives are equally false, it is forcing him to give a false testimony. But it is not even necessary to go so far as to use the dilemma. A smile, an air of doubt, a nod are sufficient to cause some children's conviction to vacillate. How important it would be to demonstrate this to the children themselves!

Now let no one believe, when we give these directions, that we are proposing hypnotism or suggestion be introduced into the schools. On the contrary, we have always been against exhibitions of hypnotism in the army, in the theater, or on the public square; we intervened to have them prohibited every time we were able to; we are all the more against introducing these dangerous practices into the schools and are of the opinion that they should be strictly forbidden in them. Our children must not be turned into automata but must be free individuals. The exercises we recommend involve suggestion, it is true, but they contain only enough of it to act as a stimulant to the will and to the common sense, and to help the child react against the depressing influence of a foreign thought. Every time we explain this influence, after its impact has been felt, we are not giving the student training in docility but rather are developing his critical resistance and decreasing his suggestibility. The large number of facts we have observed decidedly show that testimony and consequently critical judgment are educable by this method. It would be a novelty in the classroom. Why not try it? It is at least worth a history lesson.

IV. Partial Memories

We now come to a question to which, twenty years ago, overly great importance may have been attributed. Those were the times when Professor Charcot was giving his beautiful lectures on aphasia, lectures which were so clear and, we must add, so schematic. The great French neurologist had an enormous influence on all who listened to him. He insisted on the plurality of memories and on the independence of those memories in the aphasic patient. He was probably not the first to use the expressions "visual" type, "auditive" type, "motor" type — expressions which have had such an overwhelming success in the philosophical world since then — but he used them with more authority than his predecessors. Charcot's lectures brought to the order of the day studies which had been conducted a little earlier, mainly by Galton (*Inquiries into the Human Mind,* London, 1883), by Taine *(L'intelligence),* and by Ribot *(Maladies de la mémoire,* Paris, Alcan). If we add to these works a thesis by St. Paul on "Le langage intérieur," Stricker and Egger's books on *La parole intérieure,* we believe we shall have listed the most important literature related to a very interesting subject.[5]

Although these types of studies were conducted mainly on patients, attempts were made to carry them over to the field of education. It was proposed that school children be divided into the visual, auditory and motor types. It was even proposed that they be grouped into classes according to these characteristics, but this craze has decreased little by little and a more balanced view is prevalent today. There still remains the need to discuss what, in connection with these studies, appears to be workable and especially what can be directly utilized in the field of education. This matter we shall now undertake to elucidate.

First, the idea that memory is not an individual faculty must be accepted as absolutely correct. There is not just one memory; there are several memories, that is a whole series of special, local memories. The importance of this distinction is not just in the words; there is also importance in the observation that, from the point of view of development and strength, special memories are independent of one another. A particular individual's memory is better for A, another's for B. The problem, then, is to know what are the most important aspects of the subject which we must examine in order to discriminate between these various types of memory. We conclude there is reason to distinguish three main areas :

1. Memories which differ by their object ;
2. different memorization procedures ; and
3. different ideation procedures.

1. It has been well known for a long time that all people don't remember the same type of material with the same accuracy. Some are good observers and remember well everything they have seen. Others remember ideas better or conversations or theories. In the case of things we have seen, one will remember the color better, another the shape. Some remember mathematical reasoning more particularly ; others physics or chemistry lessons. It is well known that the memory for music is a special one ; we have it or we don't. Examples of great musical memory are famous and everyone remembers the often-mentioned case of Mozart. I once knew a young woman who, after attending the opera, could sing from memory several airs she had heard a single time. Her brother and her mother had the same ability. But this same person could not tell as exactly as another about the different acts of a comedy. I also know a lady who has an extraordinary memory for dates, birthdays, numbers of addresses. She sometimes forgets the name of the street but remembers the number, and this is the exact opposite of the general rule.

This predominance of one memory over another sometimes is a natural phenomenon which can be explained by interest. We pay special attention to things which interest us and consequently we remember these things better than others. A young sportsman knows by heart the names, the ancestry, the performance of a large number of race horses, but he couldn't recite a single physics or chemistry formula. This does not mean that he has memory for everything which concerns horses ; it means he is interested in races more than in science. The same is true of the memory of the politician who remembers the votes and the speeches of so many of his colleagues. But often the interest accorded certain kinds of recollections is the sign of a special aptitude, as is the case in musicians. Often too there is neither interest nor aptitude but simply a special memory of exceptional strength. The lady I mentioned earlier in connection with the memory for numbers told me she had no special interest in figures and that it was against her will that they imposed themselves on her memory. She felt this was " very stupid. " We have to suppose, therefore, that the division of memories, their independence, the superiority of some of them over others are sometimes the consequence of such other mental factors as attention and interest. Sometimes, on the contrary, they are due to some primitive cause which cannot be explained psychologically and which must be attributed to some unknown structure of the nervous system.

2. We have just seen that there are several memories and that these memories are independent. Each is special and addresses itself to a different object. We shall now describe a plurality of memories which depends on a plurality of images. It is noteworthy indeed that to remember facts or ideas or objects belonging in the same category we can use several different means cumulatively or alternatively, like so many roads leading to the same goal or like so many instruments used to do the same work.

Let us first consider the fact that being endowed with language, we are able to express verbally everything we feel. Speech is a first reproduction of all psychological phenomena. Suppose I look at the landscape. Vision and other sensations associated with vision enable me to perceive such details as the form, the color, the position of the objects I am looking at. After this sensory perception which results from the contact with nature, I can further become conscious of this same scene by carefully and verbally describing it to myself, and when I am away from the place I have looked at, I shall be able to remember it in its sensory form, for the sensations I received will become alive again in a mental image. As the novelists say : "I see it again; it is as if I were still there." I shall also be able to remember it in its verbal form : a description in words, words which I shall pronounce in actual fact or which will echo within me and which I shall listen to. Let us take another example, that of a new dance and the steps and gestures which compose it. This dance can be learned muscularly or verbally. To learn it muscularly is to dance it, that is to execute the series of movements which compose it. It is also to remember this series of movements in such a way that if my body begins to execute one of them, it has a natural tendency to follow through with the rest. I shall know this dance when motor memory will make it possible for me to execute the various movements correctly and automatically. To learn the dance verbally is to know its description as it is found in a book and to be able to recite this description verbally, pronouncing each word after the other textually or merely reproducing the meaning. Note that in these examples the two methods of representation of things are cumulative. Language is the reproduction of all the sensations and emotions we are able to experience, and consequently our whole psychic life can be lived over again in two forms, one sensory and the other verbal. This, in our opinion, is the first distinction which must be made between memories. It is the most important one of all, the one which enables us to differentiate between the two most dissimilar intellectual types, the sensory and the verbal.

In connection with this, we can make an observation which is of great psychological interest. The child is much more sensory than verbal, especially when he is young, and if we want to impress a memory upon his mind it is better to show him the object than to use the name. The visual perception of the object will be retained an incredibly longer time than the word. Show ten objects to a class of children or show ten words for the same length of time, then ask the children to reproduce what they have seen. You will be surprised at the results. It may be that immediately after the experiment they will be able to reproduce an equal number of words and names of objects. But three days later almost all the words will be forgotten and almost all the objects will still be remembered.[6]

To this first division between sensory and verbal memory is added another one which is a subdivision. Everything which impresses our mind takes five or six different forms: the visual, auditory, tactile, motor, intellectual and sentimental form. Suppose, for instance, I am trying to remember a few digits. I can either remember the way they look or the way they sound or, finally, I can remember the movement which is necessary to write them. In the first case it is visual memory I utilize; in the second case it is auditory memory; in the third case it is kinesthetic memory. The difference will be even more striking if I have to retain a musical tune. Visually I can retain it by representing the music to myself; this memory results from reading with the eyes. Auditorily I retain it by the representation of the sound; this is a listener's memory. Finally I retain it muscularly by representation of the movements of the larynx; this is a singer's memory. The same distinction is valid in the memorization of a play we have seen. Some people visualize the production, the setting, the actor's performance. Other individuals hear anew the words, the voices and their timbre. It seems that by their very nature certain things appeal to some types of memories more directly than to others; the choice is in a way imposed on us from the outside but our personal constitution brings modifications. Thus the idea and the memory of a drawing will undoubtedly be most naturally provided by visual memory. After seeing, we visualize and visualization is the logical consequence, the prolongation of vision. However, we have met artists who are not satisfied with merely looking when they want to remember a shape. They carefully follow its contours with their fingers, and when they reproduce this shape, both visual and movement memory play a role. In the same way, a material object such as a tree belongs in the visual world almost exclusively. It speaks mainly to the eyes. Its trunk is gray or yellow, rough, peeling off. It is covered here and there with small green spots, light ones, gray ones, dark ones which appear to be in movement. Instead of this visual picture, however, it is possible to have an auditory image of something which makes a slight noise when the wind passes through it. A true musician, extremely sensitive to the voice of everything, may become absorbed by this delicate sound. He may perceive its various nuances and harmonics, discover in them a world of ideas completely unknown to us, and out of these form the personality of the tree. Nevertheless, the kind of memory which most naturally comes into play for the retention of material objects is visual memory. A large number of experiments and testimonies have shown this.[7]

Are things different where language is involved? It was believed for a long time that since language is normally directed at the ear, it must be retained more particularly by auditory memory. We imagined that when we attempt to remember a lesson we have heard, a conversation, a speech or even a page of a book, we bring to life images of sounds, an inner voice. It was also observed that this inner voice accompanies all thinking processes, makes them clear and conscious. Indeed the importance of this inner language for the elaboration of abstract thought cannot be overemphasized. For instance, when I decide "Tomorrow I shall go to my laboratory," a pronunciation of this sentence actually takes place within me. When I remember a colleague once telling me, "The philosophical theory of parallelism is an absurdity," I can visualize his face and the gesture of his hand, but his words are heard again in me, as words.

It was supposed, therefore, that auditory images play a very important role in the ideation which involves language. More thorough analyses and especially numerous experiments have shown this interpretation to be in error. Analysis proved that when we believe we hear, in our inner audition, a voice which pronounces sentences, we are not experiencing a pure auditory image but rather a motor image, a weak and incomplete articulation which is accompanied by several fragments of auditory images. True language memory would therefore be a memory of articulation or, if we prefer, it would result from the acquisition of a motor habit. To learn a piece by heart is to acquire a mechanism that enables us to recite the piece at will; this recitation gives rise to very few auditory images. There are no more of them in this case than when we pronounce a sentence while taking part in a conversation. We pronounce it without needing to reproduce it auditorily. What creates confusion is the fact that the difference between motor memory and the auditory image is not very great. It is, in fact, rather small, so it is sometimes difficult to discriminate between them. Let us just say that in the case of inner speech we have less the feeling of hearing the tone of a foreign voice than in the case of inner audition; also we experience more throat sensations and have the feeling we are producing speech; moreover, speech organs can often be seen in action.

More rarely, inner language takes the form of a visualization. The case is uncommon. We remember and we represent the words to ourselves in the visual form. If we think about a dog, for instance, we see the word "dog" written in print.

Finally, it frequently happens that we see nothing, and that we do not pronounce any of the sentence we are thinking about, but we have a feeling about it, we are conscious of its meaning, we know what it means and what we ourselves want to do. It is a mysterious language without words. In spite of these variations, it is believed that the memory of language is mainly a motor memory of articulation.

In short, while we more commonly utilize visual memory to remember material objects, we usually utilize motor memory to remember words and sentences. But these rules suffer many exceptions which prove that the memories of certain senses are much more developed in particular individuals than are the memories of other senses. To take these observations into account, we differentiated between the visual, the auditory, the motor and the indifferent types. The latter represent a just equilibrium between the various kinds of memory.

3. From the study of memory we pass naturally enough to the study of ideation types. These two questions are closely related, almost confounded. From what precedes, it is possible to anticipate what goes on in the mind of a person who thinks, reflects, reasons, remembers, imagines, conjectures. The nature of the images brought into play during these operations varies from one individual to another, since each person has his own way of thinking even when he and other people are thinking about the same thing. In the case of ideation as in the case of memory we shall therefore recognize several types : the visual, the auditory, the motor, the verbal. But at this point a complication is introduced : Individual differences in education are produced not only by the personal quality of images but also by their intensity and the distinctiveness of their character. Suppose that in order to make a comparison between several persons we ask them to visualize a familiar object. We then ask them to tell whether or not the visualization resembles the real perception of the same object if it were present. The answers we obtain are quite varied. Many persons — almost half, if they are still young — answer that their representations have a strength, a sharpness, a vividness which makes them equal or almost equal to the actual perception.[8] Others find that their visual images are weak, faint, dull, faded, receding, vague, far away, very small or fragmentary, discolored like photographs.[9] These last forms are often found in the older and most intelligent children, in adults, especially in adults who are given to abstract cogitation. These special forms stand out as landmarks in the mental development of individuals and indicate which superior level they have reached.

144

In connection with this, nothing is more instructive than the comparisons we were able to make between the inner thought of a child and that of an adult man.

Young children's minds are filled with images which are representations of sensations they have experienced anteriorly. They visualize an absent object with a vividness which borders on dream and hallucination. Then, as we grow older and as our intelligence develops, we use abstractions more. Language acquires more importance and it encroaches on sensory images. An adult thinks more with words than a child; on the other hand, he does not visualize the picturesque form of things as well as the child. If you go so far as to question a scholar, he will tell you — as several of Galton's colleagues answered in his questionnaire — that he does not see anything he is thinking about, and when he thinks about one of his absent friends, he does not visualize the friend nor hear his voice to any degree but thinks about him in an abstract, free, and subtle form. If any sensory images are still evoked, they are only fragments, or they have the value of schemes or symbols which no longer correspond to the original real perception. Finally, they lose their relief and vividness to such an extent that they can no longer be recognized as representations of sensations. One more step and they disappear completely. Only the word remains. It too can come to play a secondary, fragmentary role and then fade away, as it were. Thought is now bare, reduced to a direction, a choice, a feeling, an attitude, an intellectual phenomenon which may be the most difficult thing in the world to explain and to understand.

Let us consider pedagogic applications. To have a thorough knowledge of an individual's mental type is extremely useful to anyone who needs to advise this individual. This is so because, as we shall show later, aptitudes are partly an outcome of our mental characteristics. It is evident that a visual type person will be inclined to observe things in nature. All other things being equal, he will be much more of an observer than someone whose mental type is auditory. He will be more interested in drawing, in geography and in natural history. He will become a naturalist or an artist more easily than an auditory type. But we reserve this very vast and still very poorly understood question of aptitudes for the next chapter. What we are concerned with here is memory. We have seen that there are special memories which differ either by verbalism or by the quality of sensory images. Is it not useful to be able to determine which type of memory a child has? Is it not our responsibility to put him in a position to use his most effective memory? This practical question appears to us to be of the highest importance.

I don't think it is wise to question children about their ideation. Most often they don't understand what we are talking about; they are

145

also very suggestible; finally, they do not have the ability to analyse themselves. Suppose we ask them, as we habitually do with adults, to "Imagine a rose enclosed in a box on a bed of ferns. Do you clearly see its color, its shape? Do you perceive its fragrance in your imagination? etc." Or if we tell them: "Imagine your last lunch. Do you see the table as a whole, the bottle, the dishes with their usual color? etc." I have noticed that in these cases children very often misunderstand. They think we want to find out if they know the color of a rose or if they remember particular details about their lunch. They confound knowing with imagining. If we insist on a particular question, they will very often answer "Yes," just to make us happy. And it is easy, a short time later, to get them to answer "No" to the same question asked in a different tone of voice. We cannot, in our opinion, rely on these introspection analyses. We must, instead, have recourse to an experiment. But to which one?

The experiments recommended by various authors for demonstrating the different types of memory are numerous because none of them is very easy or very reliable. Ordinarily they are recommended because, *a priori,* they appear reasonable, but this is really not sufficient. There is one method, however, which appears to us to be better, more logical, more direct than the others. It consists of evaluating the speed and the assurance with which a school child's mind registers the same facts when he uses visual memory, when he uses auditory memory and when he uses motor memory. Such an evaluation does provide an answer to some of the questions which preoccupy pedagogy. Here is a method which has often been suggested, notably by Biervliet. The teacher will read 25 words to a whole class of children two or three times. Immediately afterward the students will be asked to write down from memory what they recall. The teacher will then write or print 25 new words on the blackboard. After a presentation time roughly equal to that of the preceding test and during which they learn the words, the students will again be asked to write down everything they can recall. After having given these two tests alternatively four or five times, the teacher should see, when he corrects the papers, which children remember better what they have seen and which remember better what they have heard. Visual memory would conceivably be predominant in the first and auditory memory in the second. But we must add that, for our conclusions to be valid, they must be uncontaminated by the effects of irrelevant variables. As we have seen, however, the teacher guides the children's attention when he pronounces the words. When he writes the words on the blackboard, the children themselves must direct their work and this is more difficult and challenging for them, especially if they are young. So that — all other things being equal — the students will retain more words after a visual presentation.[10]

146

I wanted to be absolutely sure and to know exactly what such an experiment could teach us which would be useful in the schools. In our experiment, carefully supervised by Mr. Vaney, a total of 200 words was presented to 25 children ranging in age from eleven to fourteen. There were four sessions a few days apart from one another. At each session the subjects were presented a series of 25 words auditorily. They were then asked to recall these words. Immediately afterward they were presented a series of 25 new words visually and were asked to recall them. When the results were computed, we found that the children who remembered a rigorously equal number of words in the auditory and in the visual series were rare. Discrepancies were almost the rule and anywhere from 1 to 12 more words were recalled in one of the series. Can we conclude from this that the subjects who have retained a majority of the words presented visually are of the visual type and that all the others are of the auditory type? This would be jumping to conclusions. There were, we said, four visual presentations and four auditory presentations, each including 25 words.

If a child is truly predominantly visual, he should retain a majority of words not only in the four visual series considered as a whole but also in each visual series compared to the corresponding auditory series. Is this a common occurrence? No. This case presented itself only three times. Therefore, according to our data, only 3 children in 25 are predominantly visual or predominantly auditory. Someone may argue that our requirements are too stringent. We compared the results obtained on a single visual series to those obtained on a single corresponding auditory series. What happens if we compare the results obtained on two visual series to the results obtained on two auditory series? Does the group of children which has superior visual memory when we consider the results of the four sessions as a whole still retain its superiority? We find this is not so. Ordinarily our results are something like this: auditory series, 17, 21; visual series, 19, 17. We record a majority in the first visual series but in the second the contrary is true. A number of small causes contribute to these effects. Probably the most frequent one is illustrated by the case of a student who, in one of the experiments, recalled only 6 words when he habitually recalls about 10. He most likely became disturbed or distracted. It is this kind of incident which vitiates test results. After eliminating these types of cases, I find only 4 subjects in 25 whose performance consistently placed them in the auditory type category. The remainder showed no marked tendency of any kind. Now 4 out of 25 is a very weak proportion. It gives very little support to those who would classify students on the basis of imagery types. Moreover, one of the students who had been classified as an auditory type has been found to have poor vision, and he may well have had difficulty reading the words on the blackboard. This leaves 3 cases and these cases also appear suspicious, since, according to the teacher, these students have no remarkable aptitude for drawing, spelling, geography, that is to say for subjects in which "visualism" plays a dominant role. I shall provisionally conclude from this experiment, not that there are no different imagery types in school children, but that if these different types exist they cannot be recognized by ordinary means, and further that it is inadvisable at this time to group students on such a flimsy and equivocal basis.

V. The Education of Memory

Is it possible to increase one's memory? To make it both greater and more faithful? To retain what we have learned longer, or to learn new material faster? To keep our memory under the control of our will so that information can be retrieved quickly when we need it? We resolutely answer these first questions in the affirmative. For the past thirty years many memory experiments have been conducted in laboratories on adults of good will. We know now which main conditions must be met to insure the good functioning of this faculty.[11]

Strictly speaking, there is no special method, no gimmick, no marvelous secret which would enable us miraculously to amplify our memory and to retain everything we want to retain. People who maintain the contrary and who boast they can confer memory upon someone who has none are quacks. The truth is that all the advice which can be given with regard to memory has been compiled during careful observation of habitual memory errors and the best ways of avoiding them. There is nothing exceptional, nothing miraculous about these observations. Had we had a lot of common sense, we could almost have foreseen the results. But the fact that they are not transcendent does not make them any less valuable, and by learning about them we greatly increase our resources. This is so because, as we shall show later, proper memorizing methods are often diametrically opposed to our instinctive tendencies. If we adopt, automatically and without thinking, the method which appears to us to be the most natural for learning, it very often turns out to be the least effective. All the more reason, therefore, to assimilate painstakingly the scientific principles which are applicable to the education of memory. As it has been picturesquely stated: We must learn how to learn.

If we try, by consulting the literature and our own personal studies, to determine what set of conditions influences memory favorably, we find we must direct our attention to the following factors: 1) the time of practice; 2) the length of the practice period; 3) the respective action of interest and repetition; 4) the mode of repetition; 5) progression from the simple to the complex and from the easy to the difficult; and knowledge of results; 6) multiplicity of impressions through the different sensory modalities; 7) the search for idea associations; 8) the substitution of the memory of ideas for the memory of sensations.

I shall attempt to show these various factors in operation and, to do so clearly, I shall take a simple example. We shall suppose I want to learn a twenty-verse poem. I shall try to learn it so as to keep it lastingly in my memory and so it will become an integral part of my mind, of my substance. At the same time, I wish to obtain maximum learning efficiency from a minimum of effort. In this particular example we have chosen, let us see what is the best procedure to be followed, because it is essentially like a school task. At the same time as we describe the method, we shall attempt to discover the reason for its choice and its significance for memorization. In this way we shall get as complete an understanding as possible of the whole question, of what is the exception as well as of what is the rule.

1. *The best time to learn*

Let us consider first the hour of the study period. At what time of day shall I start studying the poem? The time is not irrelevant, for a memorizing act is not an act which is completed and consummated at the same instant. It must be long-lived. Nothing has been achieved if a memory has been enregistered but is not retained. Now this retention, which supposes the development of a certain neurological structure, requires suitable physiological conditions, a good circulation and a good nutrition. If I am tired, nervous, disturbed or preoccupied, I shall be able to write a letter, make an addition, pay a bill, do some mechanical work, but I shall not try to learn. Under these conditions I would become overly tired and I would learn badly. When we are tired we can entertain ourselves with some light reading, but we should not read a serious book, for we would not profit from our reading. Students who prepare for an examination while they are overworked retain little of what they have learned during this period. Overwork is not the only reason they forget but it is one of the main reasons. Another is that they learn too fast and too superficially, as we shall explain later. In connection with this, an amusing proof is sometimes given. A person who is even mildly intoxicated does not remember clearly what he has seen and heard during intoxication. Someone may argue it is because he was not paying sufficient attention, but his memory itself is weakened. If we name a number and dare him to remember it the next day when he will have sobered up, we very often win our bet. Any kind of excess has the same disastrous effect on the fixation and retention of memories. Any considerable physical fatigue, the beginning of a serious illness, anemia, chlorosis, all have similar consequences.

What we need to be concerned about here is to determine the time of day which is most favorable for memorization. This factor is important because our physical condition is not stable, changing from hour to hour, without our being aware of it. A wakeful day supposes continuous intellectual work which is sometimes heavy, sometimes light, but which is as constant as waking activity is. Fatigue therefore builds up steadily as the day passes and is at its maximum at bedtime. Sleep represents rest, not only from muscular activity but also, and above all, from conscious mental activity. It facilitates recovery from the fatigue of the day and is even successful in removing its effects completely when this fatigue hasn't attained the proportion of overexertion. Mental energy is at its peak during the first few hours following awakening. These theoretical views have been confirmed by observations and experiments. Let us begin with our observations, which were gathered mainly by questioning writers. The latter have noticed that they write most easily during the morning hours. In afternoons or evenings, notes are taken, observations are made, plans are drawn up, but work involving style, which requires a certain freshness of approach and a considerable effort, is limited to the first part of the day. The experiments were conducted on school children and were designed to investigate intellectual fatigue. This problem has been studied in many small ways which are very ingenious, very precise and which clearly show, not if a particular student taken aside from all others is fatigued — the method is worthless from this point of view — but if a whole class of students is fatigued. Several methods have been used — for instance, the dictation method, calculation exercises, cutaneous sensitivity measurements — and they show that it is during the morning classes that groups of pupils make the fewest spelling mistakes, calculate the fastest, have the finest tactile sensitivity, and are therefore functioning at peak efficiency. We shall give a single example : a group of students, which before class time makes only 40 errors in a dictation, makes 70 errors after one hour of work, 160 after two hours, 190 after three hours (Friedrich). [12]

Taking these findings into consideration, we shall choose the first morning hours for the study of the poem we must learn by heart.

But this rule is not without exception. Many persons are used to working evenings and well into the night. They get up late in the morning and are still a little fatigued, a little drowsy, disinclined to making an effort. Further — and speaking strictly from the point of view of memory — some individuals have observed that a lesson read before retiring is remembered upon rising as if the unconscious had awakened during the night to repeat it and to learn it. We shall come back in a moment to the role of this unconscious and to explain it differently. At any rate, it is essential for an individual not to decide upon a course of action without considering his own personal habits, his own way of life, his own psychological make-up.

150

2. *Length of a practice period*
   (Massed vs. distributed learning)

Let us now discuss the duration of a study session. To learn a twenty-verse poem we need about twenty minutes. We can either learn the whole poem in one study period or learn it a part at a time. Similarly we can have rest intervals of different lengths between sessions. They may be a few minutes, a few hours or even a day long. Laboratory experiments have shown[13] that much is gained by dividing a task into parts but this must be done wisely. To multiply these parts would be to forget their *raison d'être.* Ordinarily two short sessions are better than a long one because we attend better. The strength of our attention is like the edge of a blade; it quickly loses its keenness. After a short time we work automatically, without interest, and we no longer do anything well. But if the study session is too short, if, to take an extreme case as an example, we try to learn our poem in four sessions of five minutes each, we go from one extreme to the other. Attention will not wane, it is true; it will not even have time to become activated, which is an inconvenience of a different type. Any intellectual work which we begin is like a heavy machine which needs time to get under way. This initial "warm-up" will not have time to take place in a five-minute study session. A fifteen-minute session is therefore preferable.

3. *Rest after the practice period*

The study period is over. What next? After any work which requires great concentration, it is well to rest or to undertake some mechanical task, for the phase which follows active intellectual work is rest only in appearance. During this time the material we have just learned is being organized; it becomes more stable, a definite part of memory, like sediment which settles to the bottom of water. We do not realize it, for this work is done unconsciously. If we should experience a strong emotion, a shock, or be subjected to considerable strain while this is taking place, this process of consolidation would be compromised. As the American author Burnham was the first to suggest,[14] this process explains the curious phenomenon called "retroactive amnesia," which occurs following a head injury or similar trauma. While regaining consciousness the victim remembers what happened the preceding days, but he has completely forgotten how the accident occurred or even what happened a few hours before. An officer who had just fallen from a horse did not remember the visit he had made just before falling. We explain this by supposing that the memories corresponding to the recent experiences were not yet consolidated when the shock came and destroyed them. It is therefore essential, we repeat, to see to it that memorization tasks are followed by a rest period. The cramming too many students engage in while preparing for an examination represents a violation of this rule, and this explains the pernicious effect cramming has on memory.

We shall go even further. If, after having exercised our memory, we cannot get the rest which would facilitate the consolidation and preservation of what we have learned, we can at least take a precaution : we can momentarily refrain from doing work which is similar to what we have just finished. Suppose we want to learn a musical selection by heart. The work of our memory would be compromised if, after having learned it, we started to read or sing other musical selections. Numerous experiments by Cohn, Bourdon , Münsterberg, and Bigham have shown beyond any doubt that this is true. And V. Henri, who wrote a detailed report about this laboratory research, adds an interesting observation when he says :

> A lesson learned in the evening is remembered effectively the next morning. The same lesson learned in the morning to be recited in the evening is not remembered as well. This is so because in the first case the learner rests during the interval, while in the second case the learner's mind receives a large number of impressions which interfere with consolidation. [15]

4. *The two main memorization procedures : Intentional learning (attention) and recitation*

We have just discussed the external conditions of memorization, examining when is the best time to learn and how long the practice period should be, but we have not studied the actual learning act closely. Let us see which of the two memorizing procedures can best enable us to complete this act successfully : one involves attention ; the other recitation. I can concentrate my thoughts on the book, closing my ears to external noise by adopting the well-known attitude of the child who is learning his lesson. Or I can use recitation, repeating the verses to myself several times and in a low voice. I know instinctively that memory will penetrate the mind by dint of repetition.

Which of these two methods is easier, less painful? It is repetition. Which is more effective? It is intentional learning. Painstaking measurements [16] were made with trained subjects who were asked to learn about a hundred words. These adult subjects were then invited to explain with the utmost care the method they had used, and we found that some of them recited the words only once, some others twice, still others three or four times. Now, the subjects who remembered best were those who used recitation least and who paid attention most. Therefore, every time it is possible we must avoid recitation, which is often done more or less automatically. Instead, we should concentrate all our attention on the fact or the idea we absolutely want to retain. This is sometimes difficult, for we are not always in complete control of our attention. What is even more effective than voluntary attention is the interest we have in the impression or the idea which is to be retained.[17]

5. *Recitation : Whole vs. part learning*

But there is even better. If we study the question more closely we see that recitation can be done in several ways, each of which has a virtue of its own. There is reading aloud and there is mental recitation. It has been shown that the latter is more effective, probably because it demands greater attention.[18] Beyond this we must also consider the length of the mental recitation we undertake. Sometimes the poem we want to learn is read or recited in small fragments. For instance, we begin by reading only the first two verses; we read them again, and then we try to recite them without looking at the book. We constantly come back to those two verses until we are convinced we know them. This is what we have called the "fragmentary method," to convey accurately the idea that it consists of dividing the piece to be learned into very small fragments. For instance, if we have to learn this fable of Lafontaine's, we shall proceed as follows :

> An evil which spreads terror
> An evil which spreads terror
> Evil which heaven in its fury
> Invented to punish...
>
> An evil which spreads terror
> Evil which heaven in its fury
> Evil which heaven in its fury
> Invented to punish the crimes of the earth.

Another method is called the "global method."[19] It consists of reading the entire piece at one time and trying to retain it as a whole. After one or several complete readings, we make an attempt at recitation; then we return to reading without concerning ourselves about the errors we make while reciting from memory. Our reading is again global, that is to say, we read the poem through and through. There is no need to say that this global method is contrary to the dictates of our instinct and that we never have recourse to it. We loathe it for a very simple reason : it demands much more attention than the other method. When we recite two or three verses at a time, we can do the work automatically; we try to remember the sonority of the sentence. It is like music which leaves an impression on our interior audition. But if we force ourselves to read the whole poem, it is impossible to retain the sound, for this meaningless music is of very short duration; it dies away immediately the way an echo dies. It becomes necessary to find another way to arrest our attention, to compel it to probe deeper, down to the meaning, to the ideas contained in the poem. It is this small extra effort which we resent, for we are singularly sparing of our attention. Now, research has shown that the global method, in spite of its forbidding character, is definitely better than the fragmentary method for the preservation of memories. It enables us to learn a little faster and, which is important, it ensures a more reliable and a longer retention. Thus, after two years, a subject could still recite 23 per cent of the pieces he had learned with the global method while he could only recite 12 per cent of the comparable pieces he had learned with the fragmentary method. We believe there are many small reasons for the greater efficiency of the global method. But the most important one, in our opinion, is that it utilizes the memory of ideas while the other method utilizes the memory of sensations only.

Many observations and anecdotes become very easy to understand if we examine them from the point of view of the distinction between the memory of sensations and the memory of ideas. We can guess why a particular attempt at memorization is unsuccessful. I once discussed this matter with actors of the Comedie-Francaise. Actors are professionals whose lot is not enviable. They pay for their beautiful success with the great pains they take to learn their role, and those among them who are intelligent have made many observations about the laws of memory. We know they often have to learn at a moment's notice; the day before a benefit performance, or when the company is on tour, for instance, or finally when they have an engagement in the provinces or in a foreign country at a theater where the program changes frequently. When we learn fast we know our part sufficiently well to play it without difficulty the same day, but we do not retain it long, and if we have to play the same role again two years later we have to relearn it. We are told this is a fact which is quite clear and which has been frequently observed. This is true not only for actors. Many school children also learn fast and retain well but only for a short time. How is this explained? I imagine it is because attention was focused more on the sensory qualities of the sentences than on the ideas the sentences contained. Of course, this explanation is a little hypothetical and I don't guarantee its accuracy. What is more important is to prevent the child from cultivating this temporary memory at the exclusion of the other. But how shall we go about doing this?

The student will recite his lesson faultlessly whether learning has been superficial or thorough. The listener cannot tell if this apparently well-known material will still be retained in the child's memory the next day or if it will be forgotten. Lesson recitation will not, therefore, tell the teacher anything. But by taking the very simple precaution of not letting it be known when a recitation will be requested, he can insure thorough learning. The student who knows there are chances he may be asked to recite a lesson Tuesday at 8:30 prepares himself strictly for Tuesday at 8:30. He learns superficially at the last minute. If experience has taught him that the hour of recitation cannot be predicted, that it may be on Tuesday afternoon or on Wednesday or Thursday, he immediately understands the futility of learning for a particular time. Little by little he is led to make the effort necessary to learn forever. Is this not better? I prefer to know two beautiful verses all my life than to know twenty-four verses which will remain in my memory for a week, then disappear without leaving any trace. The distinction which has just been made between the memory of ideas is extremely important and will dominate everything which follows.

6. *Cultivation of the memory of sensations*

When we attempt to cultivate the memory of sensations, our goal is to increase the persistency of sensations in memory. This persistency is not increased by the strength or the sharpness of the sensation. A lesson printed with big letters will not be remembered better than the same lesson printed with small letters. What will increase the strength of our memory is the multiplicity, the chorus of numerous sensations. If three or four different sensations have contributed to our memory of element "a," we have a greater chance of retaining it than if a single sensation has contributed to it. This has been clearly demonstrated by judicious experiments conducted mainly on school children. Let us come back to this poem we need to learn. What happens when we are studying it? If we are content with looking at it, we only receive a visual impression. It is already not a simple one, it is true, and it will be all the more complicated when we shall have examined the poem more analytically. If we pronounce the words aloud at the same time our eyes go over them, two other sensory impressions are added to the first: 1) an auditory impression, since we hear our voice; 2) a motor impression, since we feel ourselves speak. Experiments have shown that a multiplicity of sensations, provided, of course, they all relate to the same object, facilitates retention. The more sensory modalities we utilize, the greater our chance will be of retaining what we are learning.[20] Consequently, we shall not be content with reading our poem with our eyes; we shall read it aloud in a private, noise-free environment so we shall not feel self-conscious and so no sound other than the sound of our voice will leave an impression upon our audition. To increase the number of sensations we shall do even more. We shall write down the poem from memory or we shall copy it. In this fashion the information will reach us through four different modalities: vision, audition, the voice, the hand. It is with this plurality of means that we teach children to read and the method is excellent. We shall go even further. Since it is the multiplicity of sensations which facilitates the work of memory, we shall strive to increase their number in each modality. For instance, we shall look for the best, the most varied, the most correct intonation so as to impress our audition and our speech organs in a great diversity of ways. If we copy, we shall use brackets, make excisions, change writing and ink in relation to the meaning of the piece and in such a way as to illustrate this meaning. And in all events, if we know ourselves and if we know our personal memory type, we shall work especially with the kind of sensation we retain best. We shall use it in preference; the others will be only a support, a complement to it. If I am a motor type, as is most frequently the case with regard to verbal memories, I shall not seek to remember the visual aspect of the page I am studying. I shall preferably set my thought on the recitation of the poem. The visual image of the page, the memory of my calligraphic effort, the auditory image of the sound of my voice are only adjuvants which will aid my interior recitation. In fact, this is how things habitually happen. When we learn a piece, we create in ourselves a motor aptitude to recite it. The visual image of the printed word intervenes mainly when we are looking for the beginning of the piece or when our memory fails us. It acts as a suggestion, a primer, a frame. The auditory image is almost never called forth. It is the memory of articulation which constitutes the substance of verbal memory.

7. *Cultivation of the memory of ideas*

It is worthy of note that when we try to increase the resources of a sensory memory, we change its nature. We make an intellectual memory out of it. To look for the proper intonation for a verse, or to calligraph this verse in a manner which is expressive, is to concentrate our attention on the idea, to take advantage of the interest this idea inspires. Consequently, it is to go beyond mere sensation. Now let us discuss the memory of ideas.

To grasp effectively the difference which exists between the memory of sensations and the memory of ideas, let us suppose we wish to retain a number which means nothing to us, for intance 2385, and a number which has a meaning, for instance 1830. The first calls forth no idea, or almost no idea. We say " almost, " for it is rare for a figure or a sensation to suggest absolutely no idea and to remain unproductive. The second number immediately catches our attention, for it is a historical date. It brings up memories about a revolution, about a change in government. We see Louis-Philippe's pear-shaped head in our mind's eye. A swarming mass of recollections is stirred up in us. It is evident that if I am asked to repeat these two numbers some time later, I shall have no difficulty recalling 1830, while the other number may be completely forgotten. The results are the same if we attempt to remember disconnected meaningless words and a meaningful sentence. Some old studies which V. Henri and I made in schools showed how poor the recollection of disconnected words is when we try to write them down or to repeat them immediately after hearing them. Suppose we ask a class of students to write the seven following words from memory after they have heard them a single time : " Jacket, money, wagon, desk, bird, house, table. " We find that children from eight to thirteen don't retain quite five words on the average. This is because a great effort is necessary to remember these particular words by their sound. On the contrary, feel how easy it is to remember a sentence like the one which follows : "The trumpeter's horse ate a bale of hay."

It is no longer the sound of words we need to retain but their meaning. The complete sentence has unity and it is not difficult to retain. Calculations — somewhat theoretical ones, I will admit — led us to say a number of years ago that the memory of ideas is twenty-five times more powerful than the memory of sensations. But I absolutely don't insist on this precise number. It will be sufficient to remember that the memory of ideas is incomparably superior to the memory of sensations and that consequently there are great advantages to having recourse to it.

It is obvious, for instance, that if we try to learn a poem by heart it is essential that we understand it. This way mostly the memory of ideas is involved. This, of course, is always the way it works when the individual who studies the piece is sufficiently intelligent to understand its meaning. If he examines himself at the time memories are evoked, he will see that it is the movement of ideas which most often dictates the evocation. When we try to remember a fact which unfortunately is meaningless, we make an effort somehow to intellectualize it. Is it a matter of distinguishing two addresses which could easily become confounded, of remembering the day of a reception, a birthday, an equation? Each uses his ingenuity to hang onto the meaningless fact a more or less artificial idea which will aid memory. Every individual who has ever had to take an examination has used some of these aids, to learn about the properties of matter in chemistry, specific weights in physics, strata and the characteristic fossils they contain in geology, the series of cranial nerves in anatomy. Formulae, stories, jokes, songs have been invented which are so many homages rendered to the memory of ideas. It is in good taste not to depend on these procedures and it would doubtlessly be wrong to abuse their use, but why not utilize them in extreme cases if they can relieve memory and especially if they can make it more precise?

These rule-of-thumb methods have been thought out and systematized by ingenious people. They have given rise to the special art of mnemonics. It consists of intellectualizing memories of sensations by hanging ideas onto them. Mnemonics especially holds good with regard to the memory of figures. As I have explained somewhere else, the rule is to replace each figure by a consonant. Vowels are added to these consonants according to our fancy. In this way we replace meaningless numbers with sentences which have meaning and which are remembered all the more easily when their meaning is more bizarre.

This is so ingenious that we would resolve to have recourse to mnemonics every time we need to memorize numbers and dates if the procedures it forces us to use were not a little ridiculous and especially if this memorization method didn't make evocation somewhat slow. Indeed, before we can evoke the number we must first evoke the sentence and effect the translation which allows us to pass from the sentence to the figure. As a matter of fact, it is this very delay which enables us to identify the subject who uses mnemonics and simulates memory.[21] No one, therefore, will take it upon himself to use this method for learning figures which are in constant use and which need to be recalled quickly; no mnemonics for the memorization of the multiplication table, for instance.

What constitutes, properly speaking, the memory of ideas is somewhat difficult to define, for there are many differences between the act which enables us to retain a particular nuance of a sensation and the act which enables us to retain a whole set of things. We need to approach each of these cases from a different point of view. When we attempt to remember a sensation, it is the very nuance of the sensation which we seek to fix in our memory, and no sentence is of any real help in retaining this nuance. When, on the contrary, we exercise our memory of ideas, it is not the nuances of sensations we are interested in but rather the meaning of things and the ideas which we associate with them. The memory of ideas is a true memory of associations. It is accompanied by language because speech, which expresses the nuances of our sensations so poorly, is admirable, on the contrary, when it comes to expressing the relationship between ideas, to bringing out the logic in it and to making us conscious of this logic. This observation gives us some indication of where the power of the memory of ideas comes from. It is like a knitted fabric; it is sufficient to get hold of a single one of its stitches for the whole fabric to reappear. Indeed, the more associations we have at the service of a memory, the more chances this memory has of living again. Now since, in the case of a memory of ideas, the number of these reviving factors is enormous, their preservation is almost infallibly insured. Let us compare two experiences so the contrast will be readily apparent. In one case we try to remember a particular red, a red of a certain quality and brightness. Regardless of what we do, the memory of the particular shade fades after a few minutes. If we are shown the same original sample in a collection of samples with the same color quality but with decreasing degrees of brightness, we shall not recognize the original sample. This is a characteristic of the memory of sensations; it is greatly affected by time. Now suppose we are told that a particular red has the purple shade of a cardinal's habit. In this case the shade we remember is not very definite but we remember at the same time the word which describes it, the comparison which illustrates it; for all this has become associated, integrated, it has become a memory of ideas. And there is a good chance that our recollection of it tomorrow, in a week, in a year, will be as good as our recollection of it today.

Being the result of a system of associations, the memory of ideas must be developed in conformity with its nature, that is, by an increase in the number of associations. It is a kind of paradox : the more numerous memories are, the better they are retained. But we immediately make a reservation : this is so provided these memories are associated correctly. There is a direction in which association can be carried on and another direction in which it must be avoided. We shall explain this tactical advice further.

First, every time we want to acquire an important piece of information we shall try making comparisons between what we are learning and what we already know. The new acquisition will thus become an integral part of our stock of knowledge. This is a very useful prescription for the preservation of a memory, useful especially from the point of view of understanding it better and of introducing method in the mind. We clearly see this assimilation phenomenon at work when a child tells about what he has learned. He tells about it in his own way, his own words, his own sentences, his own ideas, with his childish turn of mind.

Secondly, we shall try to create associations between the memory and some reference marks which will help evoke it. It is very necessary to take this precaution, for many of our memories are lost for lack of a way of awakening them. The knot we tie to our handkerchief is a naive form of these artificial reminders. The memo we jot down in our notebook is a way of sparing ourselves the fatigue of a search. It is also a means of not exercising memory and making it lazy. We must pay scrupulous attention to the methods of recall and study them in relation to each important circumstance. In connection with this I shall give a very banal example of a young lady who couldn't remember to close the piano after she was finished using it, and as a result the piano was constantly open. I advised her to practice getting up from her stool a large number of times, associating with this movement the movement which consists of closing the piano. Through repetition these two acts became one.

Thirdly, what must be avoided is making dangerous associations which bring closer together things which should be kept separate. A pedagogic rule, which unfortunately is little known, could help avoid this mistake. It holds that it is at the time of the formation of a memory that we must actively intervene to avoid making association errors. It is almost always at this particular time that they occur.

If you are giving someone your address, don't say : " Do I live at 202 K... Avenue, or at 204 K... Avenue ? " For even if you make the number clear afterwards, your interlocutor will have a tendency to substitute one number for the other because he has brought them together in his mind. I remember that the calculator prodigy Inaudi asked the spectator who provided the figures for his problems to articulate these figures without hesitating and without making an error. Even if errors were corrected immediately, they confused him. For the same reason, if you are teaching spelling, don't have the spelling of unknown words debated, don't point out spelling errors aloud, and finally, don't give your students an opportunity to make errors in dictations which have not been adequately prepared. Don't ask: " Does the word 'apartment' take one 'p' or two 'p' s'?" And don't exclaim: " This student wrote the word 'apartment' with two 'p's.' What an error! " Instead, state boldly that the word " apartment " takes a single " p, " and if you give a dictation, begin by teaching the spelling of unfamiliar words before you dictate them. These rules concerning dictation are beginning to be well known. But here are a few observations which will appear newer. When I was in Law School I had a professor of Roman Law who introduced us to Civil Law Institutions by comparing them point by point with Praetorian Law Institutions. This comparison would have been very useful two lessons later, after each separate set of institutions had become familiar and had been assimilated in our memory. The error resided in starting with the comparison. Students could not help confounding the two systems. All the knowledge became associated in a most disorganized way. Later when I studied the natural sciences I listened to a Zoology professor who described monkeys to us and passed from one type of monkey to another for each organ. It became impossible to remember the characteristics of each type of animal because we were never given a comprehensive view of the organism and because, once again, association had worked in the wrong direction. Many errors, much confusion, much useless work will be avoided if we remember that memory first consists of conferring individuality on what we learn. It is only when the new acquisition is well individualized that comparisons between similar or slightly different objects can be introduced.

8. *The training of memory*

We have just finished describing the means of avoiding memorization errors and of strengthening memories. It is fitting to add that memory, like all other functions, improves as a result of practice. We can literally increase our memory; everyone knows this. Only one author, the great American psychologist William James, has expressed a doubt about it. He practiced learning poetry by heart and observed that after a month of practice he learned neither better nor faster than at the beginning. He invited some of his friends to make similar experiments and their results upheld his. Many other workers have tried to verify James's findings, which were most unexpected and contradicted everything that had been observed about the law of mental progress through practice.[22] These workers found that memory, like our other faculties, is subject to this law. This fact has been observed in adults and in school children and the differences due to practice are found to be considerable.

To conciliate the views of the two parties, we can suppose that practice does not, properly speaking, increase the capacity of our memory, but that it refines the art with which we use it. When we learn a poem we don't bring into play only the plastic strength of the mind, that is to say this unknown physiological quality which accounts for the fact that an impression is stored and remains dormant until it is evoked. A memorization supposes beyond this that at the time it takes place we attend to the task in an appropriate manner, that we take useful rest intervals, that we make repeated readings, that we concentrate our thought on the ideas contained in the piece to be learned, in short that we make efficient use of what memory we have. Physical education increases our strength in the same way, not so much by materially increasing muscle strength as by teaching us the art of proper breathing and of using our strength efficiently.

The improvement which results from practice is even more important than we realize. If the question is examined more closely it is found that when an individual's performance improves as a result of practice on a particular task, this improved performance is carried over to similar or slightly different tasks. It is a strange, almost unbelievable fact. To learn to distinguish sounds of different pitch can help distinguish tones of different values more accurately.[23] How does this general improvement come about? Is it because in jobs which appear to us to be totally different there are elementary processes which are identical? Is it because any work involves a general thought pattern and that this thought pattern remains constant? It is not known and the matter is still being debated. But from the practical point of view the important fact to remember is that each of our functions can be improved by practice and the improvement can sometimes be carried over from one task to another. Let us develop our memory. Above all, let us develop the children's memory so that after they have become adults it will be skilled, supple, and strong.

VI. An Error of Pedagogy

I end this chapter with the description of a particular observation I made on a young lady member of my family. It will show what the memory training I advocate consists of. This training does not consist of making endless unmethodical attempts at memorization. Poorly guided efforts would achieve nothing except to discourage the learner. Unless the rules which regulate the procedure are known and respected, training will be ineffective and no progress will be made. This is what happened in the case I am going to use to illustrate my point.

Mathilda is about twenty years old. She has been taking singing lessons for several years. She sings in tune, has taste for her work and practices her singing with pleasure, but she has been distressed lately about the results she obtains. She finds it almost impossible to learn a piece of music and to sing it by heart. She can sing only if she plays the piece on the piano or if her professor guides her by humming the tune. What is the problem? Mathilda has a good, even an excellent memory for literature and for daily life events. Why should she not have any for music? It is quite possible she hasn't, the memory for music being the most special memory we know. I question her. I ask her about the assignments her professor has given her. She tells me that for the past six months she has been trying to master the "Vallon" ["Vale"] by Gounod and that she is still unable to sing even the first twenty bars without the help of the piano. The many questions I ask help her become conscious of the reasons for her failure. When she tries to sing the piece alone from memory, she has a continual tendency to sing out of tune, that is to modify the pitch slightly in the case of a few notes. She hears herself when she is singing but does not become aware of the modification she has introduced, and since memory isn't selective, she naturally retains this modification. Consequently, when she returns to her music book, she must not only continue to learn what she does not yet know but also erase from her memory the incorrect acquisition she has made during her earlier performance. She has to work twice as hard and all her attempts to master the piece have this same deplorable effect. This explains why she isn't making any progress.

What conclusions can be drawn from this analysis? Shall we say that Mathilda has no memory for music and should give up singing? No. Everyone has some memory and this is true of Mathilda. She has not as much of it, however, as the pieces she is made to study require. The method which is imposed upon her is defective. Musical compositions don't all present the same level of difficulty. Her professor should cultivate Mathilda's memory by having her learn easy pieces which are better adapted to her present development. Little by little, very slowly, the level of difficulty could be increased. This course of action could only be profitable. The student would not become discouraged and instead of damaging her musical memory, as she is now doing, she would actually increase it.

This is the advice I gave her. But this advice was not followed; it couldn't be followed because the music professor didn't accept it. This professor was a lady who, in spite of her degrees in music and her title of " First Prize of the Conservatory, " had only a very vague idea of what pedagogy is all about. When Mathilda explained to her that she was lacking in musical memory, the professor interrupted her and spoke the following words :

> If you have no memory, you are not a musician; in this case nothing can be done. Renounce the study of music. You tell me you need to exercise your memory; go ahead and exercise it by learning the composition I have assigned to you for learning. All works present the same level of difficulty for memory; they are all composed of the same notes. Finally, you tell me that you would like to practice with easier pieces; this does not suit me. Do as I say or look for another Professor.

I shall not criticize this declaration of principles point by point. I shall only draw attention to the error we make when we assert that all musical works present the same level of difficulty for the memory because they are all composed of the same notes. If this were true it would be as easy to get a child to learn a sentence by Pascal* as to get this same child to learn a sentence by Berquin** because the two sentences are composed of the same letters. The only sound statement in the lady's speech is the last one, advising Mathilda to change professors.

I related this story to show how important it is to cultivate memory by a rational training method. With a defective method we not only make no progress but we also compromise whatever memory we have; instead of getting closer to our goal we move away from it.

I shall support my statement with another example. This one relates to me and I hope I shall be forgiven for placing myself in the center of the stage. I shall not talk about music but about bicycle riding. Kinesthetic memory, however, is subject to the same laws that auditory memory is; it is still a memory and is cultivated in the same way.

I was at an age when it is already difficult to learn bicycle riding. I am told that at twelve we don't need any lesson, but at forty it is a harder task. I wanted to practice alone in my garden, which is small and planted with big trees. The path I had to use was tortuous and had sharp turns. I couldn't say how many times I fell under the trees. After

---

* Blaise Pascal (1623-1662), French mathematician, physicist, philosopher and writer.

** Arnaud Berquin (1747-1791), French writer whose elegiac plays are considered insipid and are referred to as "berquinades."

two months of practice I had made no progress and had not succeeded in going around the garden a single time. During vacations we went to live in a part of the country which is flat and has long straight roads twelve to fourteen yards across and without embankments or ditches. These roads were for me the equivalent of the very easy compositions which would have been suitable for our music student. My bicycle riding progressed in a way which astonished me. I learned to make turns at large intersections and in October, when I found myself in my garden again, I was able to follow its winding path with the greatest ease. I am absolutely convinced that if I had continued to practice all summer in my garden I would not, in October, have been able to go around it a single time without falling. Only practice on large roads had provided effective muscular training. And so, after having lost an enormous amount of time, I had finally remembered the elementary rule : Whatever we are learning, we must proceed from the easy to the difficult. The rule is so simple that mere common sense would have led to it.

FOOTNOTES FOR CHAPTER SIX

1. A. Binet, " Addition to Mr. Parisot's Report, " *Bulletin de la Société de l'Enfant,* Alcan, N° 17 (1904).

2. A. Binet and V. Henri, " The Development of Visual Memory in Children, " *Revue Générale des Sciences,* March 15, 1894.

3. E.A. Kirkpatrick, *Psychological Review,* I, N° 6, (1894), 602.

4. *Ueber das Gedächtniss* (Leipzig : 1885). See also the two important memories of G.L. Müller and F. Schumann, *Zeitschrift für Psychologie und Physiologie der Sinnesorgane,* Vol. VI (1893).

5. I talked about it in my books, *La psychologie du raisonnement, Les grands calculateurs,* and *L'étude expérimentale de l'intelligence.* The number of articles published about this subject is unbelievable. For a main source of references, I refer the reader to Titchener's *Psychology Manual* in the chapter on ideation.

6. E.A. Kirkpatrick, *Psychological Review,* I, N° 6, (1894), 602.

7. I shall only list : H. Höffding, *Esquisse d'une psychologie fondée sur l'expérience* (Paris : Alcan, 1900), p. 194 ; and the Lemaitre, Netschaeff, Kulhmann articles which sum up experimental research. The last one especially (which appeared in *The American Journal of Psychology,* October, 1907, p. 389, and April, 1909, p. 194) has shown, as we have indicated in the text, that visual images and motor articulatory images are of primordial importance.

8. Armstrong, *Psychological Review,* I, N° 5, p. 496.

9. In *L'étude expérimentale de l'intelligence,* I published two observations of ideation types in which this contrast is well shown.

10. A. Pohlmann, *Experimentelle Beiträge zur Lehre vom Gedächtniss* (Berlin : 1906).

11. See notably : V. Henri, " Education de la mémoire, " *Année Psychologique,* VIII (1902), 1 ; Biervliet, *Esquisse d'une éducation de la mémoire* (Gand : 1903) ; Claparède, *Psychologie de l'enfant et pédagogie expérimentale* (Geneva : 1905), p. 47 ; plus an enormous number of articles published especially in Germany and in the United States.

12. For a comprehensive report of methods used to measure school fatigue, see Binet and Henri, *La fatigue intellectuelle* (Paris : Schleicher, 1898); see also Binet, " La mesure de la fatigue intellectuelle," *Année Psychologique,* (1903), p. 1.

13. Ebbinghaus and Jost's experiments. See Claparède, *L'Association des idées* (Paris : 1903), p. 95.

14. Burnham, " Retroactive Amnesia," *American Journal of Psychology,* July-October, 1903, p. 118. Many other authors have also dwelled on this consolidation period ; namely, Lewy, Müller and Pilzecker; see also Ebbinghaus, *Grundzüge der Psychologie,* Vol. I (1902), 651.

15. V. Henri, " L'éducation de la mémoire," *Année Psychologique,* VIII (1902), 40.

16. Smith, *American Journal of Psychology,* July, 1896, p. 216.

17. About the comparative effects of interest, recitation, and other secondary causes, see the work of Miss Calkins, " Association," *Psychological Review,* I, N° 5, p. 476; analysed in *Année Psychologique,* I, p. 392.

18. Katzaroff, " Le rôle de la récitation comme facteur de la mémorisation," *Arch. de Psychologie,* N° 7, 1908.

19. Miss Stefens' experiments, de Larguier des Bancels, de Lobsien. See Lottie Stefens, " Experimentelle Beiträge zur Lehre von Okonomischen Lernen," *Zeitschrift für Psychologie und Physiologie der Sinnesorgane,* Vol. XXII (1900), 321.

20. *Baudrillart and Roussel, "Experiments," Bulletin de la Société Libre pour l'Etude Psychologique de l'Enfant,* N° 6, 1902. See also " Münsterberg et Bigham Experiments," *Psychological Review,* January, 1894.

21. See A. Binet, *La psychologie des grands calculateurs* (Paris : Hachette, 1894), p. 155.

22. See p. 106 for a few examples of this law.

23. J.E. Coover and F. Angell, " General Practice Effect of Special Exercise," *American Journal of Psychology,* XVIII, p. 329. For a complete exposé of the question presented with slightly exaggerated skepticism, see Thorndike, *Educational Psychology,* p. 80.

CHAPTER SEVEN

Aptitudes

I. The Correlation of Intellectual Faculties

To study children's special aptitudes is to approach one of those questions which interests us all because of the great practical significance it has, not only for school teaching but also for each child's future, since his career should not be decided upon before his aptitudes are known. It is a fact that if we took this precaution we would decrease the number of declassed and discontented individuals; by putting everyone in his appropriate place we would increase people's economic output and this would probably be one of the simplest, the most natural, the best means of at least partially solving some of the irritating social problems which are on so many minds and which threaten the future of our present society.

But what do we know about children's special aptitudes? In practice there would be two ways, if not to solve the problem, at least to get some idea of its magnitude. One would be to question the children, get them to talk about which of their studies they like best and which they like least, and having recorded their comments, see if the responses they made are in agreement with their real aptitudes. Another way would be to give them a choice between several kinds of assignments, noting which kind they consistently prefer. But has this type of study ever been undertaken? Have these aptitudes been clearly defined? Has anyone ever looked for a way of utilizing them? Has a rapprochement ever been made between children's mental aptitudes and the trades and professions these aptitudes qualify them for? No, unfortunately. All we know is that there is a problem. We have given it a little thought; we have even formed special study groups to deal with it, but nothing, or almost nothing, has been done up to now.

I open the most recent pedagogical treatise. It is dated December, 1908. Here is what it says: "Mental faculties do not develop at the same rate and to the same degree in all children of the same age. This raises the important question of individual differences which only long and painstaking observation will reveal to the teacher. Each class is made up of different intellectual types which vary according to the predominance in the children of some faculties over others. " The problem has been stated but that is all. The authors add no other word, give no example of these special aptitudes. They truly know nothing more.

Some others at least understand that a serious problem is involved, and they deal with it in the best way they can, without overlooking the fact that there is much about it they don't know. One of these authors recently wrote a series of articles in a pedagogical journal on the enticing subject of "customized" schools. A discerning man, he presented his views brilliantly. He began by recalling that there used to be a time when all children without distinction were placed in the same class. It was first observed that some children didn't profit from the program because they couldn't see, and some others because they couldn't hear; a first separation was made and special schools were created for the blind and for the deaf mute. Then it was noticed that some children couldn't follow the lessons because they were lacking in attention or because they were intellectually deficient; recently these children were also separated from the rest of the students, and special classes called classes for the abnormal are now being created for them. The author goes on to say that the same selection process should be used to remove the physically handicapped from the regular classroom and that for these, open-air schools should be created. This is not all. Carried away by his own momentum, the author declares that the normal students should also be divided into several categories on the basis of their aptitudes, which will have been identified by teachers or by specialists, and that pupils in each of these categories should be given a different training, different especially from the professional point of view. The author stops here. All his good will does not enable him to go beyond this rather vague conclusion. Notwithstanding his final reservation, I believe that he has made a serious error : to have thought it possible to divide the normal into groups which are as clear-cut as the deaf, the blind and the abnormal. He forgets that a normal individual is not someone out of the ordinary but, on the contrary, is someone whose characteristics are average. If different kinds of aptitudes are found to exist in humanity, we can rest assured that the normal subject possesses them all to some degree, and this is precisely what accounts for the fact that he is an "indifferent" [neutral], well-balanced type without distinctive characteristics. With this understood, we need not even go into the many great disadvantages there would be to giving specialized training to children too early, to giving them a training adapted to aptitudes they may not have or which may change as the child grows older, a training which also may become obsolete in the kind of unstable environment our modern societies provide. We cannot see what individual freedom would gain from the reconstitution of the old system of guild-masterships, which imprisoned workers in closed trades.

As can be seen from the few details we have given, the question we are about to take up is entirely new. Not part of the domain of pedagogy at the present time, it involves mainly laboratory work, very special research conducted by such psychologists as Stern in Germany, to cite only one of the most authoritative names. We shall draw our inspiration from this research and also from our own studies, which are already very old but which we shall present from a newer, definitely more modern point of view. Instead of treating them as psychological curiosities we shall look for possible practical applications and, after each new observation, we shall repeat the following question to ourselves like a refrain: "What can this observation be used for?"

What we are going to talk about in what follows is therefore special, partial aptitudes. What exactly do we mean when we say that certain aptitudes are special? We mean that they don't correlate with other aptitudes. Suppose we are talking about subject matter A. When we say that this subject requires special abilities we mean that students who excel in A can be mediocre in other subjects and that, inversely, students who are mediocre in A can excel in the other subjects. Consequently, if we want to get an idea about the independence of certain aptitudes, we have to study the correlations which may exist between success and failure in some areas and success and failure in other areas. This correlational analysis is very complicated, for it requires that a large number of subjects be studied if chance effects are going to be minimized. The methods used for this purpose are numerous and a few involve higher mathematics. We do not intend to go into these details but it seems only fair to give at least an idea of the simplest method which can be used. There is the "rank method" which V. Henri and I developed.[1] There is also the Pearson "correlation coefficient," and Spearmann's "rank order coefficient,"[2] and finally, the last and simplest method of all, the "method of averages" which was recently used by Ivanoff.[3] The latter method requires a lot of data but, in compensation, calculations are short. To explain how it works, let us suppose the goal is to find out if there is a correlation between an aptitude for drawing and an aptitude for handwriting. In the mixed group of children studied, 20 % had good handwriting ability; in the group with good drawing ability, the proportion of good penmanship increased to 28 %. The difference, 28 % — 20 %, equals 8 %. This difference divided by the average per cent for handwriting ability gives us 8/20 = 40 %. We have obtained a coefficient which, properly corrected, gives us the correlation we are looking for; if the correlation drawing/handwriting is 40 % and the correlation drawing/arithmetic is 13 %, it is clear that this second correlation will be much weaker than the first.

If ever a question was the object of controversy it certainly is the question of the value of correlations. Two absolutely contradictory views are prevalent today and both claim to be upheld by proof. According to one view, which has been vigorously supported by Thorndike,[4] the mind is nothing but an absolutely heteroclite collection of faculties which are as if juxtaposed but which remain rigorously independent from one another. The opposite view, supported by Spearmann[5] with impressive mathematical data, states that intelligence is one, that in each of us there exists a faculty deserving the name of general intelligence and that this faculty accounts for the relationship which is revealed by the measurement of our performance in all our activities, even the most disparate ones. There would be such a relationship, for instance, between the ability to perceive sensations and the ability to manage our life. This opinion is exactly the opposite of Thorndike's opinion. On the whole, these two views are extreme, and there are more moderate ones which such controversies do not invalidate. If we examine the case of school children, in particular, and the aptitudes they exhibit for the different subjects which are taught to them, we can make various observations about the matter which remain sound and true, whatever extreme view we choose to adopt. In the first place, it has been established that we never find an extremely small correlation — that is, an almost absolute independence — between one school subject and the remainder of the school subjects taken as a whole. The correlation system we manage to develop is much more complicated. Take drawing, for instance, since it has recently been carefully studied by Ivanoff. The aptitude for drawing is considered — and with reason, in our opinion — one of the most independent aptitudes which exists, but drawing is not equally independent in relation to every school subject; for example, while the correlation with languages and with mathematics is low, the correlation with manual skills, composition and geography is fairly high. Also there is no such thing as a negative correlation in this case; it does not follow that if a child is strong in one area he will be weak in another. The case in which a student excels in one subject only because he neglects several others is an accidental case; it is not a case which has to exist; it is not a result inherent in the nature of things. The important fact to remember, then, is that aptitudes are not mutually exclusive. This is proven by the existence of complete minds which combine them all. And finally, the most important statement of all, there is one factor which operates in a direction opposite to that of aptitudes; it is willingness to work. While aptitudes insure partial successes, willingness to work exerts a leveling action and insures success in all tasks attempted. The result is that aptitudes are less apparent in a group of studious subjects. Special ability is replaced by effort, and the results of calculations made by theoreticians in search of correlations are obscured.

II. Remarks on a Few School Aptitudes

There are several ways of studying children's aptitudes. One method consists of taking the various school subjects, one after the other, and finding out which of them have the highest correlation between them and which have the lowest. Another kind of study is more ambitious; it goes beyond school tasks and seeks to establish what the typical mental characteristics are which give rise to the various aptitudes.

We shall say a few words about these two different types of studies.

The first special aptitude is the aptitude for music. We know that music is an art which stirs up intense emotion in many people; other individuals are completely unaffected by it. Some — and this is the majority, about 90 per cent — have a good voice and a good ear for music; the others sing out of tune and are tune deaf, and this difference creates a veritable rift between the two groups. We need not add that musical aptitude is often found to be lacking in subjects who are otherwise very intelligent. There would be a lot to say about musical ability, its measurement, the particular pedagogical conditions in which the study of music should be encouraged or discouraged, but we hope we shall be excused for abstaining, for the subject appears a little special to us and space is lacking.

Drawing is also one of the special aptitudes; it is almost an innate gift. Anyone who applies himself can manage to copy a model successfully, but a large number of people find it impossible to draw from memory or from imagination. As in the case of music, this is a lacuna which may be found in very intelligent people. I remember the case of a scholar who one day felt himself incapable of drawing a picture of a sitting dog, since he couldn't visualize what the dog did with his paws. There are even painters who draw poorly and who are mainly colorists; it is interesting, for instance, to compare Rembrandt with Holbein from this point of view. It is difficult to establish which faculty is involved in drawing ability, for once the drawing act has become habitual many of its conscious elements disappear. What is true of drawing is true of speech. It is a fact that an individual who speaks fluently and easily does not know what he does in order to speak; he does not have a clear idea of the sentence he is going to use before pronouncing it; he only very vaguely knows the words he is going to employ; what he does have is an abstract feeling about what he wants to say and his speech adapts itself to this plan. In the same way, the experienced artist sees the drawing come out of his pencil, as it were. He knows what he wants to do but he finds it very difficult to explain how he represents his drawing to himself before executing it. What is very sure is that before we can draw a form we must first have an idea of it in our mind. Is this idea a visual representation and shall we say that an artist must have an exceptional ability for evoking the visual image of things? May be, and at any rate we prefer this explanation to the one which would have us view drawing as an entirely motor act, for motor memory cannot engender an ensemble of spatial relations. But it is not the natural power of visualization which is most important; it is the practice, the knowledge, the taste acquired by visualizing. Owing to our knowledge and experience, our mind contains plans and sketches. We know how to visualize the anatomy of a person in a particular position and this facilitates enormously both the execution of a drawing we want to make from memory or from imagination and our criticism of other people's art work. It is clear that a mediocre visualization associated with a great deal of knowledge is more useful for drawing than the intense visualization of someone who knows nothing and who has never studied or analysed an object from the point of view of reproducing its form.

There would be much to say also about the teaching of drawing. The principle involved is inscribed at the end of our chapter on intelligence (see p. 115). We have expressed our preference for the active method taken in its complete sense. Children who begin to draw are often made to reproduce geometric designs for the incorrectly interpreted reason that they are simpler than the human figure or familiar objects. Experience has shown this to be a bad teaching practice which discourages children. They were drawing before they began going to school and now school gives them a distaste for the task. They must be allowed to follow their natural inclination to draw freely. We can intervene later to guide and correct these free drawings. This method makes use of the natural force within them instead of destroying it, an approach American schools have been using for a long time.

In connection with this, I always remember the error I made a long time ago with my young children. At five or six years of age they were drawing instinctively. They drew a great deal and found enormous pleasure in this activity. They often looked at objects, but it was to find information which they then transferred to their own work; the thought of drawing from nature almost never occurred to them. I felt this method was deplorable; my respect for observation was shocked. It seemed to me that only direct, faithful, respectful imitation of nature could foster progress in art. Fortunately I didn't intervene, and my children continued to draw according to the dictates of their instinct. Then slowly, and of their own accord, they came back to the study of nature.

The existence of a school aptitude referred to as "natural spelling" has been reported by teachers for a long time. There are children who know spelling not instinctively, without having learned it — this would be overlooking all there is which is artificial about spelling — but with infinitely less effort than other school children who never achieve as high a level of proficiency. It is in the spelling of individual words especially that these students are superior. But how can this predisposition to good spelling be explained? We don't know. We can only make conjectures about this. Here is ours.

We learn spelling through both audition and vision but mainly through vision. The first piece of evidence in support of this view is provided to us by Belot's[6] experiments in which he compared the performance of two groups of students. The first group had learned spelling through visual presentation; the second group had learned auditorily, by listening to the teacher. He found that subjects in the first group performed better, making 65 per cent errors, while subjects in the second group made 72 per cent errors under comparable conditions. The second piece of evidence is provided by the blind; although much more intelligent* than deaf mutes, the blind do not spell as well. Why? It is because they don't learn spelling through vision.

We tend to conclude, therefore, that, all other things being equal, children who know spelling best have a better than average visual memory. But to have visual memory is not enough; it is also necessary to use it, to like reading and read a lot and, in so doing, store away the spelling of a large number of words. In this way we even learn the correct use of grammar, for repeated reading teaches us all that. It teaches us spelling as well as the application of grammatical rules, and even if we are unable to formulate these rules or think them through, we can still apply them. This is how we explain that a child is strong in spelling and weak in drawing or vice versa; in both cases he may have visual memory, but having used it differently, he receives different services from it.

The aptitude for mental calculations and for mathematics is also a special aptitude. The skill for mental calculations can be developed through practice in very young children. Calculator prodigies have started very young; indeed, some were only three. This is a faculty which essentially involves memory, for in order to solve a problem it is necessary first to retain its terms; then, when a partial operation has been completed, we have to remember this solution, not confound it with the terms of the problem, do the same thing for another partial operation, and retain everything without confounding anything until we have the final solution.

Suppose I want to multiply 122 by 122 mentally. I have purposely chosen a very simple operation; it is so simple, in fact, that it does not even require a knowledge of the multiplication table, for everyone can

_____

* See what Binet means by intelligence, pp. 102-103.

multiply by 2. The difficulty presented by the operation is therefore not inherent in the calculations but solely in the effort of memory required. I shall begin, for example, by multiplying 122 by 100, which gives 12,200. I have to make a great effort to remember this first partial product. Then I multiply 122 by 22. This is not easy for me, so I decide to multiply 122 by 10, then double the product; 122 multiplied by 10 gives 1,220; doubled, this gives 2,440. Finally, I multiply 122 by 2 which gives 244. Now the great difficulty is not to forget 2,440 while I calculate 244; also not to forget 12,200 while I calculate 2,440. I am forever obliged to retrace my steps, so to speak, to repeat to myself the partial products already obtained so as to keep them alive in my memory; even so, I occasionally forget them and have to start the whole operation all over again.

It is clear from this analysis that mental calculations require a very strong memory which can keep all the figures we need at our disposal.

Another very interesting remark is yet to be made about the quality of the memory which is necessary for mental calculations.

This memory was formerly believed to be essentially a visual memory. It was supposed that the good mental calculator made calculations in his mind the way he did on paper and that he mentally saw the paper. But it has since become known that if visual type calculators do exist, there are also some who are of the auditory type, or rather of the motor type; the latter don't see the figures but hear them or tell them to themselves, and while telling the figures to themselves, they calculate as well as if they saw them. The procedure, however, is a little different, for ordinarily while the visual type individual makes the operation as if on paper, the motor type individual decomposes it. To explain what we mean, let us suppose that the task is to multiply 125 by 142. The visual type calculator will begin his operation on the right side; he will multiply 125 by 2, then by 4, then by 1, and he will add all the partial products. The motor type calculator, on the contrary, will begin by multiplying 125 by 100 and then by 42. We have had opportunity to study these two very interesting types of calculators — the visual and the motor type — in our Sorbonne laboratory when we studied two now-famous prodigies, Diamanti and Inaudi.

It might be useful to add that most of the time we utilize both visual and motor images. The verbal repetition helps make the visual image more vivid; the latter renders a service by indicating the position of certain figures, for only the visual image includes vision in space. On the other hand, there are operations which we make in a purely motor and auditory manner, such as multiplications which are only associations of words. Finally, since intelligence never loses its rights, we make a host of observations, while we work, on the nature of figures, their relationships, their contrasts, and these observations help retain them.

In the sequence 3, 5, 7, for instance, we are impressed with the equality of the intervals; in the sequence 3, 5, 8, we are impressed with the fact that 8 is the sum of 3 and 5; and so on. These are small ways which help memory, and they depend less on its strength than on the ingenuity of the mind.

Mathematical intelligence involves a very special faculty which it would be extremely important to analyse, for it probably is the most pronounced distinction which is found in school children. All high school teachers we could consult about this matter would be of this opinion. We can even add that this mathematical sense is so important that the future of many students depends on it. Scientific and industrial careers, which are the most lucrative nowadays, attract the largest number of students. Many of them, however, are forced to give up the science courses because they cannot follow them after a time; some individuals even judge it useless to try, knowing their incompetence in mathematics. All these individuals are the waste, the sterile product of the mathematics class. Rejected by the sciences, they turn to the humanities; consequently, the result of this state of affairs today is that the audience of the philosophy class is recruited from among the students least well endowed for the sciences. This lack of aptitude for mathematics and for the sciences in general is also observed in many adults, even among well-educated individuals of superior intelligence, who acknowledge this incapacity in themselves without self-consciousness and who sometimes even take pride in it. Moreover, this incapacity, viewed in a certain way, is common to everyone, for as mathematics becomes more complex, the number of people who understand it decreases at a vertiginous rate. Someone recently remarked, while commenting on Poincaré's mathematical power, that there probably are not more than ten people in the whole world who can follow him.

What mysterious mental quality is the mathematical faculty based on then? We don't know; and although Poincaré[7] recently undertook to explain it to us, we are not quite sure, for our part, whether we have understood his explanation. The psychology of the act of understanding remains very abstruse; it all seems to be taking place in the unconscious. When we grasp the meaning of a verbal statement, each word has to play a role in the total meaning, since the total meaning depends on each of these words; but it is through reasoning that we assume this perception of the meaning of each word and the rapprochement of all the individual meanings so as to form a synthesis, for we understand the sentence as a whole; in brief, we only apprehend the synthetical result. This is why we have difficulty in understanding how we understand. This is very unfortunate, for if it were possible to know exactly what mathematical intelligence consists of, we could make a serious effort to develop it.

175

We shall not say any more about the different school subjects. Rising to a higher level, we shall now try to define a few special types of intelligence.

III. Remarks on a Few Types of Intelligence

Research conducted on all sides, either in schools or in families or among famous people, has led us to identify, in the light of our present knowledge, three special intellectual types and three corresponding opposite types. Let us give them labels which unfortunately are not very accurate but which will permit discriminating between them. We shall describe:

1. The conscious versus the unconscious;
2. The objective versus the subjective;
3. The practician versus the literary (verbal type).

It must first be understood that these types are extreme and therefore exceptional; that these different types are not in opposition to each other but rather independent from one another, for it is not rare to meet "complete" individuals who combine the conscious with the unconscious, the objective with the subjective, the practician with the literary.

The Conscious and the Unconscious

We shall make a few remarks about the methods of intellectual work, an important matter which classical pedagogy has ignored. Pedagogy has a traditional view of intellectual work which is certainly not false but which also is not true for every individual. Intellectual work is presented as a manifestation of intellectual activity which is, at one and the same time, conscious, voluntary, reasoned and personal. This is an error. There are other working methods which are every bit as effective. To the reflection method we must add, in apposition, the inspiration method.[8] Depending on the individual, one method or the other will be the most effective. We must know ourselves, try both methods, compare them, see which is more successful, and identify the particular conditions under which one must be preferred to the other, for it is mainly a question of opportunity.

The reflection method takes a precise idea as a starting point, an idea which we can formulate, an idea which we have found through reflection and the genesis, the antecedents, the continuity of which we could explain; the idea is therefore completely conscious. We undertake to work on this idea because we choose to. We begin when we

176

want to, we stop, resume and terminate the task in a manner which we judge appropriate; the work therefore stands in readiness. While it is being done we exercise our attention, our memory, our critical judgment. We examine an idea and we accept or reject it. Every time we make a decision we know why we have chosen one alternative in preference to the other; our work is therefore completely the product of reasoning. What is often difficult and even painful is the necessity of thinking only about our subject, of persevering, of concentrating our attention upon it without ever allowing ourselves to digress from it. The effort which is necessary in order for us to develop the idea we have conceived makes us conscious of our role as a creator; we have the very definite feeling that we are the author of the work and that we assume all responsibility for it, not responsibility in the legal or moral sense here, but strictly in the intellectual sense. Finally, handled in this scholarly fashion, the idea goes through a complete phase of mental evolution. At the beginning it is only an abstract seed, a vague notion, a schema; it develops slowly, it grows, it becomes amplified, it especially becomes more detailed, that is to say it becomes enriched with concrete, precise, sensory, living elements. We have an exact knowledge of this evolution as it is taking place, since it is we who, through our intervention, are causing it to occur; since often it even evolves in accordance to a script we ourselves have chosen.

If intellectual work was always of the nature we have just described, the moral of the story would be very simple. All we would need to do when we have to work would be to will; the more we would work, the better it would be. In a word, we would only need to remind students of Newton's famous recommendations which, ever since childhood, we have learned to admire: "Genius is endless patience," and we find the solution to problems by "thinking about them continually." This conception, not lacking in grandeur, exalts free will and personality, and it is characteristic of a time when a simplistic psychology viewed man as a mere collection of passive faculties at the service of a will which is always free.

But the observations which have been made, on all sides and under the most varied circumstances, on poets, philosophers, scientists and even on such very exceptional beings as spiritualists, mediums, hysterics and other patients, have shown that the intellectual work of a reasoned and reflective nature just described does not constitute a general rule. From time to time we work in a completely different way. It is a question of circumstances, of subject matter, of temperament. Especially when our imagination is involved we have a very particular way to work. The illustrious mathematician H. Poincaré[9] has recently written a remarkable report on the subject and described how the greatest part of his inventions came about. It is a very arresting, almost dramatic story.

Here is, approximately, the most common sequence of operations. He begins with a period of voluntary work. Having sat down at his desk, he examines the problem, he reasons, he calculates, he strains his attention, in brief he works consciously. He often becomes aware of the difficulty which hampers him, but it nonetheless continues to stop him, and tired or discouraged, he gives up.

Second stage. A few days, a few months have gone by. He is not in front of his desk nor even thinking about his work. He is out in the country, walking on a boulevard or boarding a bus; these commonplace events are unimportant except for the fact that they show he is not prepared to make an effort. Suddenly he has an inspiration; an idea occurs to him. It is better than an idea, it is a truth. He realizes that a particular mathematical function has particular properties or that it needs to be examined in relation to another. A solution sought in the past presents itself at a time when one is not thinking about it, and when it appears, it is accompanied by a firm belief that it is right. One doesn't feel the need to make ulterior verifications; one will undoubtedly make them eventually but for the time being it is certainty that is felt.

Third stage. A period of conscious work takes place in front of the desk. The new idea is re-examined, its contents analysed, the necessary calculations made, and the report giving the exposé of the question is written.

Poincaré emphasized the nature and the birth of this idea, and the antecedents which prepared for it. It follows a period of conscious work and probably never would have occurred if we had not first made voluntary efforts to think about the problem. The contents of the idea are both precise and vague. It is precise because it indicates the path to follow, the calculations to be made and the goal to be reached; it is truly a "pregnant idea," as Beaunis called it. But it remains vague in the sense that it does not of itself give results, and Poincaré is very right when he makes the judicious and important remark that looking at the two factors of a multiplication for a time has never given anyone, through the work of his unconscious, the product of that multiplication.

This method is therefore unconscious, and it would indeed be easy to contrast it with the reflection method: the work does not depend on us, the idea is not the outcome of a conscious effort or of a painful search; we know nothing about the idea; when it comes it surprises by its suddenness and the absence of psychological causality; it appears to be the work of an activity which is foreign to us, which develops outside of us; for our part we are passive; we let things happen and this lack of effort is all the more pleasant in that we are convinced this idea, which costs us nothing, is going to be fruitful.

But Poincaré's description is only applicable to the birth of the idea. It refers to a case in which the unconscious plays a limited role which is soon ended. In order to complete this description, I want to make a rapprochement with another case which is different only in appearance.

I am talking about the case of the dramatic actor François de Curel and the manner in which he composes his plays. He has himself described the various stages of his creative work[10] with the admirable insight of a psychologist. Like Poincaré, he begins with a voluntary work session. He has an idea about a play in mind. He writes his script and makes his characters speak by putting himself in their place, in their skin, as we are taught to do in rhetoric class, and by having them say what he himself would feel under similar circumstances. This is the reflection method; it is very painful for him and the deeper he gets into his work, the more he thinks that it is bad. After a certain time he feels he would do well to rewrite the play completely. Then, on his second manuscript, his unconscious work begins and it has some resemblance to Poincaré's mathematical creation, only Curel does not suddenly get a new leading idea, a pregnant idea which would contain his whole play. But it is during the writing that the unconscious quality of the creation becomes manifest. The author ceases to feel that he is the creator of the work, of his characters and especially of the dialogue; he no longer creates but he attends the performance of the play. It seems to him that the characters on the stage speak spontaneously about themselves and for themselves; he needs make no effort to find what they should say. He learns about their ideas and the words they use by listening to them, as it were. He is almost passive, in a position similar to that of a stenographer who takes notes during a meeting. The division of consciousness is therefore carried very far but not so far, of course, that it results in incoherence. The author remains very attentive; he is capable of intervening effectively, first to see to it that his characters stick to the script, then to guide them, prompt them, or even take their place from time to time and insert in the dialogue some words which are his own, which are truly words from the author. The feeling of this division of consciousness is so strong in Curel that he can easily, when re-reading one of his plays, distinguish between the rejoinders which are his and those which are from his characters.

It seems to me that this observation has the advantage of making the Poincaré observation more precise and, from some important points of view, of completing it, for Curel shows a different aspect of unconscious work. In the mathematician the unconscious only comes as a sudden apparition in conscious life; it brings an idea, like a devil which emerges through a trap door and then disappears. In Curel, a slower, more systematic development of the unconscious takes place; it remains in full evidence, functions side by side with the conscious and becomes for the conscious a true collaborator, like a second author who would have author rights. But it is evident that, in spite of the differences, the fundamental psychological characteristics are found in both cases. In one form or the other this truly represents an invasion of the conscious mind by something which is foreign to it. In the past this has been called an inspiration state, and poets have created a charming myth about the externalisation of the unconscious: a young and beautiful woman, a muse, was said to have paid a visit to the inspired individual; this muse is nothing but the personification of the unconscious.

Two observations which, on the whole, are a little exceptional are not sufficient to make a general theory about the method of inspiration. I believe we all, or almost all, have inspirations, but they are less dramatic than Poincaré's and less overwhelming than Curel's. We have a definite feeling that certain ideas form in our mind independently of our conscious activities, that these ideas organize themselves without our help and that we do not interfere. Often, Sourian reports, it is while we are in a dream-like state that these ideas form; the flagging of our attention which takes place under such conditions is favorable to the activities of the unconscious. Sometimes the only distinctive mark of inspiration is the involuntary nature of ideation. We feel the quality of the work produced by inspiration is neither inferior nor superior to the quality of the work produced by reflection, and we imagine it would be impossible to tell which method was used just by examining the finished product. If ever an author has used systematization to an extreme degree, it is Spencer; we would never have believed that he had consistently used the inspiration method in his work if he himself had not confessed he did.

We have wandered very far from the questions of education, or so it would seem. School is not the kind of environment where the very subtle phenomenon of division of consciousness can be found and studied; or rather, we are not familiar enough with this phenomenon to be able to recognize it in young children. We would not therefore have discussed the subject in this book on education if pedagogues had not drawn from the facts we have mentioned some conclusions which are interesting from the point of view of the hygiene of intellectual work. It is imperative that we say a few words about these conclusions, which are very sound and very useful provided their importance isn't exaggerated.

Some rebellious individuals have chosen to take an opposite view to the one expressed by Newton, that we find the solution to problems "by thinking about them continually." No, his critics answer today, we must not think about them continually; that method expects too much from voluntary and reflective work and leaves too little freedom to the unconscious. On the contrary, we must set up conditions in such a way that the unconscious will collaborate with our effort. What is recommended, therefore, is to continue the voluntary study of a difficult question until we have seen, understood, evaluated all the difficulties; when this has been done we shall stop work abruptly, in the midst of our activities; we shall rest, think about something else, and wait. We pass the deal and now the unconscious has a turn; it becomes responsible for finding the solution to the problem.

This advice is excellent, but it has a small defect; it assumes that all men are built on the same model and harbor within themselves an unconscious of great intelligence. This assumption is the error. A large family of individuals owe almost nothing to their unconscious, which is stupid and narrow; the work they produce is the result of their personal and completely conscious efforts only; and when they resume work after having let it stand awhile, they find it exactly as they have left it; nothing progresses during the night or during recreation. While we might say the "inspired" ones have more talent than intelligence, the "reflective" have more intelligence than talent. It seems to me that the dramatic author Paul Hervieu belongs to this voluntary and reflective type; he is even an admirable example of it. The pedagogy which is based on the virtuosity of the unconscious is therefore not suitable to all, only to some.

However, there is something for everyone in the advice of the theoreticians of the unconscious; some of it will be effective for reasons which are slightly different from the ones we have thought about. It is well not to prolong voluntary work beyond a certain limit and to know when to stop, thus avoiding the mental fatigue which renders our efforts sterile. When a difficulty appears insoluble, it is bad practice to persist; if we do, our attention and our intelligence lose their keenness and we accumulate a fatigue which will only delay the time of the solution. A good rest at the right time is a must. Later, when we get back to work, our ideas are clearer, our mind more alert, and sometimes we find very quickly what we had vainly looked for earlier. Is it because the unconscious has intervened? Or rather is it not, more often, because we come back to work with a mental freshness which increases our effectiveness? In some cases the first explanation is right; in some others, it is the second, but this does not matter. The main thing is that we have used a method which has worked for us.

In the preceding observations each of us can find useful indications about the best means of proceeding with our intellectual work. And when we assign work to children, especially when we assign compositions and tasks which require imagination, it is well to remember that some of them do not find ideas at will. Following his experiments on assigning compositions with or without delay, Mr. Belot gave very useful advice: Inform students of the subject of the composition ahead of time. In this way the children's ideas have time to form.

The Objective and the Subjective :
A Few Intellectual Portraits

We have shown in the preceding section that there are several very different work methods. But this dissimilarity in working methods is not the only manifestation of the differences in minds; also evident are differences in the contents of various minds. We see this if we assign children the kind of tasks which demand giving a little of themselves instead of simply reproducing, like faithful echoes, the substance of what they have been taught. Composition is certainly one of the best means there is for getting to know a mind, provided, of course, we know how to present the task and how to interpret it.

I propose that teachers who enjoy this kind of study assign themes of composition which have to do with real events; for instance, have pupils write about *a walk in the country, a dinner, a trip, a family celebration.* Or have them write about an object which is present, a material object, like *a flower, a pen, a coin;* or about a scene, such as *an interesting picture* without a title. We shall also assign compositions designed to surprise ongoing work of invention; we shall have the children imagine a story about a given theme, for instance, *the death of a dog.* Finally, we can end this series of tests by having our subjects develop a moral thought or a rule of conduct, such as this abstract truth, *Why we should not become angry;* or a moral problem presented in the form of an anecdote : *A child has committed such or such other reprehensible act. What would you do if you were his father?*

It we have the patience to dictate these themes of composition to about thirty children, and especially if we have the patience to analyse all the papers, we shall be surprised at the great variety which is manifest in them. First, there is variety in the handwriting, and also in the form; here the body of the composition has four lines, there it covers four pages. The vocabulary also is different; there, mostly substantives are used; here, there are more adjectives or more verbs; words used on one paper are commonplace and coarse; those in another are of a nobler race, have a more abstract meaning. After vocabulary we look at syntax; certain sentences are short, composed of simple clauses joined with conjunctions or such elementary expressions as *and, and next, and after, and then;* somewhere else, such words as *for, therefore, when* and *since* appear, which show that the relationship between ideas has become more complex. And in the same case, subordinate clauses are added to the main clause, still increasing the complexity. This kind of grammar and vocabulary differentiation is closely related to the child's mental evolution, and we could guess his age from the syntax he uses. But even among children of the same age, we find some of these differences, and they are due to various causes : the child's intelligence, the environment in which he lives, and also his mental type.

But let us continue our analysis and, having examined what constitutes the technique of the composition, let us look at its contents. What great variety again! What a large number of distinctions to be made! This is an admirable opportunity to become aware of the fact that each child already has his own individuality. Here is one who, describing a fair, does not know what to do with the enumeration of all the objects he has seen; he writes them down in any order without any description: "I have seen this..., that..., some horses, some cars, some clowns, some animals..., etc." Another child looks at it from a very different point of view: he tells about what he has done; he lists a series of personal actions in approximately their chronological order; he is always speaking about himself; he says, "I saw, I went, I ate, I drank, I rode the merry-go-round; later I did this..., etc." He is like the center of the world. Another child begins to describe external objects; he is impressed by their colors and their shapes; he pictures them, compares them to others, uses metaphors which are an indication of the interest with which he has looked at them. "Dogs were like this; parrots were of such a color." Comparisons and qualifications are abundant. Another, displaying erudition, includes ideas which have been presented in class in his description; he explains, he teaches. Still another attempts to interpret the event he has witnessed; he makes an effort to gain insight into the characters; he tells why someone went to a particular place, what he was looking for; or he establishes a relation, a logic, between the different facts he has observed. Another adopts a very special attitude, an attitude which is less objective than that of the preceding ones; he judges, he appraises, he gives his impressions; to him the fair is joyous or sad or noisy; he admires the horses and the cars; if the description is about a picture, he regrets the misfortune which befalls one of the figures in it; he shows himself to be imbued with emotion. It is charming, but it is well not to take too much stock in the sincerity of compositions; the children who show the most emotion in their writings are not always tenderhearted children. We can say that, even as early as grade school, "It is only literature."

I cannot at the present time treat of the vast topic of classification of mental types as a whole. The question is still too new and too little is known about it; but I shall bring the reader's attention for a moment to two different types of ideation which we find frequently if we take the trouble to look for them in a class of children. I shall discuss these two particular types because I feel I know them well, but it must be understood that they are not the only ones which exist and that they cannot serve as a basis for a general classification. These two types can be given various names, none of which are completely accurate; one can be called "objective," the other "subjective," but these expressions are a little imprecise. The first also merits the name of "observer," the second that of "interpreter." We can say of the first, too, that he is realistic, practical, unsentimental, matter of fact, and of the second that he is a dreamer and contemplative. All these differences boil down to a fundamental distinction which we must be very aware of.

By our very nature we find ourselves astride two worlds: the external world, composed of material objects and physical events, and the internal world, composed of thoughts and feelings. Depending on the moment and on our needs, we become involved more exclusively in either introspection or extrospection. At one time we need to know what is happening around us; at another time we need to withdraw within ourselves to think things over. Observe closely how an individual lives; you will see him pass, at different times, from the attitude of observer of the external world to that of dreamer. But we don't all have the same habits, the same tastes, nor especially the same constitutions. Some of us lean more heavily toward the external world, some others toward the internal world. This is what constitutes in the sciences, for instance, the two large families of observers and of theoreticians. These are two large enemy families which are never able to do each other justice. For the theoreticians, the individual who is involved exclusively in observation spends his time collecting facts which are exact but without interest, an assertion which is partly true. For the observer, the theoreticians waste their time inventing interesting but inexact interpretations, and this also is partly true. It is evident that these two ways of thinking are incomplete and fragmentary; we would need not only to get them to co-exist and be both observer and interpreter, but also to solder them together, so that each is an interpreter of what he has observed and an observer of the phenomenon he attempts to interpret. Let us take a material example. The ideal in a complete scholar is not to have both a screw and a nut, but a screw which is adapted to the nut.

It is not difficult to recognize incipient dispositions toward external observation or toward introspection in young children, but these analyses are not the kind which can easily be made in schools. We don't know individual students well enough, so that only very superficial observations can be made on them. One must have studied the psychology of intellectual types elsewhere to be in a position to make use of it with school children. Chance so ordained that several years ago, in my own family, I found two young girls who presented, in an interesting contrast, the observer and the interpreter types. These two children were almost of the same age; one was eleven, the other twelve and a half years old. They both received all their education at home, and therefore the outside influences they were subjected to were as similar as one might wish them to be; consequently, the mental differences between them were definitely due to their own natures. I might add that I was able to study them every day over several years and that I conducted a large number of experiments on them which were controlled by direct observations on the part of their parents and myself. Also it was during this study I first became convinced that the test method is a remarkable one for the analysis of the mind; it is true that I used it thoroughly and that I was never satisfied with a doubtful answer or an equivocal result.

It is first in the description of objects that Marguerite, the elder of the two children, displays her ability for observation. One asks the two sisters to describe — no other expression is used — a small object which is shown to them. One adds that the description must be made in writing, and one consistently obtains from Marguerite a description of the following kind:

Description of a chestnut tree leaf by Marguerite
(Duration : 11 minutes, 15 seconds)

The leaf I am looking at is the leaf of a chestnut tree picked in autumn for its folioles are almost completely yellow, with the exception of two, and one is half green and half yellow.

This leaf is a compound leaf with seven folioles attached to a center which ends with the stem called petiole, which fastens the leaf to the tree.

The folioles are not all of the same size ; four out of seven are much smaller than the other three.

The chestnut tree is a dicotyledon, we can see this by looking at the netted-veined leaf.

In several places the leaf has rust-colored spots, one of its folioles has a hole.

I can say no more about this chestnut tree leaf.

An exact, meticulous, dry, abundant description with a trace of erudition.

Here is the description of the younger girl, Armande, written the same day and with the same leaf.

Description of a chestnut tree leaf by Armande
(Duration : 8 minutes)

It is a chestnut tree leaf which has just fallen languidly in the autumn wind.

The leaf is yellow, but still stiff and straight, there may be a little vigor yet in the poor moribund!

A few traces of its former green color are still found on the leaf, but yellow is dominant : a brown and reddish border embellishes its outline.

The seven leaves are still very beautiful, the greenish stem is still attached.

Poor leaf, now destined to whirl about on the roads and then to decay, piled up on many others. It is dead today — and it lived yesterday! Yesterday, fastened to the branch, it waited for the fatal blow which was to carry it off; like a dying person who waits for the last agony.

But the leaf was not conscious of danger, and it fell softly to the ground.

185

Armande, the younger child, wrote less than her sister; the object did not inspire her as much. She gives fewer material details than Marguerite, and the details she reports are subordinated to a general impression of emotion, generated by the idea that the autumn leaf is going to die.

Dozens of descriptions of objects, written by the two sisters, always brought out the same difference: detail and precision of observation in Marguerite; vagueness and poetry in Armande. It is unnecessary but we say it once and for all that neither child knew about her sister's composition; they had promised not to discuss it, and I know they are absolutely trustworthy.

The description of an absent object brings out the same difference in the writings. We lived in Meudon at that time, and near our home there was a beautiful house which was always empty and which we had often visited. I asked the two children to describe it.

Marguerite's narration begins in this way:

The Lar... House

I was taking a walk in D... street the other day when a large sign attached to the gate of a garden attracted my attention. I had not been living in Meudon very long and it was the first time I had noticed this sign; I walked over and read: "Large house for sale or rent; inquire from Mr. P..., Realtor in Meudon; or from Mr. M..., 23, Rennes Street, Paris." It was kind of far, and since I was curious I said to myself: if I ring the bell here someone will have to answer, and if the caretaker is accommodating, I shall go in!

I rang the bell and after an instant the door opened although no one was behind it. (I found out later it was operated from the kitchen.) I went up a beautiful gravelled walk lined with bushy trees and with small rocks among which scotch broom grew. On each side of the door, on a small elevation, were two terraces, the beautiful walk was in the middle in a sort of a hollow, it was very straight; at the end of it a big and long staircase could be seen, above it an awning, there also a kind of terrace which windows were facing on; it was the house... Hardly had I come in that a small black dog arrived barking in a very clear toned bark; at the same moment a gray haired gardener appeared and I explained to him the reason for my visit; he agreed to let me see the house. We began with the garden; it was very beautiful, two beautiful lawns... etc.

The composition is continued lengthily. The description is surprisingly accurate. The fictitious visit is the only fiction it contains; no other detail is invented.

Here is Armande's composition:

The Deserted House

Imagine a large and superb uninhabited house which the passer-by admires when he catches sight of it at the end of a walk lined with fragrant clumps of shrubs. The garden is large and deserted. When old

January comes around and visits it he never finds anything there except trees covered with dazzling snow, walks covered with white ermine. It is sad, it is lugubrious. In back of this solitary garden are the shacky remains of an old portico on which ravens come and croak balefully when they have nothing left to do. Living in this house with closed windows and drawn curtains is deadly dull. The old pianos sleep in the drawing rooms, resting their ancient strings, the windows no longer open, everything is worn out, rusted by time and especially lack of use. Everything breathes the acrid odor of the room which is never aired. The old armchairs look at each other sadly like old companions used to living together, they look at each other with their faded gildings, and the tall statues complain bitterly about their solitude. It is cold outside and there is never any heat in the house which trembles with pain. The chairs draw near the once blazing fireplace to no purpose!

But when radiant spring comes and gives life back to trees, the lilacs and the hawthorn bloom, the sun ripens the fruits, birds warble, life stirs again in the heart of the garden which sighs, along with the breeze which caresses the fragrant heads of the lilacs.

The difference is always the same. Here more conciseness, more vagueness, more emotion, more poetry. If we ask the two sisters to describe a trip in writing, Marguerite gives a copious report filled with exact details, well observed, and without commentaries. Armande's report, on the contrary, is much more incomplete, more vague, more emotional, more interpretative. It seems evident to us that the external world is less important to Armande than the emotions she experiences in relation to it.

I tried increasing the number of tests in order to study every facet of these two curiously opposite mental attitudes. I had my two subjects write unconnected words and then I asked them for the meaning of these words; this experiment was done, repeated, continued during several years on hundreds of words. In Marguerite's list we find an abundance of names of objects which are present or of words designating her own person, also a very large number of words relative to memories of facts, but very few words with abstract meaning, very few words written without thinking about the meaning, and finally, no word denoting invention. In Armande the trend is reversed. The words designating objects which are present and reporting observations are fewer in number, and recollections are also fewer; on the other hand, abstract words, imaginative words, half unconscious words are abundant. All this proves to us that Marguerite, very conscious, little given to abstraction and dream, does not lose contact with the external world, while Armande prefers abstract words, vagueness, and, moreover, her vocabulary is finer, which in itself shows that her subjective type involves greater language development.

If we ask them to write any sentences of their choice, we see their mentalities revealed even better. This type of test has also been repeated hundreds of times. Marguerite's sentences are assertions of real facts, borrowed from her private life and consequently difficult to understand without long explanatory comments. For instance she will write : "The other day we went to Pathé's with Marguerite to buy new records. "... "When A... knocked against the shutters last night Gyp barked very well, we have great hopes that it will become a good guard dog. "... "How bored poor Armande must be waiting for me to go bicycle riding with her."

In an amusing contrast, Armande makes no allusion to her real life; she paints a poetic picture or she imagines an event which is completely false : "A car stops abruptly in front of the church. "... "While passing through the woods I saw a bird which had fallen out of its nest. "... "It is night time, a few stars shine discreetly in the sky, the quivering moon hides behind a cloud. "... "The funeral procession marches silently by and glides along the rain soaked street."

Upon a suggestion that they change their style, Marguerite becomes inventive. Her imagination gives birth to small, precise, likely events : "A small boy who was walking with his dog was grieved when he saw it being run over by a heavy cart. "... "Two carriages came abruptly in contact on B... Street and a woman passenger smashed her head against the sidewalk."

Armande passes to the entirely different domain of abstract thought or she comes back to her favorite style. "Anger is a weakness which often troubles us. "... "The walls of an old house sweat when it is raining."

Can we get them to write alike if we give them sentences to complete? Not at all. Marguerite finishes the sentence with small, precise facts; Armande with a vague and poetic idea. Given, "I walked into..., " Armande writes : "...the countryside by borrowing a shady path." Marguerite writes : "... a grocery store where I bought 2 cents worth of chocolate." This exercise was done with hundreds of sentences and the results were so clear that we could tell almost every time who the author was. Writings involving pure imagination always demonstrate the same facts and, this being so, I feel it is useless to dwell any longer on the manifestations of these two types of mentalities. What is more interesting is to see how they differ. It is evident to us that Marguerite has a more abundant, more intense, more precise imagery than her sister; she visualizes better what is suggested to her and indeed asserts that when she visualizes someone she knows, the image is as strong and clear as if she really saw that person. In this regard she is very superior to Armande, who explains that all her images are indefinite, blurred, and especially inadequate for expressing her thought. In compensation, Armande's language development is greater; she uses words which are more complicated, more select. In research on idea association, we see that she is more influenced by the sound of the word and she makes a larger number of verbal associations. Since I began writing, her verbal development has been well demonstrated; she has a way with words, has written poetry, and in conversation successfully cultivates the art of making puns. Now, as I have already indicated, her language development denotes an introspective nature; indeed I have often observed that if Marguerite, who is intelligent, can engage in introspection with profit, she succeeds less well than Armande, who has a penchant for analysing herself; one feels this is her domain. A last characteristic affixes a seal, so to speak, to the parallel we have just drawn. The external world involves space more particularly, position relationships between objects, while the internal world has neither space nor distance nor form but is subject only to the law of time. Now, a very surprising fact, I have observed many times that Marguerite, the observer, the objective type, always knows how to orient herself when she is out for a walk or doing errands in an unknown area; she can find the northern direction or her point of departure. Armande, on the contrary, is not concerned about orientation, quickly loses her sense of direction and only finds her way with difficulty. In her turn, Marguerite does not think about the hour or about the fact that time is passing, while for Armande time is of the greatest importance, one of her main concerns. She always knows what time it is; in the absence of a watch, she manages to guess the time accurately.

Before closing this discussion I feel it is particularly important to show the pedagogical conclusions which can be drawn from the above analyses. Several years have passed since I made these studies. The little girls have grown up, and I have followed closely their complete ulterior development day by day. No new fact has ever led me to question the soundness of either my previous analyses or the psychology of individual differences which I derived from them. However, a small event took place which at first surprised me greatly and which I was able to understand only slowly. Armande, the younger girl, became interested in painting at the age of fourteen and since that time painting has never ceased to be one of her main interests. Since she didn't have much aptitude for observation, I thought at first that this fact contradicted what I had observed. It seemed to me painting is truly a visual art, an external art. How could this subjective individual become engrossed in something as objective as painting? Should she not logically rather be inclined to write poetry or intimate analyses? She has done some of this, it is true, but her dominant interest remains painting, and the fact that she has been ardently faithful to it for several years is certainly proof that she has found her vocation. This, for us, represents a problem to be solved. If we question Armande at length and patiently, especially if we observe her, we manage to understand it a little. What has been most difficult for her in relation to her art is drawing; it is also the kind of remarkably realistic reproduction of the model type which

189

requires not only observation but also the keen mind of the observer. If she allowed herself to follow her inclinations, she would orient herself toward imaginative painting, representing what she loves and what she dreams about rather than what she sees, but since she does not want to yield too much to this subjective tendency, she forces herself to resist it. Then again, if she voluntarily makes a strict rule of observing and reproducing nature without modifying anything, her work becomes painful, her enthusiasm slackens, her thought becomes discouraged. Therefore an everlasting and very interesting conflict between two opposed tendencies is taking place within her. But she owes two precious qualities to her mental type : 1) a very great analytical and critical ability which is in part due to her well-developed inner language ; 2) the predominance of a state of mind which may some day direct her toward a kind of psychological painting, by which I mean the painting of what is felt rather than a representation of what is seen.

Everything considered, I am extremely happy that the ulterior development of one of my subjects appeared to have contradicted the conclusions I had drawn from my analyses. It taught me something. I am fully convinced that the value of my analyses remains intact, but the pedagogical conclusion to be drawn from them is challenged. Generally speaking, when a child is interested in observation, he should be oriented toward the professions in contact with nature ; by giving him this advice and direction we render him the greatest service. But there are exceptions to this rule which show that pedagogical rules are not inexorable or inevitable. The fertility and the adaptability of the human mind are always superior to what we have supposed. Consequently, the advice we give should always be subject to revision and nothing should ever be imposed by sheer force.

The Practician and the Literary

We now are going to discuss a last category of minds. This one is already well known in America, where professional and technical schools are flourishing and where, even as early as grade school, arts and crafts are given an appropriately large place. But in France we have remained far behind, and the ideas, so well known and universally accepted on the other side of the Atlantic, are still new here. The importance of arts and crafts is not appreciated at its just value ; there is still much prejudice against it.

Who has not in his life met very intelligent men who have general ideas about everything, who express them well, with clarity, good sense, and even with depth, who when the occasion presents itself show themselves to be eloquent speakers but who, in striking contrast, are extremely awkward with their hands, so awkward in fact that even the least talented worker would laugh at them ? I was recently given a very clear example of these partial aptitudes in the case of a government official who owes his great authority to his eloquence, to his clear, orderly, methodical mind. He could improvise intelligently on any question, but he was incapable of driving a nail into a wall. He couldn't tell if a picture hanging in his room was straight or lopsided. He was one of those bicycle riders who understand nothing about their bike and who are incapable of repairing a flat tire; he would not even have known how to tighten a screw. A classmate of mine at the Ecole Normale, whom I personally knew, had the same qualities and the same weaknesses. I never met as excellent a speaker; it was impossible to catch him unaware. President of a small scientific society, he talked with presidential taste and correctness on questions he knew the least about. No sooner had someone given him the "do" than he readied his violin bow; his speech was true music. In discussions he showed good sense, made sharp repartee, and his remarks were relevant and well timed. Furthermore he had real talent for organization. He may have lacked originality. Those who did not know him well overestimated his merits because of his volubleness; in contrast, those who had been associated with him for a long time realized that in spite of real intelligence and a very great aptitude for handling general ideas, the quality of his thought was inferior to the quality of his speech; like all people who are essentially verbal, he gave an incontestable impression of emptiness. This literary was heavy, clumsy looking and very awkward with his hands; he would have made a bad craftsman. He felt repugnance for all sports and took his revenge upon them by holding them in sovereign contempt. These are two very clear examples of literary types, or, to be more explicit, of verbal types in whom manual aptitudes are completely lacking.

By way of contrast, I shall now describe two types of practicians. One of them, oddly enough, comes from a very literary family; his father, a former congressman, is one of the orators who are most listened to today; his brothers have distinguished themselves in the sciences and in literature. As for him, even in his family he was thought of as mentally retarded for a long time, mainly because of his evident verbal inferiority. In France, as a general rule, those who don't know how to speak are looked upon as having little intelligence. When I met him, this young man spoke little and badly. I saw him try to tell stories and to describe things; it was heartbreaking. The sentences were incorrect and so awkward that his thought was not understood; most often he remained silent or spoke only in monosyllables, as if aware of his language deficiency. His letters, written in a childish script, were as laconic as his speech. And what grammar! What spelling! At the age of twenty, after having received lessons from the best teachers, he wrote compositions worthy of an eight- or nine-year-old child. On the other hand, he was a skillful and clever young man. He dressed with care, had

191

a very supple body, excelled at physical exercise. He was good at repairing clocks and executed fine manual work carefully and with good taste. I was often impressed with his talent for observation. He loved the country and made very sound remarks about animal and plant life; on that score he could teach his brothers something. His parents correctly identified his aptitudes and oriented him toward agronomy. He ranked high in an entrance examination to an agricultural school; he might even have ranked first if this examination had not included a writing test, in which he received a low score.

Here is another example. I once had a student in my psychology laboratory who, on the very first day, astonished me. He was young and knew almost nothing but he was yearning to learn. At his request I showed him how to operate several intricate pieces of equipment such as chronometers and registering instruments. He listened to me with great attention and in a slow gesture discreetly touched the components of the machine I activated in front of him. A few days later I was scheduled to make a demonstration in front of several students. I found the instruments all ready, the batteries with the wires correctly attached, cylinders well inked, drums in good working order and everything adjusted most intelligently, as if an experienced assistant had been there. My new student had set up everything. During my demonstration he operated the instruments and obtained the most difficult tracings; they always fitted within the framework of my lecture, the presentation being made at just the right time, neither too soon nor too late. After my audience had left I turned to him and, astonished, asked who had taught him the graphic method. In a tone of voice which showed surprise at my own surprise, he answered, "But Sir, you did." This means that he had learned more in fifteen minutes than students normally learn in ten practice sessions. Endowed with remarkable manual skill, this student later became one of my best collaborators. I shall not reveal his name so as not to offend his modesty, for I am forced also to mention his ingenuity in devising apparatus for experimentation, his ability for correcting the experimental method and making it more precise, and his incomparable talent as a critic. His mind is the finest, the most penetrating, the most well balanced I have ever known. Add to this a readiness of mind which I have never before seen developed to this degree and which enables him to guess a person's thought at the first word of a sentence. After all these compliments I am obliged to add that his intelligence is not a "complete" intelligence. He himself is too good a psychologist not to have become aware of this. What is a little weak in him is language. His writings do not have the same depth as his thought; in his correspondence his overly simple sentences are joined to one another by the elementary conjunction *and;* there are few subordinate clauses, few nuances. The language he uses in his articles is also elementary and this is very regrettable. His speech is lacking in refinement, in brilliancy, but it is so clear and precise that our attention becomes focused on the substance of it rather than on its form. I have heard him give lectures. To be sure, he is not an orator, he does not make eloquent gestures, his voice does not have clever inflections, he does not use piquant sentences or anything which lends an aureole to thought. His discourse is as sober and compact as that of a business lawyer. What wins his audience is the method, the order in his exposition, the ingenuity of his insights, and even the depth of his thought; he owes nothing to words.

What a large number of examples could still be given of these two so very different types of mind! I have seen eminent philosophers who were incapable of using their eyes or their hands in the simplest observation exercise, and it is probably because of their handicap that they loathed experimentation so much and spoke so much ill of it. I have seen a science professor at the Sorbonne who was so lacking in literary ability that he had never been able to learn spelling; it was a waste of time for students to listen to his very scholarly but very obtuse and disorganized lectures. By searching our memory each one of us will be able, in retrospect, to make similar observations. The distinction we have just suggested is easily verified. It seems sound and self-evident, but it only seems so when we already know about it. As for me I have known these facts for a long time, but only since yesterday have I understood their importance. My eyes were opened on the occasion I now describe.

It happened in the course of doing research on the measurement of intelligence. This kind of research, we shall remember, is conducted by means of numerous tests, about sixty of them. Among these tests are some which involve the comparison of sensations, the discrimination of sensations, the memory of sensations, the classification of sensations, or the rapid and careful execution of complicated movements and actions.

Other tests consist of defining words, remembering digits, putting words in order, understanding abstract passages, criticizing absurd statements. The contrast between these two groups of tests is evident: the first can be called tests of sensory intelligence and the second, tests of verbal intelligence. I did not realize that the difference between the two groups was very great and must even admit that the leading idea in preparing these tests with Dr. Simon had not been to separate sensory intelligence from verbal intelligence. It was the facts, the results of experiments, which forced us to make this separation.

We were indeed very surprised to discover early in our experimentation that a child is as skillful as an adult for everything involving sensory intelligence. For instance, show a seven-year-old child two boxes of only slightly different weights, one weighing 14 grams, the other weighing 15 grams; or show him two lines, one 10 centimeters long, the other 5 centimeters longer. Ask him to show you the longer line, the heavier box. Repeat the test about twenty times with different boxes and lines so as to eliminate chance errors. More importantly, and this is essential, truly try to capture the child's attention, for he ordinarily is more easily distracted than an adult. If you are successful in averting all these errors, you will, in computing the results, be impressed with the fact that the child's faculty of perception and of comparison is not inferior to that of an adult. This is only one example. It could be diversified infinitely, for as long as the experiment involves sensations and not intellectual elaboration, the child will give results equal to that of the adult. Moreover, this truly extraordinary skill in sensory perception is not limited to the normal child; the retarded and even the institutionalized imbecile also display it. While visiting Dr. Simon's service recently I saw thirty-year-old imbeciles who never could be taught to read or write because they were not intelligent enough; these imbeciles, however, were able to compare weights and lines with as much assurance and accuracy as Dr. Simon and I. Sensory intelligence is, therefore, a different kind of intelligence, close to that of the animal, and its development does not follow a course parallel to that of verbal intelligence.

From the institutionalized retardates let us pass to the school retardates, who also have defective intelligence but whose condition is less severe. We shall make the same observations on them. These children are inferior to their normal counterparts, since they are admitted to special classes only if they are three years below grade in reading, spelling and arithmetic; but as far as arts and crafts are concerned their inferiority is not nearly so marked. Their eye is reliable enough, their hand not unskillful; and when they are given a manual task to do, they do it eagerly, and the finished product is not bad. If those of their drawings which are the product of imagination show some weakness of conception, in return, their ornamentation work is not lacking in taste. We have seen our young retarded girls sew, baste, spangle in a very satisfactory manner, and make very pretty artificial flowers gracefully. As to our retarded boys, they have to be seen at the work bench. I remember that in a particular school the arts and crafts teacher refused to accept them as students. "These children," he said, "must be unruly and vicious; if I have them manipulate the scissors and the saw, they are going to hurt themselves... I shall be responsible for accidents." But the inspector, Mr. Belot, insisted and the master craftsman consented to try; after several months he had become a convert. He had taken a few good precautions; to each retarded student he assigned a skilled normal student, who guided the work by executing the tracings himself and supervising the handling of tools. After one year no accident, not even a slight one, could be reported.

Moreover, the retardates gave unexpected results from the point of view of attention, taste, and work capacity; in a class with normal children of the same age, they were neither first nor last, but about average. In notes relating to each of them we very often find the following comments: "Has a skillful hand... is fearless in the manipulation of tools... is careful and has taste." Therefore, if these retarded individuals perform poorly in arithmetic, spelling and reading, that is in tasks involving verbal intelligence, they do not perform nearly as poorly in tasks involving sensory intelligence. The teacher could write about almost every one of his retarded students: "Will make a good workman."

In the light of these remarks, the abnormal child appears to us to be an individual with a prematurely arrested intellectual development. We were undoubtedly aware of this before but did not exactly know what this interruption in intellectual development consisted of. We understand it better when we learn that the child's intelligence is sensory at first, that it utilizes imagery and concrete experiences more particularly, that verbal intelligence appears later and, with the advent of the word, permits the development of abstract and general ideas.

Among children who are normal but who do poorly in their schoolwork, the practician type is also widespread. I shall give a few of the examples which I have collected. Recently Mr. Lacabe, Mr. Bocquillon and I were making a survey about laziness in children and about the causes which are given to explain school failures. We asked several teachers to tell us something about the psychology of pupils making up the last fifth of their class in placement involving ability. Several of the teachers, believing they gave a sufficient explanation, made the overly succinct statement that the student was lacking in intelligence or in will power. But some others, who were more inspired and especially more attentive, carried their analysis further; they tried to establish which aspect of certain lazy children's intelligence is to be incriminated, and they observed that a large part of those who were not intelligent for school subjects were intelligent for manual work.

We have been told about many a child who remains completely passive in class. While he pretends to be listening to the teacher, his pencil case with its lock and its compartments, his eraser, or any other object holds a fascination for him; his thought accompanies his fingers as they palpate the object, study its contours, its edges, the physical properties of wood and rubber. This student ranks first in the workshop; his work is done to perfection. If it involves paper folding, cutouts, dimensional sketches, his workbook is irreproachable. He often ranks first in drawing and has a fine handwriting. His papers, spangled with spelling mistakes and incorrect solutions to arithmetic problems, are perfectly beautiful to look at; maps and illustrations in them are admirable.

"The young girl of the same type has marked ability for sewing, housework, cooking. In the schoolyard she may spontaneously and maternally take care of the smaller children. She is unintelligent when the task is spelling but she is more intelligent than others when the task is cooking."

The teacher who made these important observations adds, and with reason : "We must not believe that we are dealing here with types devoid of all intellectual faculty. Much observation and reflection is necessary to assemble successfully two pieces of iron, to execute a mortise correctly, to reproduce a three-dimensional model accurately on paper."

I was strongly impressed with this statement and began to wonder if unintelligent children really exist, that is, children who are completely lacking in intellectual aptitudes of any kind. I am more disposed to believe that we too often judge them from a biased point of view, literary or scientific ; that we look down too much on manual aptitudes in spite of the fact that intelligence can manifest itself in them as well as in speech. A large-scale survey should be conducted. I am convinced it would show in France what has already been shown in America, that the vocation for the arts and crafts is widespread. While awaiting the results of such a survey, I take the liberty to report the following information which I feel is already encouraging. I selected the five students who ranked lowest for all subject matter in each of three classes and inquired about their aptitudes for manual work. They are average, completely independent of their aptitudes for other subjects.

Let us support these findings with data which will add precision to our report. Half of the fifteen school children included in the above study rank in the top half of the class for manual work. Now, if we consider that some among those fifteen children are almost sure to owe their low rank to laziness and that they are also lazy where manual work is concerned, we conclude, when everything is considered, that their placement with regard to manual work is due to the fact that their aptitudes for this type of work are not merely average but superior to the average. There is a kind of compensation in them, and it is this very idea we wish to throw light on. It is a conclusion which is of the greatest interest from the practical point of view. Half or maybe even two-thirds of our dunces, the students who fail to profit from literary or scientific programs, are simply children whose aptitudes are not appreciated and whose vocation is manual work.

When the importance of this distinction between the verbal and the practician type is recognized by everyone, great progress will have been made and a great service will have been rendered. It will be understood that choosing a career must not be left to chance, that it is a choice of great consequence which must be determined by the individual's aptitudes. We shall not put a practician in a literary job, and manual work will not be entrusted to a verbal-type individual. Already, without making an in-depth analysis of these questions, we understand and can suggest how it is possible to classify various professions according to this point of view. No one is more verbal than a lawyer and also, unfortunately, a politician. The professor, the lecturer, the preacher, the actor must be of the verbal type. A physician cannot be as foreign to the manual arts; the surgeon, for instance, must be primarily a practician. Commerce also makes use of very different aptitudes: the salesman must be verbal, as well as the business representative and the agent. The buyer, the fitter, the mechanic, on the other hand, need to be practicians who work with sensory intelligence more particularly.

Let us guard against believing that a hierarchy, a class distinction should be established between sensory and verbal intelligence. Let us give up these old-world prejudices which are well abolished on the other side of the Atlantic. If an aptitude for manual work is often found in members of the working class, is it not necessary also to the scientist, to the experimenter especially? Moreover, skillfulness and adroitness do not sum up sensory intelligence; it is mainly an intelligence of images and of sensations. Do we need to enhance its nobleness? Bear in mind that it is the intelligence of the musician and also that of the painter. Painting, one of the greatest marvels, one of the greatest mysteries of human activity, is art without words; it lives with sensations, images, and feelings. Shall someone object that sensory intelligence is mainly that of children and of primitive people, while verbal intelligence marks the appearance of abstract thought and of science and belongs to a more advanced civilization? Perhaps. The remark is sound, but in what way does this constitute a depreciation of sensory intelligence? We can conclude nothing about the heights sensory intelligence can attain from the fact that its origins are more distant and primitive. Things can only be judged by their results and their destiny, not by their origin. Doesn't the novel, and especially poetry, imply the partial survival in the poet of a child's soul with its impressionability, its curiosity, its taste for mystery and its concrete imagination? We by no means depreciate poetry by recalling its origins. To classify human aptitudes according to a merit system is therefore a futile and childish preoccupation. What is essential is for them to remain numerous and infinitely varied, because the good functioning of a society requires it. Let us add also that they need to be recognized so that each individual can settle down to the job he is best suited for.

Is it already possible to determine what an individual's aptitudes are at school, at the *lycée*? It is not only possible, it is easy. All we need do is look at the children, observe them, question them. The one who only reads books about science or mechanics is not a literary type.

Neither is the one who spends his Sundays drawing. Moreover, test placements are available; they clearly indicate the children's aptitudes to anyone who wants to take the trouble to study them closely. We shall tend to see a verbal type in someone who is strong in grammar, in arithmetic, especially in writing essays, who has quick retorts, who speaks abundantly and expresses himself easily.

We would like to show in passing that it is sometimes possible to use special tests in order to determine which faculties are more closely related to the verbal type and which to the sensory type. But these tests, of very great interest to psychology, must be interpreted with the utmost care. We shall prove this while discussing several special cases.

One day three young boys presenting interesting characteristics were sent to my laboratory from an elementary school. They were thirteen and fourteen years old and all three were in the sixth grade. So as to avoid confusion we shall call them Ernest, Louis and Antoine. All three were good students, their conduct irreproachable, their application excellent, but the areas in which they were most successful were different. Ernest and Louis ranked almost last in their class; Antoine, with a brilliant and quick mind, constantly ranked first. We were told that, in return, Ernest and Louis did excellent manual work; they could draw with taste and were preparing for admission to a specialized school. Aptitudes had therefore already been identified by the teachers, but I wanted to find out, beyond this, what mental qualities such different aptitudes depended on. I gave these three young people many tests; some of the tests produced rather insignificant results, which I shall not mention, but others had all the value of a demonstration.

It became immediately apparent that Antoine excelled in tests involving verbal ability especially, and that his schoolmates' performance was constantly inferior. I first tried to establish the maximum number of words each of them could find in three minutes; Antoine gave 78, while Ernest found only 67, and Louis only 49. Then they were asked to explain the meaning of 20 abstract words, including some difficult ones; Antoine explained 16 of them, Ernest 11, and Louis 10. They were also asked to give associations to a word presented to them; Antoine found associations fairly readily in $4^m 8^s$; Ernest in $5^m 50^s$, and Louis, much more slowly, in $7^m 60^s$. Finally, I read the following challenging passage to all three of them (it is a paraphrase of one of Paul Hervieu's thoughts), and asked them to reproduce it immediately afterward from memory.

> Very different judgments have been expressed with regard to the value of life. Some say it is good, some others say it is bad. It would be more accurate to say it is mediocre, for on the one hand, the happiness it brings is always inferior to the one we have wished for; and on the other hand, the misfortunes it inflicts upon us are always inferior to those

others would have wished for us. It is this mediocrity of life which makes it equitable, or rather which prevents it from being radically unjust.

Ernest and Louis understood poorly and reproduced the statement without even the help of verbal memory.

Here is what Louis wrote :

Our life is mediocre it brings us what we are not hoping for and that if we think about something it brings us something else we can say then that our life is a struggle against chance.

There is no spelling mistake, but punctuation is missing; the idea was not understood; there is no sign that verbal memory played a role; there was no textual reproduction of words.

Now compare what precedes with Antoine's statement :

Some say life is good, some others say it is bad. Let us say rather that life is mediocre, for it always brings us happiness inferior to that we have wished for, and misfortune inferior to that others have wished for us.

In Antoine's writing we find punctuation, good comprehension, and verbal memory; his superiority is clearly overwhelming. It remained so for all tests which could be devised involving verbal ability.

Now let us look at the other side of the coin. Let us look for tests which have nothing to do with verbal ability but which are concerned with various aspects of sensory intelligence. Let us put our three young men through an exercise which requires not intelligence so much as visual memory. We have them reproduce a "capricious line," a broken line composed of straight lines and curves. We have the subjects look at it for 10 seconds, after which they must reproduce it from memory. Using a scoring system which we need not describe here, we can score the reproduction for accuracy. Louis's score is 7; Ernest's is 6; as for Antoine, the literary type, his score is only 3.5, which is proof that his performance is inferior for visual memory.

But could we conclude from these psychological analyses that Antoine is a verbal type and the other two are practicians if their aptitudes had not already been demonstrated in their work? Certainly not. We have said it before and we repeat it here : aptitudes are not identified by mental tests, or rather they can be demonstrated with performance tests, never with analytic tests. Remember the distinction made earlier, in connection with this, in our chapter on vision. Remember the observations made on Armande, the young girl who, according to a thousand analyses, belonged in the subjective type group and who nevertheless devotes herself successfully to painting. If we required one more bit of evidence in order to demonstrate the need for caution, we would add the lesson which was given us during our most recent research on painters. We conducted some experiments on a young painter who is already famous although he is not yet twenty. Young Tade Styka displays remarkable artistic virtuosity and it could be expected that his visual memory would be excellent. We had him copy from memory the models of lines we use in schools to test visual memory and we were very surprised: Tade Styka is not more skillful when attempting to make an exact reproduction than an eight-year-old child who does not yet know how to draw. Shall we deny that he has talent because he has failed one of our tests? Of course not. Aptitude for drawing is demonstrated by drawing, aptitude for singing by singing, and so on; there is no other way, no other demonstration method.

IV. Special Aptitude and General Culture

In winding up this discussion of what is presently known about children's aptitudes, I feel it is useful to examine quickly a question of general interest which has been ignored in our discussions but which is of the greatest importance: the question of utilization of children's special aptitudes. Two very different opinions can be, and have been, defended. In the first view, any child should always be given a general culture in keeping with the already-old principle which demands that an honest man be enlightened about everything. If a child has memory, especially visual memory, we shall not neglect to cultivate his auditory memory. If he is born a practician, he will not be excused from literary exercises. Two arguments, one practical and the other theoretical, are given in support of this system of integral education. From a practical point of view, we are told, it would be doing the child a bad turn to make him into an incomplete being by specializing him prematurely. To take an extreme example, if he is able to do only one job, how will he get along when economic conditions change and his job is no longer available? The second argument is based on the idea that even useless knowledge is never lost because it acts as a kind of gymnastic for the mind and expands our faculties. In this connection we can give the excellent example provided by the teaching of philosophy. It is doubtful that these teachings will find undeniable practical application in the lives of those who will not later become professional philosophers. Discussions on materialism and Kantism are useful neither in industry nor in commerce, yet many students admit that they have derived moral benefits from the study of philosophy. Their ideas became broader; problems they had not been aware of were revealed to them; they acquired two qualities which of themselves would justify spending time in a philosophy class, a little more critical judgment and a little more tolerance.

200

We believe these ideas are very sound provided their importance is not overemphasized. The first part of our answer is commonplace and we shall go over it only briefly, since it makes a point I think everyone agrees on. We shall say, on the one hand, it is good to aim for the formation of well-rounded minds so as to give each individual greater adaptive power. The present-day environment is unstable, the professions and the needs to which they respond change everyday, and mechanization makes a progress which is both salutary for the group as a whole and threatening for certain individual interests. It is therefore desirable that each student should not be confined ahead of time in one precise professional compartment from which he could not get out. On the other hand, it is certain that children's aptitudes may not be ignored, for the aptitude is a remarkable means of economizing effort, a natural instrument of progress. It permits doing better with less work. We would do well, therefore, to give a part to general culture, at least if the student's nature is such that he can profit from this training. We would do well, also, to use the aptitude, when it is typical, as the lever of instruction. If someone is a born draftsman, it is ridiculous not to have him draw a lot; but we must also use drawing to interest him in history, in geography, even in science, and maybe even in literature. In drawing maps, historical scenes, physics apparatus he will manage to acquire a general culture indirectly through his special aptitude. All this strikes me as being trite, well known, well demonstrated, definitely accepted, and I feel it is pointless to dwell upon it any longer.

What is more important is to state quite frankly what we think of studies which are of themselves completely useless and antiquated but which are jealously preserved because they are believed to constitute a kind of mental gymnastic. For this particular reason many often want to impose the study of Latin on all students. The idea seems very attractive at first. Everyone will admit that it is better to train one's mind than to fill it; it is better to have acquired good judgment than to have learned the rudiments of a particular science by heart; the school child has not wasted his time at the *lycée* if he has become used to work; the student needs not regret having studied Roman law if these courses which are useless for the practice of law have formed his juridical mind.

But let us become completely conscious of the kind of abuse a good principle can give rise to. There is no subject matter, useless, unpromising, futile as it may be, about which we cannot say it will cultivate the mind. The argument is extremely dangerous because it is tendentious and dispenses with any precise verification of facts. What proof is there that such a subject, in spite of its admitted uselessness, has strengthened my mind? This proof is never given and it would be very difficult to give.

201

Here is an example which will lend support to our view.

Dr. Simon and I have just finished a survey of unfortunate deaf-mutes who are being taught speech and lip reading by a method which is presently fashionable. From eight to ten years of extremely tiresome, costly studies, demoralizing to the student, are required to teach a congenitally and completely deaf individual to pronounce articulated sounds which he does not hear or to guess from the movements of his interlocutor's lips a few of the words the latter pronounces. When you visit a school of deaf-mutes, the professors of the institution eagerly show you some deaf-mute children who pronounce in a raucous voice a few nearly intelligible words and who can read on certain lips, those of their professors, some elementary and unvarying questions about their name and age. But there is reason to suspect that these students who serve in the demonstration and exhibition are only partially deaf or are children who have heard in the past, for under these two conditions what we call "demutization" is easier. We wanted to know if deaf-mutes, carefully chosen among those the administration itself considered as having profited from the oral teaching to an average degree, could speak orally with strangers a few years after they had left the school. In other words, we raised the question: Is this oral training, so painful to acquire and so costly to give, socially useful? Having examined about forty deaf-mutes in their own homes, we have reached the following conclusion: It is not possible for a stranger to carry on a serious, useful conversation with one of these deaf-mutes. As soon as we begin talking about something other than such banalities as name and age, as soon as we no longer use gestures and mimicry, as soon as we ask for precise information, a proper name, an address, a number, a technical word, it becomes necessary to write. We therefore became convinced of the fact that trying to demutize the complete and congenitally deaf-mute is to offer luxury training which can give these unfortunate children and their parents some moral satisfaction but which is of practically no use to them for finding a trade or practicing that trade; in a conversation with strangers they are unable to understand those strangers or to have themselves understood through the use of speech.

What conclusions were we to draw from our survey? That the oral training of deaf-mutes is to be abandoned? This is undoubtedly the first idea which comes to mind.

But in order to save demutization it was objected that, everything considered and in spite of the paucity of practical results, the training of deaf-mutes nevertheless has educational value. Here is the error, and without taking too seriously this argumentation, which is only a personal defense for a threatened tradition, we shall simply say this: To maintain that any teaching, whatever it may be, can serve to cultivate the mind is inexact and rash. This teaching must fill at least one fundamental condition, that of being adapted to the individual's aptitudes. To take eight years to learn speech and not be able to acquire it cannot be a good gymnastic. This is still one of those pedagogical errors which have done great harm and yet one which, with a little common sense, we could have avoided.

FOOTNOTES FOR CHAPTER SEVEN

1. Binet and Henri, *La fatigue intellectuelle* (Paris : Schleicher); conferer Sée, " Une formule mathématique applicable aux recherches de psychologie," *Bulletin de la Société de l'Enfant,* Paris, Alcan, N° 17 (1904).

2. Spearmann, "The Proof and Measurement of Association between Two Things," *American Journal of Psychology,* XV (1904), 72. See also, *ibid.,* XV, 201.

3. E. Ivanoff, " Recherches expérimentales sur le dessin des écoliers de la Suisse romande," *Arch. de Psychologie,* N° 30, 1908.

4. Thorndike, *Educational Psychology* (New York : 1903), p. 28.

5. Spearmann, "General Intelligence, Objectively Determined and Measured," *American Journal of Psychology,* XV (1904), 201.

6. A. Belot, " Epellation et présentation visuelle," *Bulletin de la Société de l'Enfant,* Paris, Alcan (1906), p. 147.

7. See Poincaré, " La psychologie de l'invention," *Année Psychologique,* XV (1909).

8. I borrow these two precise expressions from Souriau. See *La rêverie esthétique,* Paris, Alcan (1906), p. 115.

9. Poincaré, " L'invention mathématique." See *Année Psychologique,* XV (1909), 445.

10. A. Binet, " F. de Curel," *Année Psychologique,* I (1904), 119.

CHAPTER EIGHT

Laziness and moral education

I. Laziness

When a teacher notes that a student does not work as much as his classmates, he most often explains it to himself in the following way : " This child is lazy; if he wanted to he could do much better, but he does not want to. He has no will power ; the guilty culprit is his will. " I heard this simplistic explanation given not only by humble teachers but also by eminent professors. I was talking to a College de France professor one day about the mental differences found in school children and the interest there would be in studying these differences. In a tone of voice which admitted no rejoinder, he told me that in teaching one becomes convinced there are only two categories of students : hard-working students and lazy ones. I vainly tried to suggest that maybe the matter was not quite so simple, that will power is only a resultant and that it would be necessary to analyse each case carefully in order really to know why a student does not work, but drowning my voice, he continued repeating, " Hard-working students and lazy students, it all boils down to this. " Such an opinion could enjoy a certain popularity in the past because it was in harmony with traditional psychology. According to spiritualism there are two distinct parts in us : one is passive, intelligence and sensibility; the other is active, essentially active, the will. The will alone determines our actions and conduct, and in its manifestations is even free from any influence the passive parts of our being, our thoughts and our feelings, could exercise on it. It is a free force. Moreover, it represents a certain energy which is distributed to all in indefinite amounts, and anyone who fails to utilize this will which is at his disposal is held responsible and must be treated like someone who is guilty. But today these metaphysical ideas have been abandoned. Far from admitting that the will exists in each of us like a kind of *Deus ex machina* * which intervenes in the manner it pleases, which does everything it wishes, we are convinced that all our actions are determined by a large number of physical and mental influences, habits,

* *Deus ex machina :* an automated God.

thoughts, feelings, unconscious tendencies, hereditary antecedents, etc.; our behavior is determined by all these causes, big and small, conscious and hidden. Consequently, if we want to understand a student's psychology, correct his laziness or give him good work habits, we must not be content naively to accuse his will. We must carry the analysis further, observe, study, find explanations.

We have already seen in the preceding chapters that school failure may be due to a number of causes having nothing to do with the student's will. We have examined, one after the other, the roles played by feebleness, illness, sensory deficiencies, defective intelligence, poor memory and finally special aptitudes which make the child inept for school work. Whenever one of these causes can be incriminated, the child must not be accused of being ill-willed or of lacking will power; nor should he be accused of laziness, which, if I understand correctly, corresponds to a lack of will power for which the child would be responsible.

The lazy child is going to be the object of our discussion in all the pages which follow. He is characterized by a lack of attention which takes one of two main forms in the classroom: aimless or noisy activity, or inertia. Sometimes a little insubordination is also noted.

But if we don't take into consideration the child's school behavior or the manner in which school work is done, if, in other words, we are determined to design some test which will demonstrate a child's laziness directly, we encounter great difficulty, for it is extremely hard to make good experiments involving character.

School principals have often brought to our attention some child whom they felt was unmanageable. I remember a ten-year-old girl, truly the despair of her school, who disrupted all the classes she was ever in. Wishing to distribute the burden equitably, the principal assigned her to all the classes successively so each teacher would share in the martyrdom. This interesting child was brought to me and, in my presence, was blamed for her bad behavior. She lowered her head; her attitude was most appropriate. While I remained alone with her, she was very sweet, very well behaved, very composed. I saw no sign of instability, and had her problem behavior not been reported by several different teachers, one would have believed it was simply a case of a teacher's having taken a dislike to an obnoxious child. Let us add that this young girl had no physical defect, her corporal development was normal, she was subject to neither hysteria nor epilepsy and her natural intelligence was about average. Her school performance was well below grade level, but this is hardly surprising, since she was not paying attention in class and spent most of her time in the halls.

In my opinion the only way to study a child's character is to place him in an environment similar to the one he is used to and watch what he does without his being aware that he is being watched. The following method, which has often worked for me, consists of having a child perform a task, the results of which can be measured and which requires only attention; for instance, a canceling task. Take five children from the same class, have them sit around the same large table and, under your supervision, have them cancel all the "i's" in a text during five minutes. After five minutes have gone by, make a sign on their paper to indicate the amount of work done during this first trial; then leave the children alone, after having instructed them to continue working as if you were there. Immediately after your departure, the most easily distracted students will begin talking, disturbing or teasing their neighbor. Upon returning after five minutes, you only need to look at the work which has been accomplished to know what has happened. To obtain an accurate estimate, compare the child to himself; is his unsupervised work equal or inferior to his supervised work? If it is inferior, we can suspect the subject became distracted. We have often had the proof of this. By using this procedure we could set up a list of the children who appeared to be the most inattentive; then we asked the teachers to make a similar list using their own method. When we compared the two lists, we found they were almost identical.[1]

According to a very widespread opinion, lazy children are legion. Most students, if we are to believe teachers, are affected with laziness. Now, a very careful survey I have already made allusion to, which aims to identify the number of children who have this characteristic, has been undertaken at my request in the Paris schools, under the direction of Mr. Lacabe. Of course, we are talking about serious laziness which affects schoolwork, not temporary moments of slackening attention which are so frequent. Students who rank in the last fifth of the class in a general placement were carefully examined; it is in this group that we expected to find an abundance of lazy subjects, and indeed where would we find them if not at the bottom of the class? In carrying out this analysis it was necessary to eliminate all students whose school failure could be explained by physical weakness or by defective intelligence or memory. This having been done, the remaining group was composed of individuals whose laziness is explained by a character defect. Now this group is surprisingly small, representing only 2 per cent of the total contingent. What is this figure worth? Its value, of course, is only very approximate. It will vary according to the environment, being weaker in one particular school, stronger in another. It will vary, also, according to teachers' evaluations, for the amount of effort demanded from a student is not a fixed, invariable, predetermined quantity. What is considered sufficient by one may be considered insufficient and laughable by another. The question of appreciation and of value is what complicates the verification of moral phenomena most; we appreciate them much more than we verify them. But the notion we get is not purely arbitrary; in no way does it correspond to the answer a teacher would make if asked, "How many lazy children do you have in your class?" or "How many lazy children have you met in the course of your career?" We saw to it that the subject studied was carefully defined; all cases of slight, transitory, accidental laziness which has no serious effect on schoolwork were excluded from the study. Only students whose school failure was marked were included.

What this mainly shows us is that morally based laziness is not as far reaching as we imagine.

I read with curiosity the individual notes written about lazy students by some very good teachers who participated in our survey; I was looking for a definition of laziness, or rather I thought I would find precise details in them which would help me understand what laziness consists of. I was a little disappointed. Many analyses we are given are superficial; most often we are told about children who refuse to make an effort. Indeed, to work is not always pleasant business, especially for the child; there is nothing very entertaining about arithmetic problems and grammar lessons, and to concentrate on them requires making an effort. Some lazy children, we are told, are incapable of it; if they feel they are being watched, they read automatically with their eyes, quite absentmindedly, or they pretend to listen. Why do they refuse the challenge when the majority of their schoolmates take it up? The reason is presented to us as the interplay of small secondary causes. One child, we are told, has had overextended vacations and is no longer used to work. Another never did acquire this habit because he continually gets his family to help him; the family does the homework and works for him. Still another student copies his schoolmates' work and in so doing avoids making a personal effort. All these influences can account for a flagging work incentive, but many other students are undoubtedly subject to the same influences without being made lazy; this appears to me to be an incomplete explanation. In other cases, the teacher implicates discouragement. A child who, in spite of his work, receives bad grades and remains constantly last in his class becomes discouraged or even disgusted with his studies, especially if he does not receive moral support from his family. Several topical examples are offered. In one case the child's family is indifferent to his work; when he returns home no one is there to talk with him about what happened in school, a thing which gives a child such great pleasure. In another case, the father and mother set an example of laziness and carelessness for the child. In still other cases, school is made fun of in front of the student, and the teacher is ridiculed; or, even more common, the child is taught to view the teacher as an enemy and punishment as unkindness. In a case as marked as this one, I wonder if we are not dealing more with counter-education than with laziness. Finally, teachers give a last cause of laziness: insensitivity to the usual stimuli. The student, they say, is indifferent to everything; he is dull. They may add that he isn't accessible to emulation; this is a very serious matter, for emulation is the school child's mainspring, so to speak. This whole explanation is a little dry, a little superficial, and we still don't quite know what constitutes the substance of laziness.

As far as I can judge, we can suppose that laziness is the product of very different mechanisms; at any rate, I would propose that we recognize two types:

1. Occasional laziness

This condition is unstable; it is the result of an event which might not have happened. A child is discouraged by a bad grade or failing an examination or a classmate's bad advice; the motivation for work, which would have remained operative without this small exterior source of difficulty, is hampered, inhibited.

2. Laziness from birth

Something is lacking; there is an initial defect in work propensity. The child appears limp, apathetic, hesitant, little inclined to activity; moreover, he does not experience the pleasure which accompanies work or which is inspired by the perspective of the goal to be attained; and finally, he does not find within himself the will power necessary to overcome his apathy, to make an effort.

I once knew a young girl who, from time to time, had bouts of characteristic laziness. When in this mood she left her things lying about and would not put them in their place. She stayed a whole day sitting in a chair, yawning, spending her time reading an insipid novel; she could not force herself to make a physical effort. Fortunately for her, this condition was transitory. On other days her activity was normal; she took pleasure in her work and even put forth considerable effort. Her laziness is really of an internal and intimate nature, without any external cause. It is a general laziness, for on those days she feels indifferent to almost everything and nothing gets her out of her apathy. It is also a laziness produced by a combination of causes, for failure is noted in the areas of sensibility, activity, and the will. This is an interesting mechanism. I believe it would be wrong to think of laziness as a failing of the will only, for the will is mainly an effect, a result. Although this interpretation is not psychologically defensible, it has a real pedagogical value, as we shall show below.

II. Moral Education

We have said that teachers, when they believe they are dealing with a lazy pupil, accuse him of ill will or a deficiency of the will, and that they want to hold him responsible for this deficiency. But we have asked ourselves if this way of looking at things is very sound. First, does it agree with the views on determinism which are in vogue today? If we do not admit the existence, or even the metaphysical possibility, of free will, shall we not tend to believe that the lazy child is not answerable, since he is a victim of physiological incidents which he knows nothing about and which, besides, he has not created? Moreover, we shall say further that since these physiological incidents which explain the weakness of the will are often pathological, should we not view the powerlessness of the will as an alteration of the will and the lazy child as a patient who primarily needs a doctor? Physicians who are consulted about this do not usually declare themselves incompetent; much to the contrary, they have a professional tendency to accept the pathological theory of laziness, since they most often find in the organisms of lazy children who are brought to them constitutional weaknesses or characterized affections of the lung, heart, and especially of the stomach and nervous system. It is easy to speak of anemia and of neurasthenia.

We have consistently tried not to be exclusive in this book and to invite the largest possible number of collaborators to the great work of education. We are therefore very happy to see that physicians are often consulted in cases of moral laziness. It is always advisable to see if the condition can be explained by physiological perturbations which can be corrected by medical treatments; it is probable that this is often so but doubtful that it is always so. At any rate, we cannot approve of the physician who deliberately declares every lazy person sick and, which is worse, who always manages to verify his diagnosis *a priori* by means of an investigation which cannot be controlled. We do not want the moralist constantly to give way to the physician. We do not believe it is useful for the lazy child to think of himself as a patient; nor do we accept that the teacher think of the child as a patient whose wrongdoings are looked upon with serenity; above all, we shall never accept the idea that moral responsibility — which is so fruitful and so sound — should be abolished in the school environment. Let us end our discussion of metaphysics, for metaphysics is one thing, education is another. From the metaphysical point of view we have a right to be deterministic, because the idea of free will becomes confounded with the unintelligible conception of chance, and this particular idea by no means explains responsibility. But in practice, and especially in school, I am in favor of the student's knowing that he is responsible for his actions and for his work, and that, when he is punished for being lazy, he is justly punished. The teacher himself must also constantly assume this point of view if he wants his action on his students to be effective; one can express anger and indignation only toward someone who is responsible. Generous indignation, when it is inspired by our interest in the pupil himself, when it is kept within fair limits, and especially when it is free of any feeling of revenge, is one of the most powerful levers of education.

But then, it will be argued, you admit that education, like court action, consists of making justice reign among the children and proposes to punish them when they infringe a just law? The ideas of moral responsibility, of punishment and of justice are indeed related ideas, but I do not believe that the goal of education is to administer justice to the children. It is sufficient for education to satisfy our idea of what is just and for it not to shock. In many cases educative means are used outside of all consideration of what is just or unjust. I cannot give a better proof of this than with the following very commonplace example. A child has the bad habit of wetting his bed while he sleeps. Frankly, between you and me, it is not the child but his bone marrow which is responsible; however, if a severe punishment can be effective in correcting this habit, we shall not hesitate to give it to him. Now such a punishment, although unjust, will appear to us to be legitimate because it will have been administered, of course, in the interest of the child.

The interest of the child is indeed the goal of education, and let us insist on this, because it seems to us that in practice this goal is often misunderstood. Sometimes teachers and especially parents who admonish and punish children act because of attitudes which have nothing educative about them. Many punishments are inflicted for purely egoistic reasons.

A child yells, he is beaten; a dog barks, it is kicked. It is a kind of reflex arc, a means of defense, a relief for our state of jangled nerves. In the same way, we force a child to be quiet or stay still to protect the parents' tranquillity. No thought is given to the fact that it is very unhealthy for a small child to remain still. The great defect of all these methods is that the individual who uses them does not change his point of view. The result is that the punishment is proportional to the anger of the one who imposes it and becomes a true vengeance, for when we are angry we have to strike hard in order to feel relieved.

A second motive, which is a little more admissible than the preceding one but which still does not deserve to be called educative, consists of punishing the child to "prevent him from repeating the same error." This is still not education but a preservation system similar to the one organized by society against offenders. In this case the society is not thinking about the criminal's interest but about its own; it defends itself.

For the true educator, a repression is justified only because its goal is to improve the individual, to perfect him, to allow him to achieve a more exact adaptation to his environment. The object of the constraint is to promote self-control; the object of the restraint on his present freedom is to insure his ulterior freedom. This is the only justification for the control exerted on the individual by education.

Having thus defined the ideal of moral education, let us examine the practical result it proposes to attain: a modification of the individual's conduct. Moral education does not consist only of suggesting ideas which are just, broad and human, nor does it consist only of fostering the birth of praiseworthy feelings through the use of appropriate words. Neither ideas nor feelings are sufficient; action must follow. A morally sound individual is one whose actions are moral. A frank individual is not one who believes in frankness, praises it and appreciates it in his heart of hearts but one who practices it. A professor of ethics, in spite of all his knowledge, is not a moral being so long as his conduct is not moral. Necessarily, therefore, the goal of any kind of education is to get children to act in a certain way. This is not all. Mere action is not sufficient. Action which is backed by example and advice is not sufficient. The action must recur, become organized, effortless, natural. We have not reached our goal so long as a habit has not been formed.

Now, how can we modify a child's conduct, get him to give up habits which are judged bad and adopt good habits? How can we persuade him to concentrate his attention on something as tedious as a grammar exercise? William James, the American psychologist, is one of those who have best understood this delicate point; he has shown that we cannot build anything new in a child's soul without taking what is already there into account. A child has tendencies, curiosities, interests; he is sensitive to certain stimuli. We must take advantage of these tendencies, expose him to the stimuli he is sensitive to, so as to hang onto all this the manner of acting we want him to adopt. Consequently, first we must know him.

But how much must we know him? Need we make a very close study of his nature in order to learn to guide him? It is not indispensable, and this is a good thing, because otherwise we would never have educated anyone. It is possible to direct a child's education by relying on tendencies which are common to all children, to all men, even to all animals. We all look for pleasure and we all flee from pain. This very simple observation is the basis for training; with a whip and carrots we can have a monkey do anything we want. Replace these coarse motivating agents with more refined ones and we have the essentials of a moral education applicable to a human being.

The effectiveness of the whole educative action is determined by the teacher's personality; it is worth what he is worth. Education involves a subordinate and a superior; it involves influence, ascendance, suggestion, and, in a word, authority. But where is the authority coming from? What is its source?

Does it come from the physical person? Yes, in part. Good appearance, a good stature, very great muscular strength, a bold glance are great advantages. Professors who are short know this only too well. Even clothing is important. But I believe all the physical endowments have only borrowed value. They impress because they are usually the sign of great energy and of a strong will. They become useless when it has been discovered that character is weak. I have seen giants ridiculed by children.

The same is true of intellectual gifts; to put life into one's teaching, to keep the children's attention in a constant state of alertness, is to make discipline easy. Moreover, teachers who, because of their intelligence, have acquired a certain reputation, almost glory, have many claims on the confidence of their students; the latter are proud of their teachers. I remember examples of this. And finally, the more intelligent we are the more we use appropriateness and finesse in exercising the authority we have. But this authority is not created by intelligence. Everyone has known eminent teachers who were unable to conduct a class. For the same reason there are marriages in which it is the most intelligent spouse who obeys the other.

The same remark is applicable to the kindness, the benevolence, the affection which certain teachers display towards their pupils; some know how to give students the deep and beautiful impression that they are always treated fairly. But qualities of the heart also, I regret to say, are accessory qualities; they are useless if they are not supported by strong authority. No gratitude is felt toward a teacher who is kind if he does not have the power to have himself feared; his kindness is viewed as weakness. On the other hand, we meet teachers who are dry, cold, indifferent to the point of malevolence, but they know how to handle their class.

Authority comes uniquely from character. If we want another word, let us say the will. Let us also add strength, power, coordination. What the teacher needs is a will which is neither impulsive nor deficient; a will which is calm, which reflects, which does not fly into a rage, which does not contradict itself, which never threatens in vain. Parents who have no ascendance are those who pay too little attention to their children's education; who are prone to losing their temper; who punish excessively but remove the punishment too easily; who give contradic-

213

tory directions, first an order, then a counterorder; those especially who threaten the guilty child but never carry out their threat and who are the first to laugh at his clever remarks and at his outbursts. They should not be surprised they have no authority; it is simply because they lack character. If you want to have ascendance, begin by educating yourself; try acquiring character and the rest will follow.

Children are clever; they judge their man quickly. A teacher tries in vain to simulate the character which he does not have. I have known a few who wanted to raise their voice, who pounded on their desk like deaf men, and let punishments rain on the class. They stunned us for a time and we lived a nightmare, but soon the falsity of this simulated authority was discovered; we no longer feared them, and their punishments no longer had any effect. I would compare them to those physicians who, in spite of an abusive number of prescriptions, never manage to acquire an influence on their patients. Someone with an unfaltering will is very different. He does not even raise his voice and never seems to be involved with discipline, but when he is there, everyone behaves and there is absolute silence when he speaks. When the occasion presents itself he laughs and jokes. He becomes his students' friend, listens to their complaints, allows them to take a stand against him; nothing affects his prestige. He has a special characteristic: he practically never punishes. It is a fact that a teacher's authority is inversely proportional to the number of punishments he needs to give in order to obtain perfect discipline.[2]

We have three main ways of acting on the child's organism. They are most often combined but we shall distinguish them for the purpose of the description. They are:
1. abstention;
2. repressive means (depressors);
3. stimulants.

1. *Abstention* is almost an application of the principle referred to in political economy as "laisser faire." What it amounts to here is a benevolent and thoughtful abstention which, of course, has limits.

From this point of view, when a child engages in an action which is bad, either for him or for others, it is advisable not to intervene and to wait until he suffers the natural consequences of his action.

Legouvé told us that one day when he was traveling by train with one of his granddaughters, someone came to the window offering strawberries. The child wanted to eat some. Legouvé, concerned about her delicate stomach, said to her, "Eat strawberries if you wish, but don't complain if you are sick." The girl could not resist the temptation, she ate and was sick. This was the natural sanction of her imprudence; and an indigestion is evidently an excellent lesson. In the same way, if a

214

child wants to play with scissors, a knife, or set fire to pieces of paper, we shall warn him about the danger, then we shall let him hurt himself a little. "That will teach him."

Solicitous French parents who care about their children's health more than about the formation of their character never practice abstentionism, although Rousseau recommended it.

The British tend to do so willingly, and certainly Spencer[3] expresses a very English opinion when he teaches that children must not be prevented from experiencing the natural consequences of their actions. The more natural those consequences, the more instructive they are. He prefers nature's sanctions to the artificial ones we pin onto certain acts, as it were, by subjecting our children to punishments. Consequently, if a child breaks a toy or tears his clothing, Spencer does not advocate that we deprive him of dessert and then the next day buy him a new toy or new clothing. Rather he suggests that the child suffer by having to buy himself another toy and, if he has no money, doing without the toy or wearing the torn clothing. This is not only education but also a lesson in philosophy, for nothing is more effective in teaching the child about the meaning of life, about responsibility, about the idea that things are good or bad only because their consequences are salutary or harmful. We become angry at the artificial punishments a teacher's caprice wants to impose upon us and, as a result, we hate this teacher; we become our parents' enemy. But the sanctions of life are more easily understood; we feel their imperious logic better and submit to it more willingly.

There is much truth to this system of education. In fact, children all over the world are subjected to at least part of it, for, supervised and protected by fearful parents though they may be, they can never be completely sheltered from the consequences of their errors; lack of attention often results in a stumble and a fall. On the other hand, most children live in the company of other children the same age; their personalities confront one another, clash, become wounded; they learn to control themselves, to submit to the will of the majority. The child then becomes aware of the fact that his actions are sanctioned not only by nature but also by the social environment, and this coeducation also is an excellent education. Children who were brought up alone later recognize that they sorely missed this first lesson of life; they have more difficulty adapting to the broader social environment when they have not made their apprenticeship in the school setting.

This being granted, we find it necessary to add that the principle of abstention cannot constitute a complete system of education. First, the consequences of it would be too brutal; there are dangerous actions which a child shall never be permitted to take. If he gets too close to a precipice during a trip to the mountains, we shall hold him by the arm;

if he enters your darkroom and wants to drink potassium cyanide, we shall not let him drink under the pretext that "this will teach him." It is therefore necessary to intervene from time to time to mitigate some of the natural sanctions which are overly rigorous. Are the other sanctions as a whole sufficient to form a character and especially a morality? This is debatable. Those who believe they are must suppose implicitly that life can become a school of wisdom and kindness. We tend to believe that if life gives lessons which are sufficiently precise to make utilitarians out of us, kindness and morality, on the other hand, are based on an ideal which surpasses utilitarian concepts of living. At any rate, it is unquestionable that when our duty is to raise and educate a child or when we have to conduct a class, it is radically impossible to wait for nature to intervene and show children the consequences of their actions; we must intervene ourselves and without losing any time. In connection with this, I remember an observation reported to me which seems to have been inspired by the Spencer system but which was a ruthless application of it. A young boy had been sent to a boarding school run by priests. Not very religious, he enjoyed not only disrupting the class but also poking fun at religion. The priests could have decided to expel him but they punished him differently, in a way which was much more cruel. Nobody paid any attention to him, his work was never corrected, he was never asked to recite a lesson. When he came out of boarding school at the age of eighteen, his ignorance was complete. This was a dreadful punishment from which he suffered all his life.

What we should take from the abstentionist system is everything which helps develop a sense of responsibility in children. The formula is therefore not exactly "laisser faire" but rather to set up conditions in such a way that the child feels the consequences of his actions. Now, this new way of thinking could be introduced even in school. Inflexible rules would be made more supple; children would not be made into simple automata but would be allowed more spontaneity and given more responsibility; students would be given more freedom with regard to the amount of work to be done and the work method to be used, but what would be demanded would be results. There would not be *studies* of determined length and equal for all; each individual would be free to take the time which suits him. A similar reform could be introduced in the area of work. We should not demand that workers be present for a certain length of time during which they will gladly twiddle their thumbs, but that they produce a certain quantity of work. For the same reasons, we would like the length of military service to be adapted to the results of military education. These reforms are certainly not easy to accomplish, and should we attempt to carry them out we would encounter many difficulties. But they must be tried, for they develop initiative and responsibility to a high degree.

216

Now let us consider the case which occurs most frequently, in which the educator is compelled to intervene actively in order to modify the student's conduct. We have said he is going to use either repressive means or stimulants; these are sometimes physical, sometimes moral. But let us not be fooled by words. Just as all education is a true moral action system, so all educative procedures are mainly moral procedures. Those which appear to be essentially physical are less so than we imagine; what is material about them only has the value of a suggestion, a semblance, and their action depends on the ideas which they generate, on the value we attribute to them. A beating given a dog or a child can be effective; but it is so less because of the physical pain it produces than because it suggests an indefinite, mysterious, threatening other world. This is proven by the fact that we can laughingly give very hard slaps to a dog or a child in the excitement of a game; they love it because those slaps are not associated with the idea of punishment. In the same way, rewards are effective less because of the pleasurable sensations they provide than because of the joy which follows, as everyone will testify who, as a child, has ever been rewarded with candy or with the appearance of a " covered dish"; what made those rewards valuable was not the small gustative sensation which was experienced, so short and so meager, but rather the waiting, the surprise, the way in which the gift was offered, and all the emotions which followed suit. I believe it is useful, therefore, to develop mainly the moral means of action we have at our disposal, for they are the richest, the most varied, the most effective. The physical means, in my opinion, must only be primers, simulacra, symbols.

2. *The repressive measures.* They consist mainly of creating a disagreeable, depressing, distressing, painful impression on the student. This impression being coupled with, associated with, certain actions discourages the child and prevents him from carrying out the action; if, on the contrary, it is associated with certain abstentions, it prompts him to act. But depression is always an influence to be avoided, for it saps the organism's energy; consequently, if repressive measures cannot be eliminated completely, we must at least keep in mind that they are measures of last resort and should be used sparingly.

I am not in favor of true and complete physical punishment; it is not consistent with our ethics and it wounds our sensibility. However, I admit that a shock or surprise produced by violence or even a semblance of violence can have good consequences. I was told that in a certain boarding school there was a very irritable child who occasionally had frightening anger fits and only one person had acquired sufficient moral authority over him to quiet him down. One day the crisis erupted while this person was absent. A professor of English happened to be passing by, and without hesitating, he picked up the child, undressed him, carried him over to the pump and placed him under a stream of cold water for a moment. This little hydraulic demonstration was completely successful; the child was cured instantly, and since that time his angry outbursts have never been as violent. Here is another example given to me by one of the most eminent members of the teaching profession. When he was a *lycée* professor, he had a student who constantly adopted a sarcastic attitude toward him. One day, right in the middle of a lecture, the professor lost his patience. He ran up the steps, went to the student, seized him around the waist and shook him. In the face of this manifestation of energy, the young man remained astonished. It was only a shock, a surprise; it was not physical punishment. That very day a complete change took place. The student's behavior was altered, and he became reasonable, obedient, hard-working. Today he has become a distinguished engineer. He still remembers the salutary lesson he was given and is grateful for it.

The same depressing result can be obtained by using only the moral effect of the physical method. A reprimand made publicly in a stern and solemn tone of voice, in front of many witnesses, deeply humiliates certain children whose pride is easily wounded. In one particular school I know, this kind of admonishing is customary every Saturday, the children calling it " to pass inspection. " Demanding that delinquents apologize or make an effort to repair the damage they have done is also very good. But, of course, public disapprobation should be used only if we are sure of the witnesses' acquiescence or the effect is lost. A father is ineffectual if he scolds his son in front of a mother who deliberately sides with the son against the father.

There are many children who can be dealt with more effectively after they have been isolated. Everyone knows what enormous influence is exerted on a child when he is called into the director's office, especially if he is made to wait and then is spoken to gravely in a voice full of conviction, man to man. The child is disarmed, worried about what is going to be done to him; his heart beats fast, his resistance is at its lowest; this is the time to act strongly upon him. It is the time particularly to get him to confide in us, or to confess, by questioning him skillfully and mixing here and there the affirmative with the interrogative form. There is an art to obtaining confessions, but we shall not abuse it. Confession is a practice which is a little dangerous : It weakens; it allows the child's mind to dwell on errors which it would be better to let him forget; and it sometimes gives certain individuals an unhealthy pleasure, the pleasure of imaginative degustation. Another excellent method consists of appealing to the children's better feelings until they are moved to tears. A school director told me that having had to direct the education of young girls who, about age thirteen or fourteen, became uncouth and mischievous, he involved them in a discussion and spoke to them at length about the grief they were causing their parents. Some of them didn't cry, but if he succeeded in making a girl weep, the battle was won.

These few moral procedures in which we put a little of ourselves appear to me to be infinitely preferable to the system which includes bad grades, retention after class, and extra assignments, which some teachers hand out with as much discernment as an automatic machine would have. Obviously there are cases in which school punishments are indispensable, but let us at least give them discriminately. Let us not punish all students equally, since a little punishment is sufficient for some. Moreover, let us remember that a child who is punished too often gets used to it and becomes hardened. I recommend that we primarily use the excellent system which permits the child to repair his fault. As soon as he is punished he is warned that this punishment is noted but that if between now and the end of class time his conduct is exemplary, he'll redeem himself and his punishment will be lifted. I saw this system used in several schools and believe it is excellent. It is not based on depression but on stimulation.

3. *The stimulants.* The educative measures which we refer to as stimulants are those which act favorably on physical, intellectual, and moral activity, which increase it and, at the same time, produce a feeling of well-being and satisfaction. For *a priori* reasons, we must prefer this method to others. We even regret that it cannot be used exclusively, for it is the only one which promotes activity, high spirits and good feelings toward the teacher. It is in keeping with the spirit of all education, the task of which is to promote action while at the same time generating joyful enthusiasm.

The best stimulants are the most direct ones, those which are part of the very action we wish the child to execute. If I want a young school child to work on an assignment, I shall first try to get him interested in it. My initial task will be to capture his attention. Knowing what he likes and being aware of what Americans call "centers of interest" will facilitate this. I shall begin with a thought-provoking statement; or I shall profit from a current event I know he is aware of, a war, an accident, some ceremony; or I shall express the interest I myself have in this work, the great significance I feel it has. I shall strengthen character. I shall discuss my student's ideas with him and underline discreetly any value which those ideas may have, however small it may be. In other cases I shall take a stand opposing his so as to stimulate his interest. I shall make it a point to be optimistic, for encouragement is the main lever of education.

I have been putting these ideas into practice for a long time in my work with individuals whose education has been entrusted to me. They knew how eagerly I began following their progress, inducing it, maintaining it. Although my students have now become adults, I still feel I play a part in everything they undertake, so involved am I. There is nothing factitious about my interest; it may, at first, have been a voluntary act, but since then, little by little, I myself have been taken over by it. Truly it is with all my heart that I have become involved, and any influence I have had has been at this very price.

The stimulants we have at our disposal are not all as direct. Like the depressors, they may have only borrowed value; they may be pinned on. We shall divide them into three categories: rewards, praise, missions of confidence.

Rewards are primarily the presents and privileges parents can give their children: money, toys, candy, evenings at the theater, excursions, trips and so on. These are expensive gifts which would be out of place at school, and the teacher is forced to limit himself to more modest recompenses, such as books, pictures, pens; this does not go very far. An amusing story read by the teacher at the end of class time also has an excellent effect. But the true school rewards are marks and rank orders, only their effect is due mainly to the value we ostensibly attach to these advantages, which is an estimated value. The decorations given in the lower grades to well-behaved children belong in this category, and they have their detractors. I have seen pedagogues, holders of decorations, who spoke loudly against the custom of awarding crosses to school children; they apparently believed that it is possible to make children wiser and more disinterested than adults. In our opinion, no educative means should be eliminated as long as it has desirable consequences.

The claim has been made that rewards imply a comparison between classmates and that the child who is rewarded or who ranks first owes his victory only to the defeat he inflicts upon his rivals. It has also been said that this system primarily flatters conceited and selfish feelings and does not promote kindness and neighborly love. The problem is, further, that in practice the same children nearly always get the best ranks and obtain the prizes; the other students become discouraged and rightly so, since they are never rewarded for their efforts. It has been proposed that comparison between different students not be abused and that competition, in spite of the fact that it is a powerful motive, be played down. Our colleague and friend Mr. Boitel, Director of the Ecole Turgot, thinks it is preferable to compare the student to himself, to his past performance, giving him credit mainly for the manner in which he evolves, the way in which he outshines himself. Each one of his students records his own rate of progress by drawing a line graph showing his bi-monthly test results. Mr. Boitel feels that the rise or fall of the curve is much more meaningful than the differences between the figures representing raw scores. A man whose son is working under this system told me one day: "When my son gets home from school on Saturday, I immediately ask him, 'Well, how is that curve coming along?'"

Although this individual graphic representation method has not yet been scientifically tested — in pedagogy nothing is ever controlled; this is the rule — it deserves to be tried. However, it is important to guard against becoming too exclusive-minded an educator and thus overlooking a large number of resources. Emulation is a driving force, an incredibly strong stimulus for certain natures who are consumed by ambition. An intelligent teacher will always know how to make use of it.

After the rewards, which are like a payment for work and good conduct, let us mention the moral effect the teacher's approval has on students. A kind of tacit approbation is wonderfully effective. Well-endowed students who are still young work mainly to please their teacher, and for this reason it is well not to replace him by another too often. A vague and general feeling of contentment, a little smile are sufficient to stimulate the child's enthusiasm. I believe it is affection which most often motivates pupils to work. Add to this the influence of sheer habit on work performance, the influence of tradition and routine, the preventive action of some always possible though undefined punishment and it is sufficient; nothing more is needed.

On some occasions vague approval should become more precise, such as a praise, a compliment, a sign of our satisfaction. But many reservations are to be made here: Praise must be discreet and brief; it must be deserved; it must be proportionate to the effort which has been furnished; its justice must be completely evident, felt and approved by the whole class; it must not be repeated too often, and be more an encouragement to do even better in the future than an acknowledgment of a definite attainment. If, on the one hand, it is good to give support to the student, showing that we are pleased with him, trust him, are sure of his progress, let us not forget, on the other hand, that excess praise can excite the child's feeling of pride and that pride can easily degenerate into conceit.

What about poor students, someone will ask, how can they be encouraged? The teacher would be disarmed if he had to wait for his bad students to merit rewards before giving them any, and always punishing is not good. Fortunately we can have recourse to another method which, in our opinion, is infinitely preferable to everything we have described so far: the mission of confidence. This is the active method *par excellence*. It incites the pupil to act in a particular way; he learns that he is trusted; his self-esteem is increased. This can happen when a teacher who has to leave the room for two minutes installs the bad student behind the lectern and tells him : " When I return, write down the name of the one of your classmates whose behavior has been the best during my absence. " Almost surely the pupil, proud of his mission, will not be unfair. Or simply asking the child to distribute workbooks and pencils will be sufficient to make him very happy, especially if we have had the foresight to attach much importance to this function. Bad dispositions have been known to be improved by holding their owners responsible for the protection of younger children. A true bully can be mellowed by caring for a young handicapped child ; this protective urge, when it enters certain hearts, performs miracles. In a class of abnormal children I observed a young retarded girl who had been given the task of teaching a younger, more retarded child how to read ; the little teacher accomplished her mission conscientiously and even taught herself to read at the same time. Or, in a different category of ideas, entrust a spendthrift student with the keys and management of the cash register ; if you go about it the right way, you will see how sparing she rapidly becomes. This method gets the child to act in a certain way and forms new habits which, through repetition, may become a permanent and integral part of her nature.

In the preceding pages we have made no distinction between the various children we intend to educate. To make things simpler we have made the implicit assumption that they are all made on the same model. Many teachers behave as though this assumption were a reality. They have a punishment and reward system which they apply when the occasion arises, and they don't know, therefore, what the intimate effect is of the educative measures they use. They only maintain the kind of superficial order a police mission maintains. Many parents behave in the same way. We have already stated, and we repeat, that education is legitimate only if it is inspired by the child's interest, if the child profits from it. Consequently, we must penetrate into the child's soul, know what he thinks and what he feels. We must more or less try to study his psychological make-up.

I shall list only two or three examples of this necessity. We spoke earlier about the repressive measures which include two main types : punishment and reprimand. No teacher can do without them ; it is possible never to punish, strictly speaking, but it is not possible to dispense with reprimand, threat, intimidation. Now, the success of these repressive and depressive measures obviously depends on the resistance the child offers to them. This resistance must be taken into consideration and appraised, for there are two ways to miss the goal. One error consists of striking a weak individual too hard, of causing too great a depression. Crushed by punishment, terrorized by an overly harsh treatment, the child becomes shy, fearful, overly sensitive, sad ; he loses his self-confidence and the beautiful joy of living which is the charm of childhood. Nothing is more painful to see than the countenance of a beaten child. The other and opposite error consists of using a depressive measure which is not powerful enough, considering the pugnacity of the child we are dealing with. If a mental hospital patient is isolated in an effort to quiet him down but returns from isolation in a state of excitation, it is proof that the treatment has not been long enough. But such a patient cannot be locked up indefinitely; consequently, before prescribing the measure, the physician must ask himself if it is likely to have the desired effect. In the same way, any repressive measure fails if it leaves the child in a state of rebellion.

I was told recently about a five- or six-year-old boy who does not want and has never wanted to eat solid foods. Each day at mealtime he finds a whip beside his plate. Knowing what this means, he turns calmly toward his heartbroken father and says to him, " I don't want to eat. I prefer to be whipped. " These words prove that coercive measures have failed and that the parents will do well to look for some other means. Their defeat is all the more unfortunate, since it decreases their authority. Therefore, without compensation of any kind, they have used methods which had the great defect of arousing malicious and malevolent feelings in the child; this is infinitely regrettable, for education should be a work of kindness.

The intellectual and moral character of children is also a valuable sign. Those who know children well are aware of the fact that procedures must be diversified greatly to achieve any results. We can be content with giving orders to the very young, but we have to reason with older pupils to try to persuade them. I remember two students whose character was so different that had they been treated in the same way nothing would have been obtained from either of them. The first was both very tenderhearted and very independent. It was necessary to appeal to both his feelings and his reason; he was moved by certain words, convinced mainly by the explanations he was given, which he perceived as sound, but a sharp order caused him to rebel. The other, even though he was of the same age, was completely different. He was most certainly not insensible to appeals made to his emotions and was deeply moved by them, but it was unwise to try to reason with him for he denied the evident truth. He never acknowledged defeat; for him it became a matter of pride. The best way to handle him was to give imperious orders with no opportunity for rejoinder. In theory, one may be the adversary of autocratic argument; in fact, there are cases in which the use of this method is necessary.

I am convinced that if we could identify the various existing types of character we would fairly quickly manage to classify each child and infer which kind of moral education is suitable to his category. Instead of feeling our way in the dark and making so many errors, we could act decisively. The apathetic and the depraved child are always the main source of difficulty. But is there such a thing as a completely apathetic individual, a child who is totally insensitive to all stimuli, who has absolutely no natural propensity which we could turn to the best account? If such children exist, their number must be negligible. As for the depraved, amoral, potentially criminal subjects — those who are the educator's terror — I suppose they do not differ from other children we consider normal so much by their psychology as by their behavior. They undoubtedly are not very altruistic and are little inclined to tenderness and pity. They often even lack the sentimentality which can make up for sensibility. We know with what coldness criminals listen to their victims' heartrending moans, with what composure — sometimes even with what rapture — these brutes have caused blood to flow in atrocious situations. But even in the most hardened of these human beings we still find the rudiments of feelings which could have prevented their downfall had they been properly tended to. Almost all have vanity, a ridiculous and enormous vanity which has grown out of their egoism. See how highly they value public opinion, how they look for the publicity that court appearances afford them, how proud they are to see their name in print. We inadvertently allow this vanity to have the most pernicious effects. With the complicity of the press and public opinion this self-glorification incites them to commit crime; properly handled it could become a prophylaxis against crime. Note the kind of relations they have with their accomplices, with those belonging to the same gang. See how they boast about their skill and their courage. See how some associate can sometimes get them to commit a crime, if they hesitate, by saying to them, "Are you afraid?" or "Are you not a man?" Note also that they often keep their word, that they don't expose an accomplice, that they have their own honor system and that they have even been known to act in a generous manner out of boastfulness. Vanity, therefore, almost always motivates them, and, if the phrase does not appear too strong, we shall say that these human beings who are considered amoral or immoral do have a moral code; a very special, uniquely egoistical moral code, to be sure, but one which, I am deeply convinced, a very intelligent and experienced educator could make use of.

With such natures it is not the repressive means, punishments or reprimands, which succeed, but such stimulants as praise and especially the mission of confidence. I shall say no more about this but the commentaries can be inferred. Little by little we must replace vanity with pride and from it derive self-respect.

In order to educate the child we must take his own character into account, and also the fact that he is not isolated, that he is in a class and that this class forms a society. His society has many of the characteristics of our adult society, many of its defects especially: confusion of movements, disorder, nervousness, the feeling of its irresponsibility and of its strength and everything dangerous which results from it. The influence of the multitude, therefore, can affect the child's character, complicating the teacher's work. Indeed he must not forget that the children's society is a union formed against him. That children hate denouncement proves this; in school, denouncement is the great sociological crime. The teacher must make serious efforts to contain, to manipulate the strength inherent in this union, which is all the more active as the children are more numerous, for much more authority is needed to control forty students than to control ten. He will remember Richelieu's words: "If you would reign, divide." He will separate the mutineers. Above all, he will prevent the boisterous students from corrupting the docile ones. He will place children in such a way that the active will sit beside the indolent. He will strive to form a core of good students representing a tradition of work and discipline; remembering that example and emulation are powerful forces, he will make them work in his favor.

In certain Paris schools someone had the idea of dividing classes into subgroups composed of ten to fifteen pupils. These subgroups were given names of such great men as Turgot, Pasteur, Victor Hugo. An attempt was made in a variety of ways to give each group a different personality. In one case this was achieved mainly by encouraging competition between two groups and by giving collective awards to each group every time it obtained an average grade superior to that of its rival. When the resulting group solidarity was well established, we saw the most industrious students supervise the lazy ones in the group and even accuse them of causing their small society to lose points. Is it not ingenious and very moving to get a school child to say to another, "Couldn't you work a little harder?" The only drawback these groups have is that their character is artificial, based not on a real interest but on convention. With children, of course, it is possible to attach great moral value to a simple convention.

A last problem comes to mind. As we look over the descriptions of the means at our disposal for forging souls, we find them very trivial and wonder, with some uneasiness, if it is possible to extract a true, a high and profound moral lesson from them. This uneasiness is felt more particularly by those who were brought up to respect religious morals. They don't understand that secular morals can be taught, because to them such morals have no foundation, no rational justification and, above all, no sanction. The fact is that for a simplistic mind God's command is sufficient and the answer to everything. But since public education has become neutral and borrows no argument from the religions, by what secular procedures are we going to teach morals to children? All morals are summarized in a system of sacrifices which are imposed upon our egoism. What argument will enable us to convince children of the legitimacy of these sacrifices if we talk to them neither about divinity nor about future life, and if consequently we are forced to do without the traditional arguments which, although purely selfish and therefore not very moral, are so vigorous and so impressive?

Because of lack of space I cannot write a complete exposé of the question. I shall only show that, as a rule, moral education is possible without the help of a religious discipline.

The objections raised against secular education suppose that education is accomplished through the use of reasoning and of ideas, an ideal we dream a lot about today. We arrived at it indirectly, as a reaction against religious education, which had been accused of enslaving souls. Now, we constantly read in pedagogical journals about a child's rights of conscience. It is also stated that we must respect his reason and must not prevent him from exercising his judgment. Above all, we are told we go beyond the educator's rights when we instill in the child's mind a belief which he shall not be able to change when he reaches adulthood. These scruples are undoubtedly very praiseworthy, for they show we now understand that the child's mind can easily become stamped with indelible impressions and that the educator must not abuse his power. In connection with this I remember what a father, who was by no means a believer, told me one day, speaking about his six-year-old son: "I shall send him to the priests' school; this way he will have religious feelings which will last all his life." There is something shocking about this assault on a personality which cannot yet defend itself. But let's not go from one excess to another, or rather let us not confound the methods of education and the goals of education. The goal is to produce free men, but the method cannot consist of treating a child as a free man nor of appealing to his reason while he is still at an age when he has no reason. We have repeated, as a leitmotiv throughout this whole book, that education consists of causing useful actions, of forming habits, and consequently of making all our faculties function, that of judgment as well as others. The child's morality is not created with ideas; it does not result from arguments which are presented to him, and the listing of reasons can only serve to throw light on, guide, fortify, justify, rationalize a moral tendency which is already formed. In children this moral tendency is the result of two main factors: first, it is the respect they have for their parents and their teachers, the element of authority, the idea of duty which is necessary to any moral system if it is going to be effective; secondly, it is altruism, kindness, charity, sympathy, affection, unselfishness, all those warm and tender motives which lead to abnegation and which give a heart to morality.

Before ending the chapter I want to say a few words about a moral education experiment which has just been conducted in the Paris grammar schools. More than an experiment, it actually involves practical moral exercises. I believe the endeavor is new and since it has already had very encouraging results, I feel it is well that it be known so others can repeat it for the children's greatest good. Once again we are going to talk about the classes for abnormal children, for it is in connection with their formation that these exercises were set up. My friend Mr. Belot is given the credit for them.

It is already five years since we were given authorization to create an experimental program for young abnormal girls in a Paris elementary school. We were a little doubtful, almost anxious, for we had been entrusted with an important mission and did not want to jeopardize such a great cause. The adversaries of classes for the abnormal — there are always opponents to something which is new — claimed that it is dangerous to assemble normal and abnormal pupils in the same school. The latter, they said, were vicious children who were going to corrupt the healthy elements. Or it would be war. Normal children would make fun of their schoolmates, holding them up to ridicule; the parents would become involved; the school would soon be viewed as a school for the insane and would be discredited and deserted. From all sides we were told we must set up an impervious partition between the two student populations, plan recesses in different yards, have different school hours for the two groups; we might as well have had two different institutions. So strongly were we influenced by these fears that we chose for our experiment a school which had the good fortune of possessing two front doors; it was decided that one of these doors would be reserved for the young abnormal girls. But we very quickly dropped the idea and, in fact, the special door was never used. What appeared to be a danger at first turned out, in reality, to be an advantage. Today, under Mr. Belot's direction, contacts as numerous as possible are arranged between the abnormal girls and the remainder of the school population. Moreover, we became aware of the fact that these contacts are helpful not only to the retarded but also, and especially, to the older normal girls, who are given a marvelous opportunity to learn solidarity and unselfishness by practicing them; it is one of the best applications for the morals course given to them in school. Meals, recesses, physical education, arts and crafts and home economics programs are offered to both groups of students at the same time, in the same courtyard or in the same classes. This incessant contact allows the abnormal pupils to live with children who are better brought up and cared for, who serve as examples for them and whose behavior they imitate.

Furthermore, the higher classes provide students who become little mothers to the young abnormal girls. Mr. Belot and I saw to it that a material and administrative form was given to this cooperation, for in a school everything must be well regulated. The children's feelings must not become manifest only on the occasion of holidays, festivities, games and dances in common or during official visits. The

227

assistance the older students give the younger ones should not take the form of gifts of clothing or money too often, for once engaged on this track it is possible to go too far, taking away all spontaneity from the normal students by imposing upon them a kind of tax for the poor as it is done in England. The abnormals, on the other hand, too pampered and too spoilt, would end up taking the attention and the gifts for granted. After much groping in the dark, Mr. Belot and I decided not to do away with the festivities, the lotteries, the dances, the reunions — which are bad if they are the essential part of the program but very good if they are only the exception — but that the children's relationships must have a precise educational goal. And so, in keeping with our new regulations, the class of students who are repeating a year provides an assistant each day. This assistant stays in the special class almost all day and helps the younger children, those who are the least skillful at doing their homework and at following the lessons. The same assistant will not return to the special class again before one or two months. Moreover, twice a week, between 4 and 4:30, the little mothers come and tutor their students. One of the study sessions is devoted to instruction; the other involves object lessons, explanation and advice. Each little mother is on duty for about two weeks, at the end of which time she writes a two- or three-page report on what she has observed in her pupil. The following two weeks she is replaced by another older student, another little mother. This way the young tutors' spirited but brief enthusiasm does not become exhausted. Such a program is possible only with the very close collaboration of the school director. It demands an intelligent will, a desire to do well, and constant supervision. What has succeeded in one school must be able to succeed in another. I did not mention the curious spectacle offered by the young retarded students as they joyously await the arrival of the little mothers when the clock strikes 4; you should witness the noisy demonstrations of the young pupils and see the serious and reasonable mien of the older ones. I did not mention the letters which are exchanged, the bi-monthly reports in which so much good will is found, the interest the parents of normal students have shown in our program, the assistance they have already given us by finding positions for those of our retarded students who have now left school. All those who have been given the opportunity to observe these things, to penetrate below the surface, have been profoundly moved. We were told over and over again that similar programs should be set up everywhere, in all ordinary schools, for the benefit of normal children. Older students everywhere should learn to care for younger ones. There is much talk today about teaching solidarity. To give lessons in solidarity is good; to teach it by having it practiced is better.

FOOTNOTES FOR CHAPTER EIGHT

1. For more details, see *Année Psychologique,* Vol. XIV (1908), 177.

2. A book by Marion, *L'éducation dans l'université,* contains the finest comments about teacher authority.

3. H. Spencer, *De l'education,* p. 167.

CHAPTER NINE

A few words in conclusion

I announced at the beginning of this book that I proposed to find out if introducing experimental and rigorously scientific research in pedagogy could benefit pedagogy. Could it help improve teaching methods; could it help perfect the art of knowing children's aptitudes?

Our domain, in this case, is not pure science but real life situations. The schools exist and are filled with children, and the whole is like an organism which has been functioning for centuries. All around and related to it are officials, a hierarchy, set attitudes, traditions, personal interests and something like dogmas. This organism tends to last, resisting change even if change means progress. The experimental studies in pedagogy which are now being conducted must be considered not only in themselves but also in relation to the institutions they aim to change.

The old pedagogy, or to speak more accurately, the pedagogy which today still has dominion over education, had a primarily empirical origin. While teaching, educators made useful observations which they utilized to modify their methods; then these observations were for the most part forgotten and all that remains is certain rules of conduct, practices and habits. In this way methods were born and programs set up, always with great respect for tradition. The best that can be said about these practices is that they were designed to solve real problems, that they always remained in contact with real life and on the whole have rendered a great service. I would compare them to an old creaky carriage which moves forward very slowly but which after all still works.

From time to time reforms are made which are dictated by needs or by an intelligent educator's inspiration. They may take the form of a slight change in orientation or even sometimes that of an excellent innovation, like the introduction of professional schools in America. But all these endeavors have a general defect: they are empirical and uncontrolled. No one has ever thought about using controlled comparison experiments, which are indispensable for obtaining scientific proof. This constant lack of method prompted a psychologist to make the very sound statement: "In pedagogy, everything has been said but nothing has been proven." This general empiricism does not prevent the pedagogy we are talking about from having its own theory, its own doctrine; but this doctrine is vague and purely literary, a collection of empty sentences which is impossible to criticize, so indefinite is the thought expressed in it. It is not sufficiently precise to be false.

For the past thirty years many innovators who are, or say they are, inspired by the scientific spirit have denounced this pedagogy, wishing to destroy and replace it. These innovators are found almost everywhere today, some in France, in Italy, in England, more in Germany, most in America. They have undertaken to rebuild pedagogy on a new, scientific basis. Their work is always based on observation and experimentation. It is carried out either through surveys and with questionnaires, or in university laboratories; sometimes too, but more rarely, in secondary and primary schools. The program they have set for themselves is extremely vast; they propose, on the one hand, to introduce organizational reform in education, and on the other hand, to have the child's psychological make-up play a major role and to deduce from it, with mathematical precision, the kind of education the child must receive.

All these promises have aroused the curiosity of educators, but those who have wanted to know, to analyse, to understand the work of the new science have always been a little disappointed. Most often all they find are highly technical, forbidding-looking reports, the conclusions of which are very incomplete, and many having mediocre interest and questionable significance; they are only scattered, isolated, dismembered fragments. Teachers were especially surprised to see that, even if they absorbed all these experiments, they could derive almost no benefit from them, nothing which would be of practical value in their work. The "pedologists," at least those who became aware of the teachers' disappointment, vainly called to them: "Wait! give us credit!... We are only at the beginning!" It seemed that even this very start was not made in the right gear. I said earlier that the old pedagogy is like an old-fashioned carriage which creaks but can still be useful. Pedology looks like precision machinery, like a mysterious, shiny, complicated locomotive which fills us with admiration when we first see it. But the parts seem not to hold to each other, and the machine has a defect: it does not work.

In this book I have tried not to conciliate these two opposite systems, but rather to find my way between the two. It seemed to me that each has both a defect and a virtue. The old pedagogy generalizes too much; it is too imprecise, too moralizing, too verbal. It does too much preaching. I hate homilies and sermons; I find them ineffective, boring, exasperating. But however open to criticism its procedures may be, this old pedagogy has at least rendered some services: It had a clear idea of the problems to be solved, was involved in the life of the schools, and insisted on everything which interests us most in education. Let us at least retain its orientation, its interest in real problems. The methods of modern pedagogy, on the other hand, are tests; they are dry, narrow, incomplete, very often useless experiments thought out by laboratory people who know nothing about school or life and who seem never to have had their nose outside of their laboratory window. But these methods stand for experimentation, control, precision, truth.

It seems to us easy enough to conciliate these two tendencies by asking different services from the old and from the new pedagogy. The old pedagogy must provide us with the problems to be studied; the new, the methods of study.

In keeping with this point of view I believe we can, as of now, introduce into pedagogy a certain number of useful reforms.

Do we wish to assess a child's knowledge, to measure his level of achievement? Do we want to know how a teacher's performance compares with that of other teachers? Do we want to evaluate some new procedure and its useful effects? Do we want to conciliate the contrary opinions of a teacher and of his supervisor? We shall have recourse to the method of measurement Mr. Vaney has set up.

Do we want to evaluate a child's physical development? Do we suspect that his corporal development is inferior to the average for his age or that his health is poor? Is it necessary to take these facts into account to plan his physical education program, sports, games, to provide for school assistance, to justify a decrease in school work, and finally to request a physical examination? We have seen how to go about it, what procedure is to be followed, and what the most significant measurements are.

Is it a matter of examining sensory organs? This is a serious matter, for children whose visual and auditory deficiencies have not been recognized show a very detrimental retardation in their studies. We have reassured the teacher who is always too quick to become alarmed at his incompetence, and we have shown him that it is possible to divide the examination of sensory organs into two parts, one of which, being of a pedagogical nature, must be entrusted to him.

We have seen the many complicated and misleading circumstances in which we are called upon to make an evaluation of a school child's intelligence and how necessary it is to have a reliable method of measurement. We have described this method, which is an extremely valuable instrument, on the condition that it be used with great tact and intelligence. In connection with this, we positively stated that intelligence can be educated, there is a method for developing it and this method does not consist of oral lessons but of practical training which constitutes what we have called our "mental orthopedics program."

Memory then became the object of our attention, for it is one of the bases of instruction and it attains its maximum development in the child. The teacher must concern himself with the measurement of each student's memory for two reasons:

— so the child's memory will not be overworked.

— so the teacher will not administer, without rhyme or reason, rewards or punishments which might not be deserved. We have shown that memory is measured in a collective test as easily as visual acuity. After a word on the study and treatment of memory illusions, which are for the most part judgment errors, we have said that in the light of our present knowledge the classification of children in the visual, auditory and motor categories does not present any guarantee of being accurate and is consequently of no interest. We ended this section by describing a program for the education of memory which, just like intelligence, can be trained with the help of methodical exercises. We have insisted particularly on the necessity for progressive exercises, and a few observations have shown what errors are made when this method is not followed.

The chapter on children's aptitudes is barely sketched out. The question of correlation is still incompletely understood; this will be the science of tomorrow. We confined ourselves to asking that children who do not succeed in academic work be given access to arts and crafts programs, those programs which, today, are thought to have great educational value, and with much reason. Every time a child ranks among the last in his class, we should find out what he would be capable of doing in the wood and iron workshop.

In a last chapter on laziness and moral education, we listed the various procedures which are at the disposal of an educator who wants to influence a child. The work of tomorrow will consist of establishing relationships between the children's various character types and the most appropriate means for educating each of those types.

As a result of all these endeavors we succeed in making our knowledge of children more precise, more practical, more useful. The teachers who become familiar with these methods are in a position to avoid a few errors, to correct some of their prejudices, to set their attention on a decisive sign or to know precisely what must be done to arrive at an exact judgment. Viewed in this light, pedagogy ceases to be an outdated, deeply boring art. It gives us a closer look at our children's souls, and it already begins to teach us how we can proceed in order to insure the education of their memory, their judgment, and their will. This education is useful not only to the children; it can also be useful to us. Looking over our own infirmities and weaknesses, we see how much could be gained by applying these methods to ourselves. This should be a concern of all those who endeavor to introduce a little intelligence and art into the management of their life. This should especially be the concern of all those who hold public office. Instead of giving so much attention to material science, material well-being, material industry, they should give some thought to the fact that it is as important, more important perhaps, to see to it that moral force is properly directed and organized, for it is moral force which leads the world.

Achevé d'imprimer en septembre 1984
sur les Presses de l'Atelier Graphique Saint-Jean
10 rue Flottes, 81000 Albi (France)

Dépôt légal : 3ᵉ trimestre 1984

Nº imprimeur : 61